Objectivity in Journalism

Key Concepts in Journalism

Citizen Witnessing, Stuart Allan

Objectivity in Journalism, Steven Maras

Reinventing Professionalism, Silvio Waisbord

Objectivity in Journalism

Steven Maras

polity

First published in 2013 by Polity Press

Polity Press
65 Bridge Street
Cambridge CB2 1UR, UK

Polity Press
350 Main Street
Malden, MA 02148, USA

ISBN-13: 978-0-7456-4734-0
ISBN-13: 978-0-7456-4735-7(pb)

A catalogue record for this book is available from the British Library.

Typeset in 11 on 13 pt Sabon
by Servis Filmsetting Ltd, Stockport, Cheshire
Printed and bound in Great Britain by the MPG Books Group

For further information on Polity, visit our website: www.politybooks.com

Contents

Detailed contents

Detailed contents

Detailed contents

Acknowledgements

I hope this book honours the efforts of the many researchers and writers, historians, practitioners and critics of objectivity discussed and referred to in it. This project has benefited from the input of many individuals to whom I am grateful.

My interest in objectivity became serious in the wake of the 9/11 attacks on America and the War on Terror, a period which tested the applicability and relevance of the concept in all kinds of ways. Lelia Green was a valued collaborator in my early thinking. As my thoughts coalesced into a book proposal, and supported by research leave at the University of Sydney in 2008, I received invaluable input on philosophical questions from Chris Fleming. Richard Stanton was a wise counsel in my decision to approach Polity Press. Megan Le Masurier and Marc Brennan diligently read early drafts and provided very thoughtful comment. My other department colleagues, but especially Penny O'Donnell and Antonio Castillo, offered much appreciated advice and encouragement. I remain indebted to the three anonymous reviewers of the initial proposal who offered valuable encouragement and guidance.

During 2009, Heidi Lenffer provided efficient research support, supplied by the School of Letters, Art and Media research scheme. In the concluding stages, while on research leave in 2011, and during the final write up in early 2012, I benefited from the encouragement and input of a number of my colleagues in the Department of Media and Communications, and beyond. Many thanks to my Head of School, Annamarie Jagose, and Chair of Department, Gerard Goggin, for their support during the completion of the manuscript. John O'Carroll, Tim Dwyer and Anne Dunn all commented on different chapter drafts. Fiona Martin provided much valued guidance on objectivity, transparency, journalism and new media. Megan Le Masurier offered indispensible advice on how to blend the different historical and theoretical aspects of this research into more readable form. Her 'on call' editorial support was also much appreciated. Peter Fray took the time to comment astutely on several key chapters from a practitioner perspective. Bill Loges of Oregon State University offered invaluable comments on two chapters, and especially my approach to objectivity, ethics and new media in relation to *The New York Times* and Fox News Channel examples. I am also indebted to the two anonymous reviewers of the penultimate version of the manuscript for their astute comments and constructive criticism.

This book has benefited immensely from the support of library staff at the University of Sydney, especially the document delivery section, and I wish to acknowledge the significant contribution under time pressure of Kim Williams, Philippa Stevens, Richard Black, and John Wu, among others, as well as law librarians Patrick O'Mara and Grant Wheeler. Jonathan Seitz, Editorial Assistant for the Nieman Reports at the Nieman Foundation for Journalism at Harvard University provided generous support. I also wish to acknowledge the help of Tal Nadan, Reference Archivist of the New York Public Library; Kristina Ackermann, managing editor of *Editor & Publisher* Magazine; and Tamara Palmer, in the Office of the Clerk Assistant (Committees), Department of the House of Representatives, Parliament House, Canberra. My special thanks to Paul Chadwick for facilitating access to key past and current documents relating to the Australian Broadcasting Corporation and objectivity.

Like many other books, this one was written in between carrying out administrative and teaching duties, attending to family and friends, dashing to daycare and physiotherapy. My thanks especially to Justin Payne and Tessie Phan for their support and encouragement during late 2011–12. Since 2006, I have had

Acknowledgements

the good fortune of discussing and debating many of the themes in this book with students in the subject Media, Law and Ethics. This book has in a sense been written for, and in dialogue with, them. I have also benefited not only from the general professionalism of Polity editorial and production staff, but specifically from the patient, intelligent and rigorous editing of Andrea Drugan.

This book could not have been written without the support of my partner Teresa Rizzo, who read and commented on the final draft, but also nourished the project and myself in so many ways over an extended period of time. My thanks to my son Luc-Xuhao Maras for his patience. This book is dedicated to my father, Tomislav Maras, who loves a good intellectual and political debate, and has encouraged me to tackle issues that matter to the wider public.

Introduction

Few ideas are as contentious in the world of media and journalism as the ideal of objective reporting. The tradition of objectivity has been termed 'one of the great glories of American Journalism' (Barth 1951: 8), and considered 'beyond question the most important development in journalism since the Anglo-Saxon press became free from authority' (Brucker 1949: 269). Studies have shown that, up to the 1990s, US journalism was a 'stronghold of professional journalism dedicated to objective reporting' (Donsbach 1995: 30). For some, objectivity is the cement of good journalism, the 'cornerstone of the professional ideology of journalists in liberal democracies' (Lichtenberg 1991a: 216). For others, objectivity is a kind of deception, obscuring cultural, capitalistic or national bias behind talk of a neutral point of view; promoting faith in an external truth or ideal, an individualistic viewing position that doesn't exist. Objectivity has been described as a myth and a shibboleth (Bell 1998a: 16). It can be seen as a lifeblood, a high principle, or just a desire to be accurate.

Journalists themselves recognize how difficult objectivity, and the pursuit of it, can be (Myrick 2002: 52). They might suggest the equivalent of 'Of course, no one can be really objective. But we try to be fair' (Rosen 1993: 49; also Rosenthal 1969). In light of these reactions, if journalistic objectivity is an ideal, it is surely a complex one. What does it mean to strive for an ideal that can never be attained? Does it mean the ideal is worthless, or does it represent the ultimate journalistic virtue?

One thing to recognize about journalistic objectivity, however, is that the concept (and, indeed, the striving for it) is the product of history, linked to particular cultural formations, as well as the professional aspirations of journalists themselves. We shall explore these formations in the chapters to come. Whether the ideal is viewed positively or negatively, it has an important role in debates about journalism and the media and for that reason deserves close discussion.

Objectivity is a key concept in journalism, media and communication studies. Key works on objectivity in journalism are 'classics' in the fields of media sociology and journalism studies, such as those by Michael Schudson, James W. Carey, Gaye Tuchman, Dan Schiller and Herbert Gans (to mention only a few). This literature is broad, using approaches and ideas drawn from history, sociology, political science, organizational studies and analysis of media performance, not to mention the experiences and analyses of journalists themselves. This very diversity perhaps accounts for why we lack a book-length study of objectivity that incorporates an overview of the scholarly literature and the key research problems and questions in the area. This book seeks to fill this gap, surveying and evaluating some key issues in the rich and diverse scholarship of the area.

Objectivity is, at the same time, a key concept for media professionals and practitioners, from broadcasters to bloggers. Many figures have offered denunciations or defences of objectivity based on practical difficulties or concerns. Here, a different kind of gap emerges. An informed debate of the concept, even in practitioner contexts, falls short if we do not have a philosophically and historically nuanced view of how the concept has been defined and what it allows us to do. Few practitioners engage carefully with alternative arguments. In turn, only a few scholars address objectivity as an important aspect of media practice, and as an object of intense reflection by what Barbie Zelizer calls the 'interpretive community' of journalists (1993; see Reese 1990). We do not have an authoritative account of how this interpretive community has defined objectivity over the short and long term.

Despite an important turn in academic work to take journalism seriously (Zelizer 2004), professional and academic debates about objectivity from different eras are rarely discussed and compared. It may be possible, as Martin Conboy suggests, to look at objectivity in journalism discursively (2004: 4), but this is not often attempted 'head on'. Debate has become bogged down in competing programmatic claims that dismiss, affirm or reinvent objectivity from a particular viewpoint, leaving the reader with an often over-simplified perspective on a complex field of debate, scholarship and practice.

To overcome both of these gaps – the lack of an over-arching sense of the scholarship, and a deficit in relating theory to practice, and vice versa – I argue that we need to re-familiarize ourselves with what has been said by different scholars about objectivity, but also to extend a bridge between scholarship and practice. The task of bridging scholarship and practice is a formidable project in itself, since many scholars draw on deep insights about practice (not to mention their own experience as practitioners), while many practitioners draw on philosophical and theoretical ideas with great skill. In this context, I take a particular approach. My method is to engage with core ideas and questions and then make links to key debates from the professions, with the main project to draw out insights about objectivity as a form of media practice.

Debates around interpretation and interpretive reporting, and especially practitioner debates in the US from the McCarthy era, form a special focus here; and in what follows I encourage a re-assessment of the relationship between interpretive and objective reporting in this period. While many media historians engage in very specialized debates about objectivity and its origins, other writers no longer attempt to historicize objectivity, dealing primarily with post-McCarthy era versions in which 'straight' objectivity is regarded as passive and ineffectual. The 1950s in the US was a time when a positive connection between journalistic objectivity and the processes of democratic deliberation began to be strained: objectivity became, for many, part of the problem not part of the solution. The treatment of civil rights and desegregation in the 1950s (Davies 2005; Methvin 1975 [1970]), the social movements of the 1960s (Gitlin 2003 [1980]), the coverage and handling of the Vietnam War in the 1960s and the 1970s (see Hallin 1986), the civic disengagement of the 1980s (Merritt & Rosen 1998), further cast a cloud over the ideal of objectivity and its relevance as a norm. The consolidation of media ownership of the last fifty years (Ferré 2009: 21), combined with the promise of the Internet to provide diverse points of view and to allow collaboration, have introduced further criticism. Yet, as I argue, our assessment of objectivity since the 1950s has been influenced by views about interpretation that are not always accurate, and leave objectivity in a structurally passive position. Different waves of critique of objectivity have absorbed these views of objectivity and interpretation and frequently repeat the pattern.

In what follows I conceive of my role as both critical reader and guide, teasing out key issues in the scholarship as well as making links to different debates, such as those to do with the origins of objectivity, the status of facts, the place of values in objective reporting, interpretive reporting, the impact of 'new media', and objectivity as an international norm. As a critical reader, I see my task as being to highlight important works and themes, and to historicize and contextualize the concept. Like a prospector, this task involves fossicking through current and abandoned fields and 'passages' of research. In actuality, this 'mineshaft' is made up of a small library of works on journalistic objectivity; I shall purposefully draw on different works from this library more than once, and in different chapters, in order to link, compare and contrast different positions.

As a guide, my goal is to point out hidden or new pathways through the scholarly literature and a narrower selection of professional debates. To help with this task, each chapter of the book is focused around a key question that is often asked by newcomers to the area, including students, but also taken up by scholars researching objectivity. The questions are also linked to issues debated by practitioners. In effect, each of the questions addressed in this book could be explored differently depending on which country you live in. In posing each question, my aim is not to provide a simple yes or no answer, but to explore different issues and examine the way different writers respond to the topic.

Introduction

Objectivity as a trans-national norm?

While my primary purpose is to analyse, deconstruct and contextualize concepts of objectivity in journalism, objectivity is a practice that is institutionalized in different ways in different cultures. Here we encounter two key issues.

The first issue is how to analyse 'objectivity in journalism' across different cultures. Objectivity continues to retain a central, if disputed, place in discussions of journalism as a profession that works across national frontiers. The norm is now being recast in global terms (Ward 2011). However, objectivity in journalism did not arise in different countries at the same time, or emerge for the same reasons. In some cases it did not emerge at all, or emerged only through cross-cultural contact and diffusion. Objectivity is not discussed the same way everywhere. Stuart Allan suggests that in Britain ideals of neutral reporting tend to be left implicit, while in the US they were enshrined as a professional standard (2010: 44). In the US objectivity arises through developments in newspapers, where issues of efficiency, science and professionalization have been at the forefront (Vos 2012: 436). By contrast, in the UK, Australia, and to an extent Canada, public service broadcasting was a key site for articulating the objectivity norm. This leads to significant divergences in the way the 'drivers' or factors leading to objectivity are written about.

Allan tackles this particular problem of analysing objectivity in journalism across different cultures by treating 'objective journalism' as a trans-national norm that has distinct, recognizable form (2010: 28), usually linked to other norms (such as neutrality), or replaced by the norm of impartiality with which it is regarded as 'synonymous' (see Allan 1997: 309). Highlighting the importance of various economic, political and technological factors, Allan points to appeals to professionalism by journalists and a questioning of bias following the First World War as key factors for the wide dissemination of conventions of objective reporting (2010: 28). This book follows Allan in treating objectivity in journalism as an internationally recognizable concept that should be situated in relation to its context. It will also consider different ideas of objectivity and look carefully at the issue of how norms operate across cultures (see chapter 8).

A second issue has to do, specifically, with the question of whether the US case should be privileged. This issue is especially salient given the importance of de-westernizing media and communications study (Curran & Park 2000), but also the need to give specificity to the US case, and analyse it in a manner that recognizes the complexity of how objectivity has developed there. The American model of objectivity may be 'by far the best known professional model worldwide', but the critique of objectivity, combined with more careful attention to the 'ethnocentric' nature of journalism, makes any treatment of it as a 'representative specimen' political (Josephi 2007: 302).

Like the academic fields on which it draws, this book strives to strike a balance between trans-national and nationally bound perspectives on journalistic culture. This task is not always straightforward, however. It is important to recognize that 'there is not a singular paradigm for Western journalism, but instead multiple paradigms that grow from the national cultures in which they are embedded' (Berkowitz & Eko 2007: 779–80). There is also criticism of the elevation of objectivity to a 'universal norm' (Josephi 2007: 302). This said, debates around of objectivity in journalism in the US are often used as paradigmatic for understanding developments beyond the US. Thus, it becomes possible to look at the way objectivity is historically and culturally marked, but also explore the idea of objectivity as an Anglo-American invention (Chalaby 1996: 304). In this fashion, studies of objectivity in Canada (Hackett & Zhao 1998), Australia (Peterson 1985), France (Chalaby 1996) and the UK (Allan 1997), while highlighting important national differences in the way the public sphere and institutional structures operate, draw extensively on the rise of objectivity in the US as an important framework of analysis.

The 'linchpin' status of the US case is complex. On the one hand, the journalistic standards of nineteenth-century America can be traced back to their British and European sources (see Dicken-Garcia 1989: 3–4). On the other hand, UK penny dailies emulated mass circulation strategies forged across the Atlantic in the 1830s (Allan 2010: 34–5). There is little doubt that the hegemonic status of thinking about objectivity in the US context (and journalism studies more generally) has influenced the discussion of objectivity elsewhere; and since this constitutes a 'norm', this influence is both pervading and normative.

There is a temptation, especially when seeking to survey scholarship around objectivity, to focus on the US where the concept attracted an enormous amount of scholarly and professional attention for most of the twentieth century. While a fully comparative analysis of the development of objectivity in multiple countries would be desirable, we not only lack some of the basic historical and methodological groundwork for such a project, but there are conceptual problems with it, especially to do with how we study norms and their articulation, and evaluate their actual 'purchase' or strength in different cultural contexts (see chapter 8). This book responds to this issue by looking carefully at the problem of treating 'objective journalism' as a trans-national norm. As part of this approach, it treats the US case in its specificity, which means examining the different forces at work in the US context in some depth. It also uses US examples to tease out core issues that have wider significance. While it will be impossible to meet the needs of every reader, I broaden the discussion beyond the US where practicable and bring in cases and debates from other countries, and the themes raised here can certainly be explored and localized in greater depth.

Defining objectivity

Perhaps the most succinct definition of objectivity is provided by Walter Cronkite: 'Objectivity is the reporting of reality, of facts, as nearly as they can be obtained without the injection of prejudice and personal opinion' (quoted in Knowlton 2005b: 227). However, as with many definitions of objectivity, there are loose threads here which, if pulled, threaten to unravel the whole garment. Why does Cronkite decide to supplement the reporting of reality with the reporting of facts? What does 'as nearly as they can be obtained' actually mean? – sourced, comprehended, communicated? Defining objectivity in journalism is not straightforward. An 'inherently ambiguous' term (Tumber & Prentoulis 2003: 215), every definition depends on a different concept of what objectivity is, and how it should operate. In this study my aim is not to present a new definition of objectivity for a new media age. Nor is it a defence of objectivity in journalism. It offers, instead, a more serious appreciation of different models and frameworks for objectivity as a theory and a practice in order to create a space for more careful deliberation of the concept. This book considers the way objectivity in journalism has been defined in different ways at different times. The question of definition will inevitably become more complex as our discussion goes on, but for the moment we can draw on the following basic definition that looks at three different aspects of objectivity: values, process and language. This definition is 'basic' not because it is the simplest (indeed, each aspect could be elaborated in some detail), but because it captures 'key' aspects of objectivity in journalism, even though not every critic focuses on every aspect.

In terms of values, following Everette E. Dennis, we can link objectivity in journalism to three key aims:

1) Separating facts from opinion.
2) Presenting an emotionally detached view of the news.
3) Striving for fairness and balance . . . (Dennis & Merrill 1984: 111)

This description is echoed in Michael Schudson's view that objectivity 'guides journalists to separate facts from values and report only the facts' in a 'cool, rather than emotional' tone, 'taking pains to represent fairly each leading side' (2001: 150). It aligns with ideas of objectivity as recounting events in a disinterested or impersonal way, aligned with precepts of neutrality and balance.

Objectivity is clearly multi-faceted. It is, as a result, often articulated in a cluster of terms such as impartiality, neutrality, accuracy, fairness, honesty, commitment to the truth, depersonalization and balance. Others highlight values such as the reporting of news without bias or slant, the describing of reality accurately, presentation of the main points, even-handedness (see McQuail 1992: 184). Some go further to link the presentation of facts with an idea of mirroring or reflecting reality. Objectivity can relate semantically to a very wide field indeed. In Schiller's terms, objectivity is 'polysemic' or has many possible meanings, and, furthermore, is open to different activations. He warns us that this openness makes the concept hard to grasp: 'its universality as an ideal might shield open disparities in its application and interpretation' (1981: 196). This perhaps accounts for why it is difficult to have the final word on objectivity, and why discussion of it is on-going.

It is important to note, however, that objectivity does not just operate at the level of values, but also procedures. Jeremy Iggers suggests that the values and procedures do not always come into play at the same time, and that 'there are many journalists who practice procedural objectivity without any ... epistemological commitments' (1998: 92). In other words, journalists do not need to commit philosophically to objectivity in order to practise objective journalism. This procedural dimension might include providing a contrasting, balancing, or alternative viewpoint, using supporting evidence, ensuring close attribution through quoting, and finally organizing the story into a familiar news format (Miraldi 1990: 16; also Kessler & McDonald 1989: 21–3; Ward 2004: 18). These procedures are central to the commitment to verification and truth underpinning objective methods, but at the same time, as practices, they are open to variation across different news organizations.

There is a third important aspect of objectivity in journalism, which is arguably the least well understood. It has to do with the way objectivity forms a 'language game'. Different scholars have referred to this language game in different ways, but all of them point to the link between journalistic objectivity and specific strategies of re-presenting events, facts and details. Jay Rosen, for instance, highlights the way objectivity operates as a 'form of persuasion': 'It tries to persuade all possible users of the account that the account can be trusted because it is *unadorned*' (Rosen 2010a). Stylistically it plays to facts and not opinions. It is a 'system of signs' designed to give the impression of authority and trust, especially in core descriptions and information such as who, what, when, etc.

Schiller tackles the language game from a different direction. He argues that objectivity, at least in the sense understood from the mid-twentieth century, functions as an 'invisible frame' through which the story comes into existence on its own, independently of the reporter (1981: 1). This term captures a complex communication situation in which journalists 'report' rather than create the news. This situation is central to conceptions of the press as being above 'the "wrangling" and conflict of the public-political arena' (Kaplan 2002: 169; see also Hackett & Zhao 1998: 143; Iggers 1998: 109).

All news is constructed and governed by discursive conventions. As Schiller describes it,

> an invisible frame brackets news reports as a particular kind of public knowledge and a key category in popular epistemology. News reports repeatedly claim that, ideally at least, they recount events without the intrusion of value judgements or symbols. News is . . . a report on reality, and hence not really a story at all, but merely the facts – this is the claim. (1981: 2)

This invisible frame is not meant to be seen, or crossed. Indeed, Schiller argues it conceals 'the very presence of conventions and thus masks the patterned structure of news'. The frame is defined in terms of a commitment to the world 'out there' in which facts exist externally and independently of the observer. As such, it forms an important aspect of the procedures supporting objectivity, along with the 'reality effect' (Barthes 1986) that much objective reporting seeks to promote.

Another aspect of this communication situation, however, is that the invisible frame gives rise to reader expectations that a report will 'produce a neutral, impartial reaction in the reader' (Noyes 1953). This reaction is difficult to define categorically, and can vary greatly depending on cultural perspective. Nevertheless, if breached, it offends a sense of fairness, and gives rise to declarations of partiality, imbalance and bias. The reader is meant to decide the truth. However, the reader's sense of fairness is linked to issues of style and format, which in themselves depend on familiarity and even habit. So, although objectivity is habitually linked to the inverted pyramid form of presenting the news, an extremely impressionistic and interpretive report can meet the test of being objective if 'the reader knows what is being done to him' (Noyes 1953: 63), and issues of accuracy can be reconciled with issues of authenticity. This accounts for why the new journalists of the 1970s were able to work with 'a strange sort of objectivity' (Wolfe 1973: 66).

While heeding Schiller's advice that objectivity is diverse in its application and interpretation, these three aspects – values, procedures and language – comprise a broad, basic definition of journalistic objectivity. With all three aspects in view we can suggest that they define an 'idea-complex', that is, '*a general model for conceiving, defining, arranging and evaluating news texts, news practices and news institutions*' (Hackett & Zhao 1998: 86, emphasis in original).

Why does objectivity in journalism matter?

Given the intense discussion of objectivity in journalism by scholars and professionals, and its complex history, another question presents itself: why should we care about objectivity in journalism? Broadly speaking, there are four important reasons.

The first reason why objectivity matters is related to politics and government. Much has been written about the relationship between journalism and democracy and the role of the press – a great deal of it in dispute. Nevertheless, for Stephen J. A. Ward, 'objectivity is an essential norm for responsible journalistic communication in the public interest', and is a bulwark against authoritarianism and obscurantism (2004: 321, 318). As Schiller notes, 'with its universalistic intent, its concern for public rationality based on equal access to the facts, objectivity harboured a profoundly democratic promise' (1981: 181).

In the 1920s Walter Lippmann draws a direct link between journalism, democracy and objectivity, when he suggests in

Liberty and the News that 'the present crisis of western democracy is a crisis in journalism'. He observes that questions were arising about world affairs that demanded facts not readily available (1920: 4–5). His solution involved, in part, turning to objectivity. Lippmann highlights a 'loss of contact with objective information. Public as well as private reason depends upon it' (1920: 57). He advocates better journalism training around the 'ideal of objective testimony' (1920: 82). Lippmann's argument points to the importance of the provision of impartial information in society, and defines one key way in which objectivity has mattered, and (depending on one's point of view) may continue to matter.

A second reason why objectivity matters relates to 'media power', a term which means more than just 'the power of the press'. I use it in several senses, including: the capacity of the media to 'do' certain things, its power within (and some would say 'over') society, also power struggles between different parts of the industry and profession. Media power describes how the press and journalism occupies its field, and has to do with the way public discourse is imagined, and promoted or controlled, via terms such as objectivity.

Power also operates on the level of professional standards. Every standard relies upon, or is defined by, a realm of 'hack' work that is disparaged. However, the line between the professional and hack can be difficult to determine. Objectivity has long been linked to a move away from the excesses of sensational and 'yellow' journalism towards 'respectable' journalism. But this movement can be viewed as part of a deeper struggle for power in the mediasphere. Historical research on objectivity is crucial here because of the way it shines a light on the links between objectivity and commercialism and the popular press, and provides a fuller picture of the interaction between the so-called 'respectable' and 'popular' press.

Even today, debates between quality and tabloid newspapers take place within what Pippa Norris terms a 'media malaise' framework in which the popular press is linked to moral decline (2000: 5). They ignore or downplay the historical ties between objectivity and the tabloid commercial press (see chapter 1). Yet, arguably, the bullying tactics and 'moral wars' (Pray 1855: 264) around the penny press of the 1830s–1840s are still evident in debates around objective versus sensational reporting.

The third reason why objectivity matters relates to media performance. As Andie Tucher notes, 'Clearly people want the press to appear objective. The best proof of that lies in their frequent complaints that it doesn't' (1994: 202). For all of the criticism of the concept, the 'effort at objectivity and neutrality is important' (Glasgow University Media Group 1976: xii). In the 1940s, when the Commission on Freedom of the Press, better known as the Hutchins Commission, stated famously that 'It is no longer enough to report the *fact* truthfully. It is now necessary to report *the truth about the fact*', this was in the context of a debate about objectivity as not just a goal, but a fetish (Siebert et al. 1956: 88). 'Objective' is currently an active criterion of evaluation for each Wikipedia site. Denis McQuail makes measuring objectivity a core task of his book *Media Performance* (1992). He notes that, despite the controversy surrounding the concept, objectivity is 'valued by the news audience for its practical benefits, since it is key to trustworthiness and reliability and plays an important part in assessments of performance by the media public' (1992: 183).

Within the area of media studies known as 'media performance' analysis, objectivity is seen as a core communication value, helping to situate the public interest claims of different agents (1992: 28). McQuail reminds us of the difficulty of the task of assessing objectivity, both in relation to audience expectations and the standards of performance in place: which makes 'application of objectivity as a criterion of performance itself less than fully objective' (1992: 191). This explains why other terms such as 'accuracy' and 'impartiality' are taking its place. The latter are regarded as more directly measurable, allowing the researcher to place to one side the very difficult organizational and cultural factors that McQuail discusses as part of his judgement that objectivity has an 'ambiguous standing' as a standard. He writes:

> Objectivity itself can only be assessed, with varying degrees of approximation, by way of indicators. All the research procedures described call for value judgements about priorities, criteria of performance and

13

choice of indicators. The 'objective assessment of objectivity' is only possible within severe limits set by another set of values (our own or those we adopt). (1992: 236)

Evaluating media performance occurs within 'cultural settings' that are defining and delimiting. However, despite its 'ambiguous standing', objectivity remains for many a key concept when discussing the responsibility and accountability of the media.

A fourth reason why objectivity in journalism matters has to do with ethics. An important aspect of ethics relates to judgement, especially in terms of the selection of sources, and the application of 'news values'. While it is common for objectivity to be described in terms of ensuring that value judgements do not intrude on the story (White 2000: 390), objectivity also operates as a form of judgement. This judgement refers not only to how stories are handled, and deemed newsworthy, but also to the way some events or facts are deemed to fall inside or outside of the category of 'news'. Judgement relates, then, to how news journalists construct their 'news net', and navigate the web of facts, and gossip (Tuchman 1978). Of course, some facts are very difficult to verify, which leads, potentially, to a series of disputed claims from different parties, none of which are authoritative. Judgement comes into play in seeing the relationship between the facts and the truth, but also the facts and the shape or momentum of the story. Bad judgement can lead to a crossing of the 'invisible frame' whereby the journalist inserts him or herself into the story, or even becomes a 'player' in the story (an occupational hazard for the political reporter).

Ethics also relates to the 'compact' between readers, journalists and news organizations (Fray 2011). William Morgan, ombudsman for the Canadian Broadcasting Corporation, suggests that 'objectivity', 'balance' and 'fairness' are really just words. 'None of them is easy to define or to guarantee or even to achieve' (1992). He reminds us that beneath the debate about words, however, is a more important issue to do with norms. He connects objectivity to what can be termed a 'regulative ideal', which has to do with the way journalists shape their work to fulfil their responsibility to the organization, their subjects, and their readers and audiences. Jaap van Ginneken sees this as an important aspect of objectivity: 'the notion of objectivity . . . is always implicitly related to the notion of (an agreement between) relevant audiences' (1998: 43; see also Kieran 1997: 46).

There is no doubt, as we shall see in the next section, that while objectivity may have once defined credibility, the ethic of objectivity is today contentious as a norm or standard of journalism. But that is not to say that it holds no lessons for us, or is not useful (given its still wide public recognition), or indeed, cannot be re-crafted into a meaningful ethic. Indeed, if objectivity in journalism can be said to embody, in a particular time and place, a compact between writers and readers in a relationship to do with the production and consumption of information and the public good, then it seems that a compact of this nature can still be vital in an age when information travels at the speed of light and via innumerable networks. In the late nineteenth and early twentieth century, objectivity in journalism represented a response to a particular set of technical, economic, cultural and social problems and issues. While those problems may have taken on new forms, we can still gain a great deal from looking at objectivity as a certain kind of invention, one that can inform the way we tackle the technical, economic, informational, discursive and cultural problems of our own time.

An unpopular ethical touchstone

One of the dilemmas that confronts any study of objectivity in journalism is that the term is infrequently codified into legislation or regulations. Objectivity is currently not a popular concept in regulatory circles, and 'less secure in the role of ethical touchstone than it has been' (Overholser 2006: 11). Ward notes that objectivity was not put forward as a principle or guideline when the Canadian Association of Journalists redrafted their code in 2002. 'Instead, members cited related concepts: accuracy, credibility, fairness, independence, and so on' (2004: 251). This accords with a sense that these latter terms are more amenable to evaluation and measurement through surveys, economic and political study, or content analysis.

The code of the UK National Union of Journalists, last amended in 1998, does not include objectivity (National Union of Journalists 2011). The Society of Professional Journalists in the US did not have objectivity in its code until 1973, when it finally drafted one after borrowing its original code from the American Society of Newspaper Editors in 1926. The now superseded 1973 code includes the concept of objectivity in the preamble, where it declares that 'responsibilities carry obligations that require journalists to perform with intelligence, objectivity, accuracy, and fairness'. Also in Part IV Accuracy and Objectivity, after declaring 'Truth is our ultimate goal' in the first article, the code states in the second article that

> Objectivity in reporting the news is another goal, which serves as the mark of an experienced professional. It is a standard of performance toward which we strive. We honor those who achieve it. (Society of Professional Journalists 1973)

Surviving the 1984 and 1987 revisions of the code, objectivity remained in the code until September 1996, when it was replaced by a broader commitment to professional integrity and the ideal to 'Seek Truth and Report It: Journalists should be honest, fair and courageous in gathering, reporting and interpreting information' (Society of Professional Journalists 1996).

Objectivity has never appeared in the Australian Journalists' Association code of ethics (the association incorporated into the Media, Entertainment and Arts Alliance in 1992) despite revisions of the code in 1984 and 1999 (Media, Entertainment & Arts Alliance 1999). In the Australian context, the sole regulatory appearance objectivity makes is in the legislation governing the Australian Broadcasting Corporation (ABC) (see chapter 8). The British Broadcasting Corporation's 2006 Royal Charter and Agreement does not require objectivity explicitly, although it appears in editorial guidelines around use of language in the discussion of terrorism (British Broadcasting Corporation 2011b).

Polish media workers embraced 'a principle of objectivity' in their 1995 Media Ethics Charter, 'which means that the author depicts the reality independently of his/her own views, reports reliably different points of view' (Polish Journalists' Association (SDP), et al. 1995). The term also appears in South Africa, where the Independent Broadcasting Authority Act 153 of 1993 (as amended in 2002) states in its regulations for Party Election Broadcasts and Political Advertisements 7.3. 'Every broadcaster who transmits news or current affairs programmes in respect of the elections shall do so in an impartial and objective manner and in a manner which treats all parties fairly'. It has nevertheless attracted controversy for the way it is perceived to be linked to Western, liberal views of media freedom, and also because of the way it was used to discredit reporting by black journalists in the apartheid years (see Mazwai 2002; *BBC Monitoring Africa* 2003; Harber 2003).

Allan suggests that the meaning of concepts such as 'objectivity' and 'impartiality' are historically specific. Accordingly, 'It follows that each concept . . . will continue to evolve as the constellation of these forces changes across the public sphere'. Indeed, Allan provocatively suggests that with the rise of reality TV and 'infotainment' programming, 'the end of "objectivity" and "impartiality" as the guiding principles of an ethic of public service may soon be in sight' (1997: 319; see also Turner 1996). Iggers suggests, however, that an 'obituary for objectivity may be premature' (1998: 91). Before we consign objectivity to the code of ethics graveyard, we should note the way that other terms, perhaps more suited to the legal climate of the day, such as impartiality, work alongside the norm. Indeed, Geneva Overholser notes that ethical concepts such as accountability are increasing in importance (2006: 11). Such terms can either work to bolster the objectivity norm, or work as the regulatory 'face' of the norm.

Starting points

More than most topics, the study of objectivity in journalism is influenced by one's starting point. These are, indeed, abundant.

You can start with the philosophy, or newsroom practice. You can start with bias, or 'just the facts'. You can focus on the innovations of editors in a 'great man' approach to history, or focus on social processes. You can look at the topic from the perspective of the editors and publishers, or through the experience of the reporter. You can focus on great metropolitan papers in New York, or train your eye towards papers in smaller cities and towns. You can start with the formidable scholarship in the area, or follow the cut and thrust of professional debates. The different ways into the topic can be bewildering.

Indeed, the different chapters of this book represent different ways of entering into the topic of objectivity in journalism. Some focus on history, others philosophy, or ethics. The reader is open to engage with the chapters in the sequence of their choice. So, for example, some readers may choose to begin with the chapters on the objections and defences to objectivity, before considering the history in detail. Others will benefit from having a deeper historical background before considering the other chapters.

One starting point that I shall decline at the outset is any simplistic binary of objectivity and subjectivity. Talking about objectivity in journalism usually leads to a discussion of subjectivity. Turning to subjectivity is, in some respects, a good idea. It raises issues of direct relevance to objectivity: neutrality, observation, perception and experience. However, it can restrict discussion by placing objectivity and subjectivity in too neat and static an opposition, leading to the seemingly inevitable conclusion that objectivity is impossible because we are all subjective and biased. What can disappear from view are more complex ways of approaching the concept of journalistic objectivity: its origins and histories, the philosophies and institutions behind it, its relationship to practice (see Nolan & Marjoribanks 2006).

Another starting point that I am mindful of is the concept of objectivity itself. This book has a clear focus on objectivity in journalism, but the fact is that objectivity 'in general' is a powerful cultural idea, one that has its roots in the foundations of Western science and the enlightenment. Indeed, the precise meaning of this broader idea of objectivity is still being debated. Objectivity as an idea has a wide-ranging influence across a number of different areas, philosophy, science (Daston & Galison 2007), law (Kramer 2007), history (Novick 1988), and of course journalism. The characterization of objectivity as a form of 'knowledge that bears no trace of the knower', a kind of 'blind sight, seeing without inference, interpretation, or intelligence' (Daston & Galison 2007: 17) will describe for many readers its main features.

Yet, close inspection of the nature of objectivity in specific contexts can yield important insights. It is interesting to note that in the seventeenth century the terms 'objectivity and 'subjectivity' in fact had the opposite meaning. '"Objective" referred to things as they are presented to consciousness, whereas "subjective" referred to things in themselves' (Daston & Galison 2007: 29). As Lorraine Daston and Peter Galison show in their study of scientific objectivity, the description of objectivity as 'blind sight' may capture objectivity as a form of perception but misses something: namely that objectivity is also an 'ethic', one dedicated to preserving the 'artifact or variation that would have been erased in the name of truth'. Blind sight is not, therefore, an end in itself, but a way to attend to detail and the character of the object. As an 'epistemic virtue', to use their term, objectivity as a form of knowledge is not the same as truth or certainty, but an ethic of study itself, a safeguard against false assumptions and filters, affirming values such as truth and variation, binding the conduct of the scientist.

If 'classic' scientific objectivity aspires to a knowledge 'unmarked by prejudice or skill, fantasy or judgement, wishing or striving' (Daston & Galison 2007: 17), objectivity in journalism finds a different ground, producing variants of objectivity focused on facts of public interest, the 'story', the separation of fact from opinion, or at other times focusing on political neutrality. Underpinning these are precepts about democratic discourse, and the public interest. Any study of journalistic objectivity should strive to look at what makes these forms of objectivity distinctive and unique.

Objectivity in journalism can be a difficult concept to grasp not just because of the long history of objectivity, but also because it is closely linked to others such as bias and impartiality. In what follows I trace out the particular identity and development of objectivity in journalism beyond what has been dubbed the objectivity–bias 'paradigm' (Hackett 1984). Objectivity is very commonly raised in discussions of bias and balance, but not always closely examined in its own terms. Bias and balance are, as Guy Starkey insists, 'mutually exclusive' terms. 'Put simplistically, balance is the absence of bias, and bias is the absence of balance' (2007: xvi). Balance requires objectivity. 'Being objective means not placing undue emphasis on one part of a representation, in order to distort it, for whatever motive' (Starkey 2007: xvi). Bias is conventionally seen as inimical to objectivity – although objectivity has itself been seen as biased (Glasser 1992; McQuail 1992: 191). However, this matrix represents a somewhat one-dimensional view of objectivity, which can be explored in relation to procedures of selection, and presentation of news, as well as a norm of ethical behaviour and professional ideology. Bias and balance are arguably not mutually exclusive from the point of view of media practice, where the work of relating facts and the statement of views of different parties is part of the same procedure (see Iggers 1998: 93). Following Robert A. Hackett this book seeks to reach beyond the bias 'paradigm' and make objectivity itself the object of investigation (1984: 253).

This introduction to journalistic objectivity tries to summarize a range of arguments and perspectives from what has become an expansive, but also very fascinating and rewarding area of study. Readers of this book may find it unusual that, although it draws on critical theory, it does not simply denounce objectivity as impossible. Although I do not deny that critical theory can offer a position from which to legitimately object to objectivity – and, indeed, I discuss numerous critiques of objectivity in what follows – my main purpose is to historicize and contextualize objectivity in journalism through discussion of key texts and debates. In doing so, I have attempted to not only give greater perspective to objectivity but also to the critique of this concept and practice in order to highlight gaps or unresolved issues. I also look at some of the ways objectivity is being defended and reinvented. What I try to show is that objectivity in journalism is not simply a philosophy that can be denounced or secured. It defines or actualizes ways of knowing that have impact in the world, influence the nature of reporting, and shape the professional underpinnings of journalism. In each case, objectivity is constructed or constituted in different ways, opening up (or closing down as the case may be) different possibilities for media practice.

Note on terminology: *Because objectivity operates as a concept in history, literature, law, and the social sciences as well, I refer to journalistic objectivity. I use this concept, rather than the idea of 'objective reporting', firstly because the idea of reporting has a history of its own, and secondly because questions of objectivity extend beyond a particular approach to reporting.*

1

Why and when did journalistic objectivity arise?

Perhaps no question is as central to an understanding of objectivity in journalism than that of its origins. Objectivity in journalism cannot be traced to a single 'magic moment' (Schudson 2001: 167). Media historians have put 'great man' versions of history into disrepute, questioning the fetish of singular origins (Winston 1999). Nevertheless, 'why and when did objectivity arise?' remains an essential context question without which our understanding of objectivity in journalism will lack a link to history and culture. However, the question of origins is a challenging one, both on the level of the factors driving the development of objectivity and also the dating of objectivity. This chapter teases out the debates around these two core issues.

What follows draws extensively on the work of James W. Carey, Michael Schudson and Daniel Schiller, as some of the foremost historians of objectivity in the US. But it also weaves into the discussion significant work by Stuart Allan in *News Culture* (2004); Stephen J. A. Ward in *The Invention of Journalism Ethics: The Path to Objectivity and Beyond* (2004); Richard L. Kaplan in *Politics and the American Press: The Rise of Objectivity, 1865–1920* (2002); Gerald J. Baldasty in *The Commercialization of News in the Nineteenth Century* (1992); and Robert A. Hackett and Yuezhi Zhao in *Sustaining Democracy? Journalism and the Politics of Objectivity* (1998), all of which engage deeply, and often divergently, with the same research questions even if their projects are different.

The drivers of journalistic objectivity

Objectivity in journalism emerges out of a complex of factors. A full account of these factors immediately confronts the two key issues discussed in detail in the introduction, the difficulty of studying objectivity in journalism across cultures, and the treatment of the US case.

Several arguments have been put forward to explain the development of journalistic objectivity in the US and beyond. Building on Allan (2010: 28) and Michael Schudson (1978), the key arguments that will be discussed here have to do with professionalization, technology, commercialization and politics. None stands as a clear master-narrative and all of them have been contested, or subject to further work. These arguments work in quite general, deterministic and abstract ways; and in that sense they have limitations. Nevertheless, they remain useful in forming a broader picture of the different forces at work in the development of objectivity in journalism.

While my focus in the discussion that follows will be on the US case, which has been explored in depth by media historians, each of these 'drivers' point to broader research trajectories that can be drawn on to open up wider analysis of objectivity in journalism, regardless of national context. It should be stressed I am not advocating a point of view that objectivity was an 'inevitable outcome' of any of these particular forces (Schudson & Anderson 2009: 92). Rather, surveying the different arguments allows us to engage with the complex forces influencing journalistic objectivity, and to explore their interaction.

The professionalization argument

This argument sees professionalization of reporting as a key factor in the emergence and development of objectivity. As such it is tied in with standards of good practice and the status of journalism. Professionalism and professionalization are themselves large areas of study. Surveying the literature, Michael Schudson and Chris Anderson chart an important disciplinary orientation away from 'traits'-based research that seeks to determine whether journalism is or is not a profession on the grounds of its knowledge base and area of expertise, towards an approach that looks at the conditions and circumstances 'in which journalists attempt to turn themselves into professional people' (2009: 90).

The professionalization argument is often localized around the state of reporting in major US cities in the late nineteenth and early twentieth centuries (see Baldasty 1992: 89). As journalists came to consider themselves professionals, the issue of an appropriate model of professionalism arose, with objectivity playing a key role (Janowitz 1975: 618). 'Best practice' suggested the reporter presents the facts, preferably covering all sides of the issue, allowing the reader to decide (although there is disagreement over whether this represents the highest standard of professional performance; Carey 1997 [1969]: 138).

The argument that objectivity emerges and develops through professionalization is powerful because it helps explain the nature of modern journalism, but also the context in which it operates. Professionalization is considered a pre-requisite for, but also the goal of, debates around objectivity. Another strong aspect of the professionalization argument is that it foregrounds issues of occupational and industrial uplift and integrity: it allows us to think of objectivity in progressive ethical terms such as virtue, standards and excellence. It permits us to focus on issues of education. It also works in relation to concepts of objectivity as an ideal (Schudson 1978; see below).

Carey provides one of the most useful characterizations of the professionalization argument in the following passage:

> Objective reporting became the fetish of American journalism in the period of rapid industrialisation. Originally the development of this form of journalism was grounded in a purely commercial motive: the need of the mass newspaper to serve politically heterogeneous audiences without alienating any significant segment of the audience. The practice apparently began with the wire services. ... This commercially grounded strategy of reporting was subsequently rationalized into a canon of professional competence and ideology of professional responsibility. (Carey 1997 [1969]: 137–8)

Servicing 'politically heterogeneous audiences' demanded a radically new commercial approach that was (for Carey) subsequently rationalized into an image of the professional (see also Bennett 1988: 123).

Why did this rewriting occur? Carey suggests that in the late nineteenth century reporters were trained largely under an apprenticeship system and reporting was seen as a trade. Professionalization was part of an effort by journalists to gain increased status, credibility and, indeed, trust. The pay-off for professionalization can be seen as social, but also corporate. Objectivity marked the work of journalists as organizationally distinctive, more highly developed; news was special, and different from advertising (which itself forms a kind of news). Objectivity arises in this work situation as what has been described as a kind of contract: it is a 'bargain' in which 'journalists gain their independence and in exchange they give up their voice' (Rosen 1993: 48; see also Hallin & Mancini 2004: 221; Gans 1979: 183; McDonald 1975 [1971]: 69).

With college training, journalists had greater appreciation and awareness of scientific values and developed what could be seen as a worship of facts (Schudson 1978: 68). Objectivity at this time was sweeping across a number of academic disciplines, and justifying journalism in social science terms thus proved attractive as a means of gaining institutional legitimacy (Beasley & Mirando 2005: 184). The emergence of journalism schools cemented the link between an emphasis on facts and science and new models of journalism. As Carey puts it, the 'conventions of objective reporting were institutionalized when they were developed in universities beginning in the 1890s' (1997 [1969]: 138). In a unique alignment of interests, 'the press moved to show the public that it was serious about improving practices by bolstering professional training and enacting codes of ethics', while educators sought to meet the demand for 'reporters who were ethically sensitive as well as technically proficient' by focusing on journalistic ethics (Ferré 2009: 19; see also Vos 2012). In this manner, objectivity was fast-tracked as a way to characterize the profession, as well as indicating a point of mutual interest for practitioners and educationalists.

One of the benefits of the professionalization thesis is that it links objectivity to broader social change: firstly, to what James W. Carey terms the 'communications revolution' and, secondly, to the rise of professions. In relation to the former, Carey sees this 'as a revolution in commercial and popular culture which reorganized the basis on which art, information, and culture were made available' (1997 [1969]: 129). It leads to the rise of a national media and a 'mass' audience but also the emergence of a 'new social role' which Carey terms the 'professional communicator'. 'The professional communicator takes the messages, ideas, and purposes of a source and converts them into a symbolic strategy designed to inform or persuade an ultimate audience' (1997 [1969]: 133). Advertising executives, public relations practitioners and journalists all qualify as professional communicators, albeit with different degrees of professional autonomy and freedom.

In terms of the rise of the professions, in the late 1890s to early 1900s, US society, especially the new middle classes, underwent a widespread professionalization (Wiebe 1967: 127; see also Bledstein 1976). The growth of university education in journalism, and rise of professional associations, gave further impetus to professionalization (Carey 1997 [1969]: 136). Skills and cultivated talent became the new basis for social order. With professionalization came the need to define a field and assume authority or control over a discipline.

One significant aspect of the professionalization argument is that it can be studied focusing on positive, but also negative impacts. Indeed, Carey's account of professionalization is important precisely because he points to its adverse effects.

> It is important to recognize that the canons of objective reporting turn the journalist into a professional communicator, from an independent observer and critic to a relatively passive link in a communication chain that records the passing scene for audiences. (1997 [1969]: 138)

For Carey, objectivity impacts on the literary and interpretive aspects of journalistic work. He writes of a 'conversion downwards' whereby the 'role is de-intellectualized and technicalized' into a mere reporter (1997 [1969]: 137). Objectivity compromises the independence of the journalist, giving new prominence to sources. This leads the reporter into a subservient and technical 'lapdog' relationship to political and corporate authority (Kaplan 2002: 193). For Daniel C. Hallin and Paolo Mancini, the dominant form of professionalism in North America has a particular impact on the autonomy of the journalist. Objectivity has a key place in placing boundaries on autonomy in a way that is not replicated in the UK, for example (2004: 226).

There are three main weaknesses in the professionalization argument. The first is its explanatory power. As Dan Schiller notes, 'journalistic professionalism can not constitute a sufficient explanation for the appearance of the convention' (1981: 3). Which is to say that commercial, technological and political factors are equally important to the development of objectivity.

This is related to a second issue, raised by Schudson, which is that journalism is an 'uninsulated profession' lacking the forms of advanced training and social control that other professions use to protect their autonomy. Unlike professions such as medicine or law, journalism is a difficult occupation to 'close off' intellectually and in practice, and it has an unusually 'public' relationship to the client and to politics. This 'uninsulated' character impacts on the professional status of journalism, and constantly complicates professional aspiration.

A third issue with the professionalization argument is that it tends to treat the space of journalism as uniform: publishers, editors and reporters are seen more or less on equivalent terms, when in fact there exists significant levels of criticism and negotiation between these different actors in 'the profession' (Tuchman 1972). There is a potentially wide gap between aspirational statements of codes of ethics and the lived reality of reporters and editors. In this respect, the professionalization argument requires a more critical account of labour politics. This is important, for example, to understand the 1930s when objectivity is linked to the struggle against unionization and organizational control. These conditions 'gave publishers reason to promote the objectivity norm even if they had done little or nothing to invent it' (Schudson 2001: 163; see also Morrison & Tremewan 1992: 124). Hallin and Mancini highlight how, in this context, 'objectivity provided a mechanism of control over journalists' (2004: 221).

The technology argument

Advocates of the technology argument see technology as a key causal factor in the development of objectivity in journalism. Technology has been an ever-present consideration for journalism. As Allan notes, 'the use of the steam press in the 1830s was followed by the introduction of the Hoe rotary press in 1846, thereby enabling the mass production of newspapers on a scale never seen before' (2010: 35). Perhaps no technology has been given greater significance than the telegraph, which is closely intertwined with a shift in our understanding of communication and geography, the development of national railway systems, and the dissemination of market information and commercial news (Carey 1989: 201–30; Pray 1855: 364). Introduced in the 1840s, with the first inter-city experiments in wiring stories dating from 1844, the telegraph rapidly found a place in news transmission. The Mexican–American War (1846–48) gave impetus to its use (Allan 1997: 305), as did the founding of the news cooperatives such as The Associated Press in 1946. For Donald L. Shaw, in a study of Wisconsin newspapers that is regarded as a keystone of the technology argument, 'increasing emphasis upon impartial gathering and reporting of news' and 'growing independence from party control' correlate with 'increasing amounts of wire news' (1967: 4).

However, there is another layer of the technology argument, specifically focused on written language and the form of journalism itself. Indeed, perhaps one of the most valuable aspects of the technological thesis is to encourage reflection on our understanding of the *form* of the news (see Conboy 2010: 137–8). The wire services supposedly led to a lean, unadorned 'objective' style; a form of writing stripped of locality, regional touches and colloquialisms. This is understandable given that the price per character was one cent (Kielbowicz 1987: 35). Wires employed factual, denotative and functional language, leaning towards the inverted

pyramid form. Andrew Porwancher suggests that 'because telegraph lines were expensive and often failed in mid-report, journalists transmitted the most important information first so that
their papers could still print the stories even if they failed to receive
all of them. Editors also preferred the standardized format of the
inverted pyramid because they could easily rework an article'
(2011: 191).

Carey argues 'the telegraph reworked the nature of written language' but also 'the nature of awareness itself' (1989: 210). Over
time, our sense of the facts became linked to this informational
form of language, so that we know 'the facts' mainly through this
'code'. As a result, the language of news becomes standardized,
which is to say that different styles of reportage and storytelling no
longer counted for news in the same way. 'By elevating objectivity
and facticity into cardinal principles, the penny press abandoned
explanation as a primary goal' (Carey 1997 [1986]: 161). This
style has limits: it restricts the extent to which one can express a
perspective in the story, or explore the world as an essayist might
(see White 2000). It sets up explanation and analysis as separate
activities and, in doing so, dampens reflection on alternative framings of the story, as well as overt reflection on factors such as
ideology, class or politics.

Carey's work is commonly associated with the technology argument. Although he is no straightforward advocate, his research
into journalism history, technology and communication takes
him deeply into the topic. Carey highlights how the wire services
stripped the local, the regional and the colloquial away from
journalism, demanding something closer to the scientific or informational mode of journalism. He famously states 'the origins of
objectivity may be sought, therefore, in the necessity of stretching
language in space over the long lines of Western Union' (1989:
210).

There are risks with a technologically deterministic account
of social change; namely that it can discount other factors. One
might think that the speed of information being sent over a news
wire would lead to a new emphasis on timely information, the
latest news. But it was the penny press that promoted the move

towards the daily news, and a focus on timeliness and breaking stories as a selling point. It was through the penny press that all news started to be treated as though it came out of a stock market ticker machine. As Carey puts it, 'the telegraph cemented everything the "penny press" set in motion' (1997 [1986]: 160). Nevertheless, while we should remain wary of technological determinism – and indeed some have called for a re-examination of the idea that objective reporting was the result of increased use of telegraph and news wires (Stensaas 1986: 58) – the technology argument highlights often-neglected organizational arrangements, such as the way correspondents become 'stringers' who supply bare facts, and issues to do with the increased volume of news (see Carey 1997 [1986]: 160–1).

Some caveats should be placed around the technology argument. The first has to do with the assumptions regarding the technology. Early services were not restricted to the telegraph, but combined pony express, stagecoach and telegraph (Pyle 2005). Richard L. Kielbowicz describes the telegraph evocatively as a 'tangle of technologies' (1987: 34). 'Even in the face of instantaneous communication by telegraph, the comparatively primitive postal service continued to be of great value as a news relayer' (1987: 26). The language of dispatches could vary depending on the rate and time of day, from simply dropping common words such as 'the', to inverted pyramids, to in fact adding details (Schiller 1981: 5). Indeed, biased and false dispatches were known to be sent (Schiller 1981: 4; see also Sinclair 1919: 150–75). On top of this, it was accepted journalistic practice of the era, as Edwin Shuman explains in one of the first handbooks on journalism, to turn bare announcements into articles by supplying 'the missing details from . . . [one's] imagination' (1894: 120). In other words, the introduction of the telegraph did not occur in a vacuum and did not lead to a total uniformity in style and format.

A second caveat has to do with the risk of confusing the technology with the development of cooperative newsgathering associations, the history and development of which are complex (see Shaw 1967: 9). For Edwin Emery, the agencies became the 'common denominators' of a standardized conception of impartial journalism. Their influence was also felt on the level of style and news writing (Emery 1972: 465–6). From these non-partisan accounts 'grew the concept of objective reporting which has permeated American journalism to the present' (Siebert et al. 1956: 60). Schiller disputes this theory, arguing that wire services were integrated into newsrooms that already valued factual accuracy (1981: 4; see also Schudson 1978: 5).

Of course, wire services are not the only technology that impact on journalism, although they have a special place in the literature on objectivity. Medium-specific issues need to be kept in mind. In the UK and Australia objectivity emerged in the context of radio broadcasting (see chapter 8), and Martin Conboy argues that 'radio's immediacy as a technology threatened the greater claims to factual objectivity which had been gathering credibility . . . in newspaper journalism' (2004: 191). In the US, televised news put new emphasis on the objective eye-witness account (McQuail 1992: 186). It has been argued that broadcast television news 'has reinforced objectivity', and that the supposed unmediated-ness of television 'probably breathed new life into the public expectation that news media could be neutral and objective windows on the world' (Hackett & Zhao 1998: 47).

The commercialization argument

With close links to the technology argument, the commercialization argument is focused on news as a commodity, and in broad terms holds that objectivity developed as a way to service advertisers wishing to reach politically heterogeneous audiences (Carey 1997 [1969]: 137). But underpinning this is a crucial issue to do with the relationship between the newsroom and the business office within a news organization.

There has, arguably, always been a commercial element to the news, both in terms of reader interest, but also the alignment of business cycles and journalism. 'Every day there is business to be done and there are prices to be posted' (Carey 1997 [1986]: 158). Stuart Allan, drawing on Jürgen Habermas's work on the rise of the bourgeois public sphere, highlights how 'early capitalist commercial relations necessitated the distribution of news in a far more public form than that which had been provided by the "news letters" printed in political journals' (1997: 298). Central to the commercialization argument in relation to the emergence of objectivity in journalism is the aim of not offending or alienating readers on the basis of political affiliation. As E. Barbara Phillips puts it:

> Letting the 'facts speak for themselves' instead of offering an interpretation of events avoids controversy which, in turn, avoids offending news (and advertising) customers who may reject the news (and advertised) product along with the unwanted interpretation. By 'sticking to the facts' and eschewing explicit explanation, journalism in the objective mode skirts the problem that one person's truth is another's propaganda. (1977: 68)

Because the commercialization thesis has to do with the partiality and party orientation of newspapers, it could be suggested that it is wrongly named. But the reason for highlighting commercialization is to focus on issues of the market, distribution and especially advertising.

While the commercialization argument seems relatively straightforward, it is at the centre of a number of different research problems. The first of these has to do with the relationship between objectivity and commercialization or business, which cannot be explained as a simple dichotomy. Indeed, objectivity can be regarded as a commercial strategy for news organizations as much as a matter of high principle transcending the profit motive (see Ognianova & Endersby 1996: 3). In his study of Adolph S. Ochs, editor of *The New York Times* from 1896, Porwancher notes, objectivity was 'a set of ideal interests used to camouflage or even further the press' material interests: increased profit, advertising, and circulation as well as protection from legal sanctions' (2011: 186). Here, objectivity is less an ethical principle than a marketing strategy: 'Trustworthiness was a central tenet of objectivity, and the *Times* traded on this perceived trait to attract advertisers' (2011: 190).

The importance of the commercialization argument is that it

reminds us how impartiality is not above commerce, but tied in with a business strategy. As Robert A. Hackett and Yuezhi Zhao suggest, 'a number of analytically distinct but interacting forces of the dominant commercial logic – cost-optimization, homogenization, non-partisanship, depoliticization, consumerism, marginalization of progressive alternatives, specialization and legitimation – help to constitute journalism's regime of objectivity' (1998: 65). Thus, 'the nineteenth-century ideal of objectivity was at once a political stance *and* a commercial imperative' (1998: 67).

The second research problem has to do with the influence of productivity considerations on journalism. With the penny press, news organizations needed to be able to construct journalism in ways that it could be handled and processed as a commodity, and economically so. Theodore L. Glasser links objectivity to this highly organized industrial form by focusing on the idea of efficiency (1992: 177). In effect, objectivity can be seen in terms of cost saving. As William B. Blankenburg and Ruth Walden note, 'the more interpretive the story, the more costly it is in reportorial time. Or conversely, objectivity is cheaper' (1977: 594; also Hackett & Zhao 1998: 66). That is, within constraints of money, time and people, reporters can file stories by sticking close to what is stated by sources without having to sift through mountains of evidence or having to sort out what is truth, and also without having to be specialists in a field. Objectivity frees reporters from the need to acquire expert knowledge and also allows inter-changeability of reporters (McQuail 1992: 185).

The commercialization argument is, of all the arguments, one of the most demanding in terms of historical knowledge about the media, especially concepts such as the market (Schudson 1978: 58; Schiller 1981: 9–10; Allan 1997: 304), and different phases of economic and political activity (see Kaplan 2002: 104). The arrival of the penny dailies in New York has been the main focus of attention, although the metropolitan dailies were acknowledged as being 'a small minority among American newspapers' (Crawford 1924: 3). The commercialization argument is not solely used in historical studies, but has been used to suggest that objectivity is an important way that news organizations not only create efficiencies, but define a centrist middle ground with which to attract and preserve a mass audience (Ognianova & Endersby 1996).

The political argument

While often treated as a minor theme in the other arguments, politics has also figured in its own right as a key theme in research on objectivity in journalism. As Schudson summarizes the case, 'since the Associated Press gathered news for publication in a variety of papers with widely different political allegiances, it could only succeed by making its reporting "objective" enough to be acceptable to all of its members and clients' (1978: 4). It is a long-standing trope that the turn to commercial media and objectivity represented a turn away from direct party affiliation or sponsorship, and also that the rise of news was tied to a decline in the power of the editorial (for a summary of both views, see Park 1923: 283). Schudson gives the political argument a strong place in an overall narrative about US journalism, when he suggests that the 'very concept of politics changes from 1880–1920' (2001: 160). Just as reformers were criticizing party loyalty, newspapers were able to claim independence from parties.

Politics finds a place in research into objectivity in other ways. The issue of 'news management', whereby the government sought to control news for the purpose of publicity, has been important (Schudson 1978: 164–6; 2001: 163). The public good represents another important element of the political argument. For Schiller, 'Objectivity developed in tandem with the commercial newspapers' appropriation of a crucial political function – the surveillance of the public good' (1979: 47).

Stephen J. A. Ward gives politics a unique, almost transcending role. He explores how objectivity arises from economic and other factors, but is not 'reducible' to them. He goes on to foreground the way objectivity provides a political justification for the business of news, 'for a journalism of objective information'. Tying this to liberal philosophy he argues 'The marketplace of ideas needed not only the free combat of ideas but also objective information'

(2004: 193). In his view, 'journalism, at its best, is one of the arts of democracy' (2004: 9).

Richard Kaplan's research defines a different kind of political argument. Kaplan focuses on the partisan rather than the commercial press per se, and in this field he plots the rise of objectivity as occurring between 1865 and 1920. Kaplan's argument is framed as an alternative account of the rise of objectivity (for him, really impartiality) in journalism. Questioning the adequacy of the commercial and professionalization arguments, he argues neither 'alterations in the urban newspaper market' nor 'the journalist's desire for professional autonomy and prestige' adequately explain the development (2002: 141).

In their place, Kaplan puts forward a political theory of press-reform (2002: 142). In order to do this, he follows the partisan press right up to the twentieth century, rather than leaving it in the 1840s as some redundant pre-commercial press. Unlike other critics, Kaplan delves more deeply into how partisanship works. A central aspect of Kaplan's research is his exploration of the 'ritual' dimensions of the way the partisan press interacted with its subscribers and readers. This was not a simple commercial transaction.

> The relationship between subscribers and journal did not consist in just an anonymous exchange of money for product in the market but, rather, a mutual vowing of commitments and duties as members of a political community. The individual journal was the organ of the political community, and commissioned with the task of expressing the group's ideas and its interests. Ties of solidarity and identification bound readers to their papers. (Kaplan 2002: 23)

Viewing the nineteenth century newspaper as an 'expressive organ of a pre-existing political community' (2002: 24), Kaplan gives us a fuller picture of the partisan press. Two key inter-related aspects are noteworthy here. Firstly, the press played a key role in the experience of politics, and was 'centrally implicated in the construction of the parties' issue agenda and in the formation of the citizenry's political preferences' (Kaplan 2002: 25). Secondly, this is why the end of party subsidies did not necessarily mean the end of party orientation. The latter was ingrained in journalistic culture, and the papers were partners rather than slaves (2002: 56).

Kaplan, whose focus is on Detroit newspapers, disputes the idea that market progress leads inevitably to neutrality and objectivity. He is not alone in this view. Baldasty charts a general decline of political culture in the US from the mid-nineteenth century (1992: 44), leading to a general de-emphasis on politics (1992: 127–30). For Kaplan, changes in the political culture were crucial to editors and publishers disaffiliating from parties. Certainly market forces gave the newspapers a base from which to make decisions, but the key determining factors come from the political culture. Following the Civil War, the agenda of the partisan press under-serviced public debate and discussion, trading instead in tired party positions. The 1893 depression severely damaged the standing of Democrats who were in control of both the White House and Congress (2002: 143). Long-standing emotional grievances from farmers pushed their way into the political stage resulting in calls for economic relief and reform, especially around currency standards. The election of 1896 was bitterly fought around 'new class and sectional issues' (2002: 144). Reform proved contentious, and the grip of partisanship loosened. The political culture had transformed sufficiently that newspapers began to issue declarations of independence 'renouncing all partisanship' (2002: 145). From the 1890s, disinterested impartiality became the dominant mode.

Other factors

These four arguments do not exhaust all of the possible theories and hypotheses around the development of objectivity (see Mindich 1998), but they provide a useful outline and point to the extraordinary nature of the development of objectivity in journalism.

There are some additional 'factors' worth mentioning briefly. Firstly, in the UK and Australia, reluctance to grant the public broadcaster a role in delivering news (and therefore 'trespass' on the activities of the existing press) were an important factor. In both cases, the public broadcaster defined an 'impartial' role for itself under intense scrutiny by government and established press interests (see chapter 8).

Secondly, in terms of the US, an important factor to consider is the American Civil War (1861–5) which, as well as fuelling partisanship on the issue of race (see Kaplan 2002: 22–54), is linked to developments in technology and the speed of newsgathering (see Mindich 1998: 64–94). Kaplan suggests that much debate in the partisan press in the late nineteenth century was intimately bound up with the war and questions of race, and the citizenship rights of African-Americans (2002: 22–54). The Civil War has been seen as a 'pivotal event of American political and social history' and 'among the primary agents of social and intellectual change during the nineteenth century' (Shi 1995: 46). Following this line of discussion, it has been argued the war was a turning point for all aspects of journalism (see Schudson 1978: 202, note 7 for a summary of the debates; also Irwin 1969 [1911]: 12). For Ward, many of the advances in reporting of the 1900s in the US were 'already evident during the American Civil War' (Ward 2004: 189).

Schudson is more sanguine about the influence of the Civil War: 'it is often taken to be a turning point in the history of the American press. It was not. It did not "turn" the direction of journalism; its impact was to intensify the direction in which journalism had been turning since the 1830s' (1978: 66). He does not suggest it had no impact, however. It was 'not so much different as bigger, more prominent, and, as people anxiously followed campaigns that involved their husbands and brothers and sons, more important to ordinary people. The war pushed the newspaper closer to the center of national consciousness' (1978: 67).

A third factor to consider is what I term the 'nexus factor': namely, the interaction or meeting point of many of the arguments described above in the early 1900s. If the early twentieth century can be considered an era of fascination in research on objectivity then arguably it is due to the intersection of these different lines of research. The expansion in the advertising market, consolidation of ownership, as well as rising class and professional consciousness, and sensitivities over issues of political influence (especially around labour matters and aggregated capital) contributed to a strong sense of press criticism. Ward makes a similar point when he notes that 'objectivity is not the result of just one factor, such as the desire of newspaper editors for neutral copy or the impact of a new technology such as the telegraph' (2004: 33). Combining all of our arguments Ward suggests that 'new technology, the commercialization of news, fears about the manipulation of public opinion, and the advent of "objective" society were among the many motivations for the construction of objectivity' (2004: 33). Fusing these arguments together, Ward sees objectivity as part of a new episode in the journalist–audience relationship: 'the journalist as impartial mass informer' (2004: 33).

Dating objectivity in journalism: the 'Schudson–Schiller' problem

The key arguments to do with the development of journalistic objectivity help us understand *why* journalistic objectivity arises, but it leaves the issue of *when* in a more ambiguous position. Following Harlan S. Stensaas, it can be said that the origins of the term 'are hazy at best' (1986: 52). The difficulties here have to do with variation between countries, but also the difficulty of establishing a clear timeline from the different arguments that have been put forward. Placing the focus on explicit discussion and articulation of the objectivity norm, we can say that objectivity began to be discussed in the UK from 1926 (and in the context of the BBC's role in the General Strike of that year) and in Australia in the 1940s (in the context of debates over the role of the Australian public broadcaster). In-depth discussion of the UK and Australian cases can be found in chapter 8.

The first mentions of the term 'objectivity' in relation to journalism textbooks in the US date from 1911 (Mirando 1993; Dicken-Garcia 2005; Vos 2011). This goes against Streckfuss's view that 'journalists did not use the word "objective" to describe their work until the 1920s' (1990: 973). The term appears in

Charles Ross', *The Writing of News* (1911). Taking a cue from an editorial in the *St. Louis Republic* that states the 'three notes of modern reporting are clarity, terseness, objectivity', Ross argues that the ideal news story is 'written from an impersonal, objective viewpoint' (1911: 18). 'News writing is objective to the last degree, in the sense that the writer is not allowed to "editorialize"' (1911: 20). It should be noted that Walter Williams and Frank Martin's, *The Practice of Journalism* (1911) refers to the same editorial but does not link it to an objectivity norm. Early journalism texts 'did not advocate objectivity fully or exclusively' (Vos 2011: 442). Thus, Streckfuss' observation is not without merit, for it is primarily in the 1920s that the term becomes more common, with most scholarly attention focussing on Nelson Antrim Crawford's *Ethics of Journalism* (1924) and Harry Harrington and Theodore Frankenberg's *Essentials in Journalism* (1924) (Streckfuss 1990: 974-975; Beasley & Mirando 2005: 186; see also Vos 2011: 442).

The second part of this chapter examines the issue of dating objectivity in the US context. My justification for this focus is that media historians in the US have uniquely tried to examine the history of their press in relation to the development of objectivity. This project has not been attempted to the equivalent scale in other countries. In Britain, for instance, different coordinates for media history exist: often framed by concepts of impartiality or the fourth estate, parliamentary reporting, and with a much stronger focus on securing independence from government, the influence of media owners, the role of the radical press, and a critical approach to the idea that market democracy or advertising is a handmaiden for the development of the media (see Curran & Seaton 2003). A different inflection thus arises. For example, in a 1978 essay 'The Long Road to Objectivity and Back Again', Anthony Smith describes a 'rubric of objectivity' at work in the twentieth century, focused on 'structuring reality, rather than recording it' (1978: 168). Surveying the work of different Royal Commissions in the twentieth century, James Curran notes that one response to problems in the marketplace, and the liberal theory of the press itself, is to focus on social responsibility and objectivity. But he notes that 'in a British context it has radical implications, since it upholds impartial journalism and professional autonomy in a way that challenges the partisan, hierarchical character of the national tabloid press' (Curran & Seaton 2003: 353–4). He goes on to note a disjuncture between professionalization, educational institutions and the industry in Britain that is very different from the US (2003: 357).

Even with the US as our focus, there is a further complication. While the four arguments we have examined have a prominent place in the literature, there is growing awareness of their limitations. Schudson and Anderson identify a shift in scholarly focus away from 'wide-scale' accounts of the development of objectivity towards more specific accounts of the different 'claims to occupational authority', built around particular norms (Schudson & Anderson 2009: 92). Concepts of professionalization in particular, as well as other 'macro' level drivers, are increasingly being questioned as inadequate to account for the way objectivity is linked to the shaping of journalistic work and group identity (and its boundaries). This work forces a re-think of the already complex task of how we approach the history of objectivity in journalism, and especially the task of dating.

In the US case, dating is itself a uniquely controversial issue because of what I term the 'Schudson–Schiller problem': named after media sociologists and historians Michael Schudson and Dan Schiller. The problem has to do with the fact that each scholar puts forward a different thesis about the origins of objectivity in journalism. For Schudson, it emerges in the 1920s (1978); for Schiller, the 1830s (1981). As Steven R. Knowlton comments, 'although both Schudson and Schiller believed they had determined when objectivity took hold in American journalism, both cannot be right, for their answers are clear, certain and nearly a century apart' (2005a: 4).

Alternative accounts of the development of objectivity do exist (see Calcutt & Hammond 2011: 106–7; also Williams 2005: 29). For example, Stephen J. A. Ward contests key aspects of the Schudson–Schiller problem. Writing from a philosophy of journalism perspective he traces the history of objectivity back to

Ancient Greece, and the discussion of journalistic ethics back to seventeenth-century England (2004: 6). Ward makes a strong case for locating a proto-objective era in the UK from the seventeenth and eighteenth centuries. He identifies a focus on 'factual techniques'. 'The early press was not unfamiliar with the five "Ws" of journalism – who, what, when, where, and why' (2004: 107). When in 1702 the *Daily Courant* declares that it will ' "relate only Matter of Fact, supposing other people to have Sense enough to make *reflections for themselves*" ' (Ward 2004: 148), Ward sees this as 'one of the earliest statements of news objectivity'. The nineteenth-century paper, building on this history, 'sets the stage for the arrival of objectivity early in the twentieth' (2004: 174). Ward suggests that 'Historians usually treat journalism ethics as a development of the early twentieth century, with the establishment of schools of journalism and professional associations. In fact, journalists were talking about their social roles, norms of practice, and public duties long before the written codes of ethics in the 1920s' (2004: 100). However, as Ward notes, while we can trace the operation of concepts such as impartiality, news and truth much earlier, 'we should not read modern values into the past' (2004: 100). The 'ethical lexicon' of the seventeenth century shares terms with the present, but 'had meanings that do not necessarily correspond with modern senses' (2004: 116).

In light of this scholarship any historical investigation of the origins of objectivity is faced with a decision about when to start the story. A parallel problem exists in the history of philosophy of science, where there is an argument that the entire history of rational thought is a history of objectivity, what Daston and Galison call 'an identification of objectivity with science *tout court*' (2007: 28). Their argument for a much shorter history of objectivity in general (dating from the 1800s) influences my own decision to work within the period identified by Schiller and Schudson. Daston and Galison's argument suggests that, firstly, it is important to focus on issues of evidence and use. Secondly, it is important to avoid a kind of conceptual synecdoche where this or that trait stands for all of objectivity in journalism. Thirdly, any approach should be 'non-teleological' where possible, meaning some ideal and final concept of objectivity should not be projected back into the past and cast as an inevitable end-point.

The specific issues of dating posed by the Schudson–Schiller problem, combined with the demand for much more nuanced accounts of the historical foundations of the way objectivity is linked to the shaping of journalism, represents a real challenge to any attempt to explore the question of when and why objectivity arises. When Dan Schiller refers to objectivity as a 'canon of expertise' (1981: 3), and Michael Schudson to an 'ideal', are they speaking about the same thing? Furthermore, does the argument that the 'ideal' of objectivity in journalism dates from World War I mean that we should ban any mention of the term prior to that date? Meeting this challenge, I want to suggest that what is required is a careful approach to the nature of objectivity itself. Objectivity in journalism does not operate like some software program that is executed by the system in order to address some professional, technological, commercial or political need. Different conceptions arise within, and respond to, a complex set of commercial, cultural and organizational conditions. In other words, the very concept of objectivity in journalism shifts and changes in different periods.

Exploring this idea, I contend that since the 1830s 'American journalism' has operated within an 'orientation' towards objectivity – broadly speaking, an approach to news production disposed towards the facts – but that within this orientation specific forms of objectivity become dominant at different times. This allows us to draw together, but also respect variations between, different conceptions and even *layers* of objectivity. The following forms are drawn from Schudson's discussion in *Discovering the News* (1978), which is frequently linked to the professionalization argument and the idea that objectivity arises in the 1920s, but also presents a social history of the development of American newspapers in the nineteenth century.

The proto-objective era of news as commodity, 1830–1880

The period 1830–80 can be characterized as a proto-objective era of news as commodity. It led to a 'triumph of "news" over the editorial and "facts" over opinion' (Schudson 1978: 14), with values of accuracy, analysis, liveliness and timeliness underpinning the 'collection of news at any price' as the 'first duty of journalism' (1978: 51). My discussion follows Schudson in the assumption that in the eighteenth century 'no norm of objectivity appeared. . . . The occupational preconditions for a modern concept of objectivity simply did not exist' (2001: 154–5). But, as Schudson highlights, this does not diminish our interest in this era which placed the facts, news, technology, advertising, and crucially readers, in a new configuration. As Ward notes, 'A proto-objective journalism that believed in factuality, independence, and impartiality existed by the late nineteenth century' (2004: 254).

Working within the low cost 'non-subscriber' penny press model of this era, editors such as Benjamin H. Day of the *New York Sun* (established in 1833) and James Gordon Bennett of the *New York Herald* (established 1835), were forced to innovate. In general, the penny press was cheap, bright, avoided politics and focused on gathering news rather than political commentary and advocacy (Baldasty 1992: 46). In terms of subject matter, crime, the business of the local police, the courts, the goings on of society and street reporting, all became a new focus of attention (Schudson 1978: 91). This approach consists of more than the sheer 'recording of facts' and emphasizes instead 'the analysis of the shape of events' (Schudson 1978: 53) – a formula that complicates setting any simple 'rule' of objectivity. Indeed, Bennett suggests a 'dull record of facts' is useless (quoted in Schudson 1978: 54).

It is important to provide a sense of the shape of the press at this time, even though it evolves over the period in question. The 'commercial revolution' in the press leads to a product quite distinct from the collection of political editorials and shipping news on pages 2 and 3, often with minimal headlines, wrapped in columns of advertising on pages 1 and 4, that formed prior practice. While the rise of the commercial press is often described as a battle with the partisan press, Baldasty notes that 'not all newspapers of the 1820s and 1830s . . . were partisan. In the larger cities, literary and commercial papers had flourished since the eighteenth century' (1992: 6). The shift away from annual subscription sales to street distribution is perhaps the most well-known feature of the newspaper in this era. The changing commercial conditions drew the ire of six-penny papers due to the advertising policies of the penny press, open to 'quack doctors' and abortionists (Schudson 1978: 20). Later, this period also saw wide experimentation in the display of news and of advertising, including self-advertising by the press, illustrations, cartoons, large headlines sometimes crossing single columns (1978: 95–6).

Of course, this readership, and the world they lived in, was in transformation on many fronts. The telegraph, railway and trans-atlantic cable were transforming the communications landscape. In the face of enormous social and cultural upheaval the role of the newspaper in this period was broad, aspiring to teach, guide, inform, interpret and entertain (Schudson 1978: 98–9). Schudson highlights a unique connection between the newspapers of this period and the life of the city, including the arrival of new immigrants, the development of urban populations, and a rising middle class (1978: 106; Schiller 1981: 10). In this period, the aristocratic values of land-holders were being challenged; the conditions of tradespeople under threat from larger scale 'aggregated' industry: crime coverage was an indicator of this, linked to shifting property interests and concerns over 'law and order' (Schiller 1981: 23). Another indicator was the rise of women's pages and the changing status of women, especially as a target for department store advertising and advice columns (Schudson 1978: 101). The style of news became simpler, more accessible. With a new focus on consumption and the market, an emphasis on entertainment and leisure emerged, and with it the Sunday supplements 'featuring notes of the fraternal orders and women's clubs, . . . mild write-ups of the picturesque features of city life, together with such embellishment of fiction and beauty hints as they could afford' (Irwin 1969 [1911]: 18). The Sunday supplements became the space for exploring colour pictures and comics, but with it an entire 'economy of attention' that eventually spread out across the week in the form of experimentation with headlines and column boundaries (Irwin 1969 [1911]: 18; Schudson 1978: 99).

The use of the prefix 'proto' in my description of this period is meant to suggest not just the first, but also a precursor. Political independence or impartiality is often held up as a key value of objectivity, but the penny press had a mixed record in this regard. They were *laissez faire* in terms of their advertising clients, and were formally independent from political parties, but the papers themselves ranged from the neutral, the indifferent, to the politically motivated. Horace Greeley, editor of the *New York Tribune* (established in 1841), criticized the 'gagged, mincing neutrality' of some of his rivals (Schudson 1978: 22).

The penny press did not always offer a separation of 'news' and 'views'. This is central for Schiller, because it points to the way the penny press serves as a forum and *vox populi* for the anxieties of a 'new public', namely the tradespeople and to a lesser extent the labourers and merchants of society. (The interests of the affluent classes addressed by the six-penny press.) Schiller has argued strongly that broad terms such as the 'middle class' do not necessarily give us a sense of this new public and their interests. He suggests that, by 1830, 20 per cent of the urban population of the US lived in New York, which then had a population of 200,000 people. Some 40–50 per cent of New York's wage-earning population were artisans and mechanics (1981: 13, 16). The penny press assumed a 'new and important role within political society, . . . urged upon it by the new public' (1981: 15). The penny press responded with a journalism 'free of the insidious obligations born by the elite press' (1981: 53). 'Independence, virtue, impartial defense of life, liberty, and property' were core values (1981: 76). It was a journalism of exposure, highlighting corruption, collusion and vested interest when it threatened to undermine the public good.

It would be an overstatement to suggest the penny press was a labour press – especially since there was a pre-existing labour press in the US, one highly critical of the party press (Schiller 1981: 36, 45, 71). Schiller goes to great lengths to recognize the contribution of the labour press (see also Hackett & Zhao 1998: 23). At a time when consumption practices were changing the branded space of advertising, changes to the conditions of production helped shape the very concepts of rights, justice, public interest and public good pursued by the papers. As Schiller reminds us, the penny press borrowed heavily from the discourse of the labour press. (In Britain the radical press served a similar function, 'the attempt to shift policy through public causes' rivals, according to Conboy, the 'much-heralded arrival of objectivity' as a marker of journalism (2004: 91; and Curran & Seaton 2003: 8–17).)

Many practices associated with objectivity become evident in this period. 'The lead' sentence is an example, closely linked to the rise of the telegraph in the 1840s and economical use of language, but also to the reading practices of the middle class. Or, as Schudson puts it, 'pushed by the high cost of telegraphic transmission of news now pulled by abbreviated moments in which newspapers were being read' (1978: 103). While this era saw the triumph of news and facts over editorial, and a linking of reporting with the public good, Schudson warns about the risks of defining this as an era of objectivity: 'But in 1840 or 1850 or 1860, American journalism did not yet have clearly common ideas and ideals. American journalism had not yet become an occupational group or an industry' (1978: 60).

Objectivity as democratic realist epistemology

No professional or occupational norm develops in a vacuum. In keeping with this idea, it is appropriate to refer to another form of objectivity stirring in American culture: this is *objectivity as democratic realist epistemology*. Objectivity as a way of seeing the world permeated the art and culture of the day. America embraced photography enthusiastically from the 1830s. It gave impulse to a realist imaginary, such that Isaac Pray described the *New York Herald* as 'the daily daguerreotype of the heart and soul of the model republic' (1855: 412; Schiller 1981: 88). Journalism and popular science entered into a supporting relationship, via declarations of the new journalism as allied to 'truth, public faith, and science' (see Schiller 1981: 80), but also coverage of scientific achievement (the periodical *Scientific American* began publication in 1845). From the mid-nineteenth century 'positivism nurtured widespread acceptance of a uniform, objective world' (Schiller 1981: 83) accessible through common sense examination of the facts observed. Schiller suggests 'this world became the newspaper's fundamental business' (1981: 87).

As Schudson notes, it would be an error to see objectivity as simply the articulation of journalism as a science. Instead, it is an interaction between reporting and the realism of the day. 'Reporters in the 1890s saw themselves, in part, as scientists uncovering the economic and political facts of industrial life more boldly, more clearly, and more "realistically" than anyone had done before' (1978: 71). Political and social reform was increasingly tied to better information about social issues. There existed a 'public demand for facts' (1978: 72), and realism as an aesthetic philosophy rose to meet this demand. Literally so, for, as Schudson notes, this realism, focused on the streets, parlours and courts of the city, was attuned to the needs of the democratic market society. Human beings became 'objects about which facts could be gathered and studied. The human mind externalized or objectified the human bodies, and, ... human beings objectified themselves' (1978: 75). As Carey puts it, 'in the 1830s society took on an objectified existence; it became a realm apart from and other than the individual' (1982: 1184; see also Ward 2004: 187).

In this mode, far from being a specific professional ideal, objectivity is a way of knowing the world which journalism interacted with. The turn to realism and empirical thought suited a democratic age questioning the basis of religion and the social order (Schudson 1978: 76). This was a world that journalism was uniquely positioned to analyse, report and commodify. It may seem inane to suggest that the concept of objectivity in journalism relies on a concept of objective reality; but this is to miss the more essential point, which is that objectivity in journalism is part of a broader societal objectification, and objectification of social and cultural relations through facts (see Calcutt & Hammond 2011: 118–46).

Objectivity as a reporter-focused occupational or organizational ethic, 1880–1900

A third form of objectivity can be identified circa 1880–1900, which is *objectivity as a reporter-focused occupational or organizational ethic*. As Carey observes, 'nineteenth-century journalism was dominated by the printer and editor until the reporter emerged as a distinctive figure late in the century' (1982: 1185). With the telegraph, 'the reporter who produced the new prose displaced the editor as the archetype of the journalist' (Carey 1997 [1986]: 161). As divisions of journalistic labour emerged (Schiller 1979: 53) and as the era of news as commodity matured, the reporter increasingly became the focus of attention and control.

The penny papers not only published but sought out news to a greater extent than its competitors. Full-time reporters and correspondents had begun to be hired in the 1830s (Schudson 1978: 23), but 'it was only in the decades after the Civil War that reporting became a more highly esteemed and more highly rewarded occupation' (1978: 68). Tensions emerged between the 'old type of American reporter', the bohemian journalist, 'prying, overcurious, unclean of person, dissolute, reckless, counting life and honor no whit against the latest news' (Irwin 1969 [1911]: 12), and the new reporter, often college-educated, who wielded the 'real power of the press' (Irwin 1969 [1911]: 40).

The role of the reporter in the process of newsgathering became more publically noticeable; and while the 'beat' or 'scoop' remained important, the conditions of the newsroom changed, placing an emphasis on news essentials and sound judgement. Staying with the facts became an imperative. In this period objectivity functioned organizationally as a disciplining practice, applied in the exchanges between editors and reporters. Editors policed principles of accuracy and a rigid separation of fact and editorial opinion – although with substantial room for colour or sparkle, and also sensationalism. While not termed as such, objectivity permeated the culture of editors and reporters, both in the workplace and in the emerging press clubs and reporters' drinking holes. 'Reporters came to share a common world of work; they also shared common ideas about how to conduct their work' (Schudson 1978: 70). Schudson informs us of 'a sign in the office of the *Chicago Tribune* which read, "WHO OR WHAT? HOW? WHEN? WHERE?", which points to the codification of news as information in the form of newsroom maxims, later to be extended by early handbooks on reporting dating from the late 1800s (1978: 78). Schudson suggests that, perhaps despite themselves, reporters were forced into an attachment to facts 'by the organizational pressures of daily journalism' (1978: 81).

It would be mistaken to suggest that this variant of objectivity as an organizational ethic focused on the reporter fully supplanted the proto-objective era of news as commodity, as clearly there are close ties between the two. Commercialism intensified. This was, after all, the era of yellow journalism, the crusading against public 'evils' of Joseph Pulitzer (of the *New York World*, which he assumed control of in 1884), the 'gee whiz' sensationalist news values of William Randolph Hearst (of the *New York Journal*, purchased by Hearst in 1895), among others. Nevertheless, the rise of the reporter focused journalism in particular ways. In the late 1800s, different genres of journalism and forms of reporting 'dramatized' the news and gave expression to the realism and reformist agenda of the day. Journalism of different stripes sought to capture the life of the city world 'without interpretation, with complete mirrorlike accuracy' (Schudson 1978: 85). Arguably inspired by the courage of the sensationalist press, in the early 1900s muckraking journalism resisted the separation of fact and opinion in narratives about the great human drama of urban experience and spectacle (Miraldi 1990). Objectivity may have been an inspiration, but not a strict template. As Hackett and Zhao note, 'even in its heyday, the pursuit of facts – the information function of news – never completely overrode the desire for pleasure and the drive for persuasion' (1998: 37).

Objectivity as informational ethic, circa 1900

The diversity in style and approach in relation to objectivity in the late 1800s has been overshadowed by another significant strand of objectivity, namely *objectivity as an informational ethic*. Associated with *The New York Times* – although other papers lay claim to the accurate dissemination of information in the 1840s (Schiller 1981: 104) – this ethic relates to the organizational/occupational disciplining of reporters, but also addresses the sensationalism of the 'new' or yellow journalism of the late 1800s by proposing an alternative approach to news. Schudson traces the success of the *Times* in this period to its ability to function as a 'Business Bible' (1978: 108), as well as the decency and propriety of its approach. The slogan 'All the News That's Fit to Print' embodied this approach (but even more so an alternative phrase that emerged out of a competition run by the paper, 'All the World's News, but Not a Sheet for Scandal'). The *Times* was, through its political conservatism, able to play to the rich (1978: 109), but also functioned, once its price had been dropped from 3 cents to a penny, as an emblem of respectability for lower but aspiring classes (1978: 112).

When Adolph S. Ochs bought and assumed the editorship of the *Times* in 1896, he published an announcement. The description of news would resonate with most modern understandings of objectivity: his aim was to give 'all the news, in concise and attractive form', to give it 'impartially, without fear or favor, regardless of any party, sect, or interest involved' (Ochs 1896). The paper would be 'non-partisan' – albeit within a program of tariff reform, low taxes and limited government! Editorially the language of decency, cleanliness, earnestness and common sense, was pitched in terms of a struggle against the new journalism of the day. For Schudson, 'The *Times* in 1900 trusted to information' (1978: 120), and in a sense this inaugurates a key paradigm for discussions of objectivity up to the present, as well as the performance of the paper itself, especially in the area of foreign news (see Lippmann & Merz 1920; Reifenberg 1982: 27). While earlier journalists had combined realism and entertainment, under the influence of the informational model, realism and entertainment information and story became opposites (Carey 1982: 1184–5). Of course, both models of journalism draw on stories and provide information, and to some extent the distinction is flawed; but what it points to is the way the frame of the news shifted to define the news as a form of information rather than entertainment, with the informational ethic becoming central to the 'we report, you decide' approach to news.

The informational model of objectivity has assumed an important role in contemporary ideas of quality journalism. Take, for example, the case of sensationalist journalism. Martin Conboy suggests that 'the contemporary popular press has reasserted much of the sensationalism and distraction which erode the discursive objectivity of the press' (2002: 139). Like many forms of popular culture, the sensationalist media tend to be cast as morally dubious, and indeed the penny presses were capable of hoaxes, trial by media and invasion of privacy (see Tucher 1994). But in many cases they were also morally engaged, often exploring new aspects of the ethical landscape and ideas of the public good. Indeed, professional antipathy to the commercial press can lead us to forget that the penny papers 'invented a genre which acknowledged, and so enhanced, the importance of everyday life' (Schudson 1978: 26), helping to redefine the moral boundaries of communities (Schiller 1981: 7). Objectivity has complex links to yellow journalism, even though the informational ethic of objectivity makes it hard to acknowledge this in the way the code of ethics for the *Springfield Union* in the 1920s does, advising us to 'avoid all that is yellow in journalism, but emulate the enterprise that characterizes the yellow journalist' (Crawford 1924: 220).

The informational model of objectivity has long been a powerful force in objectivity debates, but this should not lead to false assumptions about other forms of reporting. As Schudson notes, 'Newspapers which stress information tend to be seen as more reliable than "story" papers. But who makes this judgement and on what grounds? Who regards the information model as more trustworthy than the story ideal, and what is meant, after all, by "reliable" and "trustworthy"?' (Schudson 1978: 90).

The ideal of objectivity, post-World War I

Up to this point we have drawn on Michael Schudson's scholarship as a matrix for reading different periods in the development of news and objectivity. However – and here we run into an aspect of the Schudson–Schiller problem defined above – there is a difficulty with this approach, insofar as Schudson's own argument is based on the notion that the formal ideal of objectivity arose strictly post-World War I, during the 'famine of facts' (Lahey 1924: 135) of that time. This is different from other scholars who see objectivity as a fact-based philosophy dating from the 1830s, 'publically certified' on a 'microcultural' level within newspapers (Schiller 1981: 76–95). Although his work clearly lays a framework for considering the rise of journalistic fact-mindedness in the 1800s, Schudson, for his part, is stricter around the specific conditions of the concept:

> It would be a mistake to read contemporary views of objectivity into the fact-mindedness of the 1890s. Objectivity is an ideology of the distrust of the self. . . . The Progressives' belief in facts was different from a modern conviction of objectivity. . . . (1978: 71)

For Schudson, the objectivity ideal, fully articulated, points to a development in the 1920s and 1930s when, following the impacts of propaganda and public relations, journalists felt that the facts themselves could not be trusted. A response to an increasingly relativistic and complex world, objectivity arose as a moral and political/democratic commitment designed to bolster the factual basis of reporting as long as facts were 'submitted to established rules deemed legitimate by a professional community' (Schudson 1978: 7).

While the development of propaganda and public relations are key areas of concern, Schudson points to a wider cultural malaise. Through objectivity, journalists sought to address the scepticism and 'drift' of the post-progressive era (see Lippmann 1914). Other scholars, such as David E. Shi, also identify this period as an 'epoch of confusion', referring to artistic developments in Modernism which questioned representationalism and also theoretical physics 'which ruptured conventional notions of a stable and uniform reality' (1995: 275).

Schudson's scholarship on the objectivity ideal creates something akin to a tectonic shift in our understanding. Through the lens he provides, objectivity in journalism becomes less a science as much as an article of belief or faith. Objectivity is less an expression of professional excellence as an expression of professional anxiety. Whereas 'objectivity' suggests the facts can speak for themselves, objectivity as an ideal assumes they cannot. He also gives us a different account of the ascendance of the informational ethic of objectivity, which masks a questioning of the very ground upon which the reporter stands: 'That ground, on which both advocates and opponents of "objectivity" in journalism stand, is relativism, a belief in the arbitrariness of values, a sense of the "hollow silence" of modernity, to which the ideal of objectivity has been one response' (1978: 158). On the surface, objectivity may look like naïve empiricism, but it addresses a different set of circumstances, and is no longer simplistically aligned with a realism based on facts as external phenomena subject to laws.

> Facts here are not aspects of the world, but consensually validated statements about it. While naïve empiricism has not disappeared in journalism and survives, to some extent, in all of us, after World War I it was subordinated to the more sophisticated ideal of 'objectivity'. (Schudson 1978: 7)

This 'sophisticated' ideal operates partly as moral philosophy, partly as political tactic, presented as a discourse on 'the facts'. Needless to say, it is in this period that the ideal of objectivity gains renewed force as a discipline for the separation of facts and values, one immediately recognizable as part of the modern 'disinterested' discourse on objectivity based on a 'distrust of values' (Schudson 1978: 5–6), but also out of a profound concern for democratic government and the public function of the press.

The full story of the articulation and codification of objectivity, the accretion of concepts of impartiality, balance and style into an orthodoxy, remains to be told – although several scholars in addition to Schudson have made important contributions (see Schiller 1979; Carey 1982: 1187; Streckfuss 1990; Hackett & Zhao 1998; Mirando 1993, 2001; Vos 2012). Few, if any, company codes of ethics in the 1920s referred to objectivity. It is a long way from what Schudson describes as a 'precarious faith in procedure' (1978: 185) to the highly institutionalized understanding of objectivity defined in terms of 'inverted pyramids, non-partisanship, detachment, a reliance on observable facts, and balance' found in journalism schools and their core textbooks (Mirando 2001: 30).

While Schudson places the major emphasis on the rise of public relations and propaganda, and a general cultural crisis or feeling of drift, there is increasing evidence that other factors specific to the 1910s and 1920s prompted a form of reckoning from editors and publishers – especially from those not based in New York and protective of the press as a public institution. We should remain mindful that 'the last decade of the nineteenth century and the first three decades of the twentieth were a period of extreme social conflict in the United States and a high point of American Radicalism' (Iggers 1998: 61). Schiller suggests 'a stream of harsh criticism began to descend on the practice of journalism' (1981: 187). The advertising revenue of newspapers in the 1910s and 1920s, as a proportion of income compared to circulation, seemed to have spiked, prompting fuller reflection on business ethics (Schiller 1981: 185; see Crawford 1924: 3–24). Concern over the impact of regarding the press solely as a commercial business arose, and with it talk of a 'wall' between newsrooms and business operations (see Ward 2004: 221–2). There was a strong trend towards monopoly between 1910 and 1950, 'exactly the period when the professional norm of objectivity was taking root in American journalism' (Hallin & Mancini 2004: 220). All of these factors impacted on journalism, with the new codes of ethics considered 'a defense against the rising influence of advertisers, government officials, and others who had begun to see the value of the media as a tool of persuasion' (Kelly 2005: 158). Barbara M. Kelly captures the dilemma well when she asks: 'How were the editors and publishers to handle this new genie that was not only out of the bottle, but buying space and supporting the industry?' (2005: 158).

Duelling doctrines: bias and credibility, 1960–present

Debate over the ideal of objectivity was an important fixture of journalism debates through the 1950s, with interpretive reporting forming a special area of concern (see chapter 5). The post 1960s period has been even more turbulent. In his overview of the period,

Steven Knowlton suggests it is a time that journalism entered the crucible (2005b: 221–35). It is one of the ironies of objectivity in journalism that an ideal developed to maintain the reliability of facts over values itself succumbs, by the 1960s, to a 'distrust in values'. For Schudson, this shift in the treatment of objectivity stems from a range of factors: generational change in journalism, broader political developments such as McCarthyism, Vietnam and Watergate. Schudson especially focuses on intense 'news management' by government in the post-World War I period, and a critical 'adversary' culture. These factors combine together in what Schudson calls a 'critique of conventional journalism' (1978: 183).

For our present purposes we can suggest that this period can be characterized as one in which two 'doctrines' of objectivity work in parallel, but also jostle with one another. The first sees *objectivity as a biased doctrine*, and the second *a doctrine of credibility*. In terms of objectivity as a biased doctrine, as Schudson suggests,

> objectivity in journalism, regarded as an antidote to bias, came to be looked upon as the most insidious bias of all. For 'objective' reporting reproduced a vision of social reality which refused to examine the basic structures of power and privilege. It was not just incomplete . . . it was distorted. It represented collusion with institutions whose legitimacy was in dispute. (1978: 160)

The notion that objectivity is a biased doctrine takes many forms, and it has also been cast as a myth (Morrison & Tremewan 1992; Klotzer 2009; Taflinger 1996) and an ideology. This latter idea is perhaps most clearly expressed in Theodore L. Glasser's essay, 'Objectivity and News Bias', which figures objectivity *as* a bias. 'Today's news is indeed biased – as it must inevitably be – and this bias can be best understood by understanding the concept, the conventions, and the ethic of objectivity' (1992: 176). We shall examine Glasser's argument in more detail in chapter 6.

The notion that objectivity is a doctrine that supplies credibility has also been put forward. In a 1969 memo to staff of *The New York Times*, then Managing Editor, A. M. Rosenthal, stressed a link between the basic character of the paper and objectivity. That character indeed rests on 'The belief that although total objectivity may be impossible because every story is written by a human being, the duty of every reporter and editor is to strive for as much objectivity as humanly possible' (Rosenthal 1969).

A key concept in the academic literature on objectivity, Gaye Tuchman's notion of 'strategic ritual', makes the link between credibility and bias (1972). For Tuchman, news people diffuse pressures, criticism and reprimands in relation to their work, especially in relation to deadlines and libel, by appealing to objectivity. Objectivity safeguards credibility while diffusing concerns about bias. Procedures relating to sources, facts and attribution are, in Tuchman's view, *actually strategies through which newsmen protect themselves from critics and lay professional claim to objectivity* (1972: 676, emphasis in original).

Debates around the rise of public or civic journalism in the US reveal the complex nature of the link between ideology, credibility and objectivity. For advocates of public or civic journalism, objectivity leads to a loss of credibility and, more importantly, a loss of connection with readers and their broader communities (Rosen 1993). This has an impact on the quality of democratic life for all. As James Fallows puts it, much unhappiness lay with 'the concept of "objectivity" because it promotes the illusion of detachment from public life' (1996: 260). However, at the same time, public journalism was heavily criticized by established media as a departure from the objectivity norm. Editors of the *Washington Post* and the *Times* argued that public journalism goes against the impulse to separate feelings from facts. Fallows notes that there is in fact a 'hidden consensus' where much of public journalism can be read as simply good journalism, but the sticking point is objectivity as a doctrine and its role in journalism.

Conclusion

If objectivity in journalism was a river, it would have many tributaries. Tracing the origins of objectivity is thus a complex task, demanding attention to a veritable tidal system of commercial, cultural and organizational drivers and conditions. Indeed, the very concept of objectivity in journalism shifts and changes in different periods. Academic, popular and professional discussion is not always careful in delineating which concept, era or strand of objectivity is being discussed. To remediate this situation, using the case study of US journalism, within a broad orientation towards objectivity commencing from the 1830s, I have discussed a number of distinct forms or layers of objectivity: a proto-objective era of news as commodity 1830–80, objectivity as a democratic realist epistemology in the late 1800s, the rise of objectivity as a reporter-focused occupational or organizational ethic from 1880–1900, and objectivity as an informational ethic at the turn of the twentieth century. Circa 1920 we see the rise of the ideal of objectivity as defined by Schudson, which unpacks in two directions as it were, objectivity as a biased doctrine, and objectivity as a doctrine of credibility.

Answering the question, Why and when did journalistic objectivity arise?, the formal response would be 'it depends on the concept of objectivity you are talking about'. However, in terms of the approach taken in this chapter, we are in a position to say that since the 1830s objectivity in journalism has emerged in a number of different ways and at different times, varying according to different professional, technological, commercial, political and organizational conditions, although not fully articulated as an ideal until the 1920s. Engaging with this history, and grasping the fuller picture, can give us a better picture of the shifting nature of objectivity and debates surrounding it. It can also give us a sense of the grip of history on our present discourse. Attentiveness to variation and change, and the ability to see beyond a particular position, are important pre-requisites in the study of objectivity in journalism. Teasing out these debates and arguments is on the one hand the task of scholars, but, on the other hand, this work is crucial to assessing the capacity of journalism to re-invent itself, which is a task of vital importance to readers and groups of all kinds, not just journalists.

2

What are the main objections to journalistic objectivity?

'Objectivity may be dead, but it isn't dead enough' (Iggers 1998: 91). As this quote suggests, objectivity in general, and journalistic objectivity in particular, is a term that invites dispute. For Iggers, the desire for an extra nail in the coffin stems from his view that objectivity is an obstacle to journalists 'playing a more responsible and constructive role in public life' (1998: 91). In this chapter, I attempt to describe the different kinds of objections to objectivity in journalism, while leaving specific critiques associated with the journalism of attachment, peace journalism, and public journalism (among others) for later chapters. It is not difficult to put the concept of objectivity into crisis. But, it should be noted that just as there are many concepts of objectivity, there are many objections to objectivity; and not all of them directed at the same target. Before launching into the objections it is important to underline the fact that the stakes are high. Tackling the various objections to objectivity is a serious business. If the assumptions upon which journalists carry out their work are suspect, then this can impact negatively on public confidence. In other words, it can impact on the credibility with which social and intellectual problems are discussed. To paraphrase a concern voiced by E. Barbara Phillips, how can journalists transmit insights if they don't approach the world from a reflective, theoretical mental attitude? (1977: 71).

Values

The objection to objectivity based on values is wide-ranging, encompassing the question of whether ethical and political values can co-exist with journalistic objectivity (see chapter 6). John C. Merrill links this critique to the idea of 'subjectivizing': every story is always 'judgemental, value-loaded, incomplete, and distorted as to reality. That is the nature of journalism. That is the nature of *any kind* of communication' (Dennis & Merrill 1984: 106). Denis McQuail summarizes a range of concerns about values when he links objectivity to 'fragmentation, individualization and "secularization" – the withdrawal from value commitments. In the most critical view of objectivity, the practice is viewed as actively serving, whether willingly or not, the interests of agents of an established order and as reinforcing a consensus which mainly protects power and class interest' (1992: 188).

This linking of objectivity to a 'withdrawal of value commitments' raises questions about the ideological basis of objectivity. This in turn has fuelled an ardent set of criticisms around 'selectivity'; of sources, frames and even purpose. Armand Mattelart, writing in the Chilean context, raises concerns around selectivity when he suggests that 'as a practical concept "objectivity" presupposes on the part of the journalist perceptive powers capable of selectively penetrating reality and determining what is important and what is not' (1980: 37), but in reality the journalist offers an 'interested selection', by which he means a class-ideological selection. Far from being value-free, objectivity is thus a 'consecration of an ideology and class interest as a universal value' (1980: 37). While objectivity puts forward a conception of facts as *what they are in themselves*, and not what the journalist *sees* them to be', the description of events does not emanate in the external world but in an 'interpretative grid' which is implicit in selection itself. Mattelart raises a further, related concern to do with science. The celebration of objectivity on scientific-technical grounds has an effect of alienating the journalist's labour. Facts are thus decontextualized, 'deprived of the conditions which would explain their conditions and detached from the social system which endows them with meaning' (1980: 39).

Stephen D. Reese puts forward a different approach to ideology when he uses the idea of a 'paradigm' – an 'accepted model or pattern' guiding information-producing tasks – to explore the principle of objectivity. He places objectivity in a larger ideological framework to do with the occupational ideology of media workers. In doing so he shifts the focus away from objectivity as a way to know 'external reality', towards the forms of knowledge allowed by the paradigm and its ensemble of rules (1990: 394).

One of the most famous discussions of objectivity and values, and objectivity as a value, is to be found in the work of Herbert Gans, whose seminal 1979 study, *Deciding What's News*, analyses values in the news, and the values of journalists. As Gans notes, 'journalists try hard to be objective, but neither they nor anyone else can in the end proceed without values' (1979: 39). Gans' work is not necessarily presented as an objection to objectivity per se – he is, rather, interested in the 'workings of objectivity'. However, in the last chapter of his book, Gans introduces a concept of perspective that seriously complicates objectivity. He writes: 'In the prototypical homogeneous society, which has never existed, everyone shares the same perspectives; but in a modern society, no one sits or stands in exactly the same place. Consequently, perspectives on reality will vary' (1979: 310). Gans does not deny that it is possible to cut across and take on other perspectives, but journalists and intellectuals are themselves 'attached to organizations, class, and other positions' (1979: 311). Furthermore, 'no one can synthesize all perspectives'. Gans concludes that rather than constitute some position beyond the realm of values, objectivity itself is a kind of value (1979: 39).

Crucial here is a process Gans terms 'value exclusion', which refers to the conscious exclusion of values: journalists do this in three ways: through objectivity, the disregard of implications, and the rejection of ideology (as they define it)' (1979: 183). Extending Gaye Tuchman's research (Tuchman 1978), Gans sees values exclusion as a practical consideration defending journalists 'against actual or possible criticism' (1979: 183) as well as a way to safeguard journalistic integrity (1979: 186).

Values exclusion puts a different cast on the common view that it is important to strive for objectivity. It also allows us for a more complex idea of what is commonly seen as 'detachment'. Through this concept one strives not for one transcendent standpoint, or even solely to escape partisan views, but to apply judgements about what values to exclude and which to include, often in reaction to the news or perceptions of fairness. This means that, on occasion, journalists will regard themselves as free to include values, show solidarity, take stands, and form reality judgements according to their 'paraideology' or workplace and professional ideology (Gans 1979: 203).

Gans argues that values exclusion provides a way for journalists not to become overly focused on the implications of the news, and the broader consequences of their work, as the main focus is on conveying facts. Values exclusion is learnt, and practised, but also linked to perceptions of legitimate controversy, consensus and deviant perspectives (see Hallin 1986: 117). Organizations can 'reinforce' values exclusion, while class or racial background and financial position can provide a different inflection on the 'feeling of objectivity'. One complex and contentious area of values exclusion is ideology, for while journalists may be conscious of values that should be excluded, they are (by virtue of the very nature of ideology) less conscious of their own ideological positionings, and vulnerable to what I term below 'frame-blindness'. Gans's conclusion is that journalists do not always practise good 'ideological editing' (1979: 194).

Scientistic journalism and empty facts

A strong criticism of journalistic objectivity has to do with its hollowness, especially when it stages balance or neutrality through a convenient juxtaposition of opposing viewpoints. This line of criticism relating to scientistic journalism and empty facts goes further, and focuses on the way modelling journalism on science and facts has some detrimental effects. Namely, it affects what James Carey calls the 'conversation' journalism has with its public, or how journalism fits into the conversation that is public society. The conversation Carey has in mind is imagined as an exchange between thinking citizens leading to more certain community direction based on shared values of common sense and democracy. For critics in this category, objectivity has a detrimental effect on civic problem solving. For Doug McGill 'the ideal of objectivity . . . has become a crutch for journalistic practices that work against civic aims' (2004). For Jay Rosen, 'objectivity is a very bad, unworkable philosophy for that task of re-engaging citizens in politics and public life' (1993: 51). It has, in other words, contributed to a deficit of deliberation and democracy.

Within this line of argument, the provision of more information, the reporting of a greater number of experts, the emphasis on facts, leaves the public less involved – bored and agitated onlookers on the game of journalism (Carey 1999 [1987]: 51). The journalism of fact, the ritual airing of different views, the way facts filter down from experts on high, limits understanding. Scientistic journalism leads to a demobilized or immobilized public. 'It is above all a journalism that justifies itself in the public's name but in which the public plays no role except as an audience' (1999 [1987]: 51).

There is a sense that objectivity is not up to the challenges of contemporary public life. For Carey, the conventions of objective reporting were developed to 'report another culture and another society' (1997 [1969]: 140). In this argument, science, in itself, is not the main concern. Facts exist as facts only in particular universes of discourse, and with skill these can be translated and passed around (Park 1940: 679). The problem, rather, has to do with the high-minded educational assumptions behind the scientistic approach. The assumption is that it is intellectuals that have the greatest access to facts, and that the journalists and experts are educators of the audience. In effect, what is handed down is a dialogue between experts on facts to audiences, leaving audiences on the outer. A conversation with the public falls by the wayside.

The antidote for Carey is to question the vocabulary of facts, and objectivity, and imagine journalism in other ways: as poetry, as diary, a repository of culture, a journalism of record of community life (1999 [1987]: 52).

As well as renewing a relationship with the public, there is another important side to this line of criticism which has to do with the very identity and independence of journalism. Objective reporting on one level gives a very precise role to the reporter, a process of putting words, actions and events into simple language. There is a craft to the construction of non-partisan reports, but in some ways journalism becomes a form of technical writing. It becomes a form of professional communication, where journalists adapt information from one source (say a government report) to another (the reader). The journalist becomes a relay point in a larger system of news transmission. This sits at odds with more 'inquiring' ideas of journalism and reporting.

For Carey, the idea that journalism becomes technical writing and a non-independent relay point is something to be concerned about. It means losing an older idea of journalism as a literary genre, as creative and imaginative work, and journalists as independent interpreters of events. Just as this 'conversion downwards' was happening (1997 [1969]: 137), objectivity became a central idea in explaining the professional competence and responsibilities of journalists. As a result, older ideas of journalism (as advocacy and criticism) begin to be side-lined or made secondary to the main ideal of objectivity. An 'essentially utilitarian-capitalist-scientific orientation towards events' prevails, where perspective, the 'role of personalities or actors' is privileged over information (Carey 1997 [1969]: 141).

Objectivity as biased and irresponsible

One of the hallmarks of journalistic objectivity as a professional ideal is that it allows the journalist to rise above bias and aspire to a higher level of responsibility. A powerful line of criticism of objectivity turns the tables on this view by arguing that objectivity is itself a form of bias and is not responsible. This line of argument suggests that despite the fact that objectivity is linked to higher standards of professionalism, questions of morality and responsibility do not always get fully addressed, or are evaded. Thus, as Theodore Glasser suggests – echoing arguments that date from at least the 1950s (Carroll 1955: 25) – 'objectivity in journalism effectively erodes the very foundation on which rests a responsible press' (Glasser 1992: 176).

For Glasser, objectivity is biased in four ways. Firstly, it is biased against other advocacy or 'watchdog' roles for the press, sometimes associated with the 'fourth estate'. This is quite a serious criticism as it goes to the role of journalism in society, and the way one idea of journalism can work to constrain this role. Secondly, it is biased in favour of the status quo, because of its reliance on official sources and establishment institutions. Thirdly, drawing on Carey's work, Glasser bemoans that objectivity is biased against independent thinking. Fourthly, objectivity is biased against the very idea of responsibility. It allows journalists to shift responsibility by arguing they are the reporters, not the creators of news, and therefore the consequences of what they report is not their concern (1992: 183). The picture of objectivity that arises from this critique is one that is especially passive and aligned with the status quo. For Glasser, objectivity has brought about a 'disregard for the consequences of newsmaking', and the task today is to 'liberate journalism from the burden of objectivity' (1992: 183).

One of these burdens is an artificial commitment to balance. For example, when journalists focus on balance, on giving both sides their say (as though there are only two sides), they may 'inject' a sense of fairness into the piece but may do a disservice to 'actual' truth. There is a concern that objectivity has morphed into what the contributors to the manifesto 'On Behalf of Journalism' call 'false balance, a tyranny of evenhandedness. Little more than "He said, she said" journalism' (Overholser 2006: 10). For Jay Rosen, balance can be seen as 'a flight from truth rather than an avenue into truth' (1993: 49). Discussing aspects of the reporting of lynching and war, Doug McGill notes, 'the norm of objectivity often has allowed serious social wrongs to continue unabated, while reporters misguidedly pursue the goal of "balanced" coverage' (2004).

Source dependence

As a form of professional communication, in Carey's terms, objective reporting impinges dramatically on the independence of the journalist, and their traditional roles of advocacy and critique (1997 [1969]: 138). Under this new regime, the reporter encounters a complex division of labour in the newsroom (indeed journalism becomes closely bound to the function of reporting). Also, they became a 'broker' between audiences and sources. Carey's analysis of this situation focuses on issues of source dependence and reliance on official sources, with new protocols and contexts transforming the journalist–source relationship. As Carey notes, 'the net effect of the press conference, the background interview, the rules governing anonymous disclosure and attribution of sources, and particularly the growing use of the public information officer within government is to routinize the reporter's function and to grant the source exceptional control over news dissemination' (1997 [1969]: 138).

The reporter's situation can be seen as a pushing and pulling between different obligations: those belonging to workplace, audience and source. However, Carey feels the source pulls on the psychology of the reporter in a unique way: reporters dependent on sources often inhabit the same corridors and receive direct feedback from them. This in turn translates into a particular 'sympathetic' orientation towards official sources. 'Reporters do not seek independent confirmation or use a critical method to test the statements issued by officials. . . . There is no real attempt to balance the official version against the contextual evidence' (Koch 1990: 174–5). As Todd Gitlin notes, with little actual contact with readers and viewers, 'reporters tend to be pulled into the cognitive worlds of their sources' (2003 [1980]: 270). He goes on to make the stronger claim that structurally, 'journalists are trained to be desensitized to the voices and life-worlds of working-class and minority people' (2003 [1980]: 269).

Frame-blindness

Frame-blindness describes a situation where journalists fail to recognize the ideological nature of their own framing of issues. As noted in the introduction, a key feature of objectivity in journalism has to do with an invisible frame being presented around events, allowing them to be 'reported' rather than 'constructed'. While framing theory is a vast area, for our present purposes I draw on Gitlin's definition of frames as 'persistent patterns of cognition, interpretation, and presentation, of selection, emphasis, and exclusion, by which symbol-handlers routinely organize discourse' (2003 [1980]: 7). News reports claim to 'recount events without the intrusion of value judgements or symbols'. News is 'a report on reality', and not a 'story' (Schiller 1981: 2). In political reporting it has been linked to a 'mirror' or 'messenger' analogy, with the reporter as journalist a neutral professional 'standing above the political fray' (Hallin 1986: 5). This claim to an invisible frame does not guarantee a thorough or even unbiased report, with one of the most startling examples being the racist reporting of lynchings in the US in the late nineteenth and early twentieth centuries in *The New York Times* (see Mindich 1998: 113–37).

Framing relates to a key dilemma in journalism (Hallin 1986: 72). On the one hand, reporters provide just the facts. On the other hand, they are teachers and storytellers compelled to draw on frames to educate, persuade and entertain. Between these two poles journalists can rely on different frames and discursive patternings. Conflict, for example, can be constructed through 'law and order' or 'injustice and defiance' frames (Fawcett 2011). Events and actions can become enlarged or even distorted through particular frames (a particular problem in political reporting of scandals and speculation over leadership, for example).

The issue of frame-blindness raises important concerns to do with the relationship between journalism and the social order. It does so because 'framing' implies that language has a key role in mediating and constructing the social order. As Robert A. Hackett notes, '*language* itself cannot function so as to transmit directly the supposedly inherent meaning or truth of events' (1984: 234). In other words, framing does leave the message transmitted by the report unchanged. Nevertheless, news journalists operate as though direct transmission was possible thanks to routines that

> decisively shape the ways in which news is defined, events are considered newsworthy, and 'objectivity' is secured. News is managed routinely, automatically, as reporters import definitions of newsworthiness from editors and institutional beats, as they accept the analytical frameworks of officials even while taking up adversary positions. When reporters make decisions about what to cover and how, rarely do they deliberate about ideological assumptions or political consequences. Simply by doing their jobs, journalists tend to serve the political and economic elite definitions of reality. (Gitlin 2003 [1980]: 11–12)

News routines, including those around objectivity, enable reporters to distance themselves from the ideological and political frames influencing their work.

Gitlin points here to a complex professional situation. Objectivity 'insulates' reporters from various interest groups, which range from 'direct political pressures of specific advertisers, politicians, and interest groups', and even publishers. Objectivity also 'tunes' reporters into 'the expectation and experience of news executives and high-level sources', so that 'they systematically frame the news to be compatible with the main institutional arrangements of the society' (2003 [1980]: 269).

Here, what I am terming frame-blindness intersects with source dependence. For Daniel C. Hallin, writing about coverage of the Vietnam War, the same routines Gitlin highlights leaves journalists open to manipulation. Reporters focused on 'just the facts', 'but they were not just *any* facts. They were *official* facts ... The effect of "objectivity" was not to free the news of political influence, but to open wide the channel through which official sources flowed' (Hallin 1986: 25). In something of an indictment of the relation between objective reporting and official sources, Hallin argues 'official sources fill an important void left by the ethic of objectivity: they fill the vacuum of meaning left by the journalist's renunciation of the role of interpreting reality' (1986: 73).

There exist 'hard' and 'soft' versions of the framing thesis in regard to journalistic objectivity. In the hard version there is a concrete, pre-given reality that we judge the media against. We can say that frames distort or fail to measure up to a reality (see Hackett 1984: 234; also Gans 1979: 305): they 'transmit' something about actual events. Ideology is a factor insofar as it provides a skewed picture of the world. The 'soft' version is more challenging, because it questions the pre-givenness of social and political reality. As Tom Koch argues, the idea that the frame distorts real objectivity is a chimera since 'being involved in an event – even as a recorder – we influence it' (1990: 20). So-called events are constructed, pre-mediated. In a sense our worlds are constructed via a layering of frames of different power and form. In this domain, rather than speak of distortion, reality is *all* ideology and discourse, with frames embedded within a 'gaseous' cloud of social and economic relations.

Another example of the soft theory that applies to objectivity is Hallin's theory of 'spheres of consensus, controversy and deviance' (1986: 117), which describes different forms of public discourse. Hallin pictures these as regions of a concentric circle, with consensus being the inner core, legitimate controversy the middle layer, and the sphere of deviance the outer layer. The sphere of consensus is the 'motherhood and apple pie' layer, where core values are not contested. Consensus values are rarely subject to opposing views and disinterest need not be maintained. The sphere of legitimate controversy is the region in which journalistic objectivity is most at home, sounding out different perspectives in electoral contests and legislative debates. This sphere is bounded by the sphere of deviance, where some views are ruled to be beyond those of legitimate controversy, and objectivity works in a political way to disqualify some views from being heard. 'Here neutrality once again falls away, and journalism becomes . . . a "boundary-maintaining mechanism"' (1986: 117). The fact that much of the commercial media are funded by advertisers places extra considerations on definitions of consensus, legitimate controversy and deviancy.

Ideology and hegemony are commonly evoked terms in studies of framing, although they can be operationalized in different ways. Ideology can be linked to a naturalization of social relations, with news declaring 'that's the way it is' when in fact 'the way it is' is constantly being contested (Hackett 1984: 248). The ideological function of news and norms of objectivity in this sense are to 'reflect and represent the prevailing structure and mode of power' (Hackett 1984: 249). For John Hartley, 'the impartiality, objectivity, neutrality and balance which form the bedrock of editorial ideology are no sham. They are required if news is to act alongside the other agencies in naturalizing dominant ideology and winning consent for hegemony' (1982: 61–2).

Hegemony, as understood by Italian political scientist Antonio Gramsci, is accomplished through the educational and media systems (Hall 1977: 333). It can be described as a process of coercion or domination by consent, whereby the dominant classes, operating in a field of meanings, expectations and desires, 'succeed in framing competing definitions of the reality within their range, bringing all alternatives within their horizon of thought' (Hall 1977: 333). The media operates within this field to give events social intelligibility, to translate the real into symbolic forms according to codes and conventions like objectivity (Hall 1977: 343).

The work of framing is masked, Stuart Hall suggests, by professional routines and norms which construct the work of encoding 'within the bracket of a professional-technical neutrality'. The concept of neutral reporting, for example, distances the reporter from the ideological content of the material he is handling and the ideological inflexions of the codes he is employing' (1977: 344). Hall is quick to add that this does not mean that the media does not have some 'relative autonomy' – which is 'enshrined in the operational principles of broadcasting – "objectivity", "neutrality", "impartiality" and "balance"' (Hall 1977: 345) – but thus autonomy ultimately works in a broader sense to support the 'structured ideological field' on which consensus or disagreement is formed.

Objectivity as contradiction in terms and dangerous myth

The argument that objectivity in journalism is a contradiction in terms belongs to Hunter S. Thompson, famous for his use of fictional devices, first person, sarcasm, satire, cursing and exaggeration in books such as *Fear and Loathing on the Campaign Trail '72* (Thompson 1973; McLaughlin 2002: 163–6). Thompson regards the rules of objectivity as constraining on the very act of journalism because the subjective observations of the journalist are crucial to truth-seeking. Thus his view that

> So much for Objective Journalism. Don't bother to look for it here – not under any byline of mine; or anyone else I can think of. With the possible exception of things like box scores, race results, and stock market tabulations, there is no such thing as Objective Journalism. The phrase itself is a pompous contradiction in terms. (Thompson 1973: 44)

Whereas some journalists will acknowledge objectivity as an impossible ideal, but strive towards it nonetheless, Thompson gives up on it. Total coverage is difficult. Balance unrealistic (Hahn & Thompson 1997). If objectivity is premised upon a distance between the event being reported and the reporter, subject and journalist, then Thompson can be said to dissolve the distinction between the two.

Thompson was tuned into the way objectivity leads journalists to look for particular kinds of facts: these facts can be supplied by those in power, and in this sense journalism can be manipulated. Thus, his comments on Nixon: '"It was the built-in blind spot of the Objective Rules and dogma that allowed Nixon to slither into the White House in the first place"' (Keil 2005: 60). 'He seemed so all-American, so much like Horatio Alger, that he was able to slip through the cracks of Objective Journalism. You had to get

Subjective to see Nixon clearly, and the shock of recognition was often painful' (Thompson 1994: 243).

Thompson found objectivity inadequate to cover American politics, but more than this, in the play of facts and information, he regarded it as almost complicit in the problems of American politics, the illusions it creates, the superficiality and staged responses. It is not that objectivity is just flawed, but that we cannot afford it. 'Not even the Pope can afford "objectivity" in a US election year. It is . . . a luxury and a cop-out, a holding tank for bystanders' (Thompson 1994: 243).

Some can find gonzo journalism indulgent, tiresome – easy to mimic badly but difficult to do well – a particular product of the excesses of the 1960s and 1970s. Others appreciate (for all its flaws) its honesty, its insights into power, its inventiveness with language and its (often long-term) immersion in its subject – a return to good research and groundwork (Ricketson 2001).

Leaving Thompson's particular style to one side, this line of criticism shares some aspects with the criticism that objectivity is overly scientistic. What is shared between the two is an idea that alternative forms of journalism offer more in the way of explaining how the facts fit together than sheer reporting. As one editor of an anthology of literary journalism puts it, in an increasingly complex society, readers 'demand not just information, but visions of how things fit together now that the center cannot hold. . . . Literary journalism couples cold fact and personal event, in the author's humane company' (Kramer 1995: 34).

Gonzo journalism is but one expression of the 'new journalism' of the 1960s and 1970s, which sought to disturb the 'pale beige tone' (Wolfe 1973: 31) of standard journalism, and fuse non-fiction techniques with a commitment to reporting. Another figure equally concerned with objectivity was Tom Wolfe, although he is less overtly critical of objectivity. As a form of reportage he felt that the basic unit was not information per se, but the scene (1973: 35, 66). This shifts the focus of attention of the journalist but also provides a new 'stage' on which to act and participate in the story. It allows for 'an egotistical objectivity but an objectivity of sorts in any case' (1973: 66).

In many objections to objectivity, the concept is seen as something that needs correcting, or improving. For others it is a mindset that conceals how subjective they are (Morrison & Tremewan 1992: 124). But there exists a more stark line of objection we should consider. Namely that it is a dangerous myth, and that a belief in objectivity can have outright negative effects. Thus, rather than strive for a difficult ideal, we should admit that absolutes are beyond us (Klotzer 2009). William Morgan of the Canadian Broadcasting Corporation undertakes a version of this criticism when he suggests that

> objectivity in journalism, perhaps as in academic work, seems to me to be at the very worst a dangerous myth and at best a distant and mostly unattained goal, towards which we strive when we remember. I even tend to doubt that the word has a place in a book of journalism policy, being probably unachievable and certainly unverifiable. (Morgan 1992)

From this line of criticism, objectivity emerges less a noble striving for truth than a staging of facts and numbers to achieve an objectivity-effect. Objectivity here is linked to rhetorical devices, such as being precise in relation to time, places, objects, numbers.

Debate over the 'dangers' associated with objectivity have taken on a complex form due to developments in cable news: 'more personalized, more interactive, more opinionated, more communal, less objective?' (Kinsley 2006). Pictured against a new backdrop, detachment begins to look like lack of attachment, critical disinterest, uninteresting. Current affairs with a twist of comedy, documentary or opinion, seems more informative than the 'straight report'.

> More and more, Americans are trusting the information they get from sources with a voice, including comedy programs like *The Daily Show*, documentaries like *An Inconvenient Truth* . . ., and Fox News's remarkable growth stems in significant part from its clear point of view (Overholser 2006: 10–11).

While honesty and factual accuracy remain core values for journalists, the pretence of objectivity has become an issue for audiences and consumers. Former reporter for *The New York Times*,

Doug McGill, identifies pseudo-objectivity as the danger (2004). The concern here is that a journalist might compile a story of opposing points of view, and thus fulfil the ritual of objectivity, but do nothing to advance understanding of the issue beyond an initial acquaintance with it. It is becoming less common, in McGill's view, for journalists to base their reports on the facts rather than take sides in a debate. But political journalist Michael Kinsley goes further, questioning what he calls 'artificial objectivity'. 'Objectivity – the faith professed by American journalism and by its critics – is less an ideal than a conceit. It's not that all journalists are secretly biased, or even that perfect objectivity is an admirable but unachievable goal. In fact, most reporters work hard to be objective and the best come very close. The trouble is that objectivity is a muddled concept' (2006). The argument that objectivity is a dangerous myth suggests that striving and falling short may not be so virtuous after all.

Objectivity as a bystander's journalism: the journalism of attachment

A persistent critique of objective journalism is that it is a form of moral spectatorship (Ryan 2001: 7). Journalists working in the specific area of war reporting have mounted their own critique of notions such as neutrality and detachment. This leads us to what has been called the journalism of attachment, a journalism that 'cares as well as knows' (Bell 1998a: 16; McLaughlin 2002). Schooled in a BBC tradition of distance and detachment, foreign correspondent (and later British MP) Martin Bell comes to see objectivity as an 'illusion' (1997: 8); although he holds 'more than ever' to values of 'fairness and impartiality, and a scrupulous attention to the facts and a determination to pay heed to the unpopular spokespeople of unfavoured causes' (Bell 1998b: 102). A similar questioning of objectivity has been put forward by *Sarajevo Times* editor Kemal Kurspahic (1995) and CNN's Christiane Amanpour (1996). However, by contrast, both seek to stick with the concept of objectivity. Amanpour writes,

I have come to believe that objectivity means giving all sides a fair hearing, but not treating all sides equally. Once you treat all sides the same in a case such as Bosnia, you are drawing a moral equivalence between victim and aggressor. And from there it is a short step toward being neutral. And from there it's an even shorter step to becoming an accessory to all manners of evil; in Bosnia's case, genocide. So objectivity must go hand in hand with morality. (Amanpour 1996)

The idea of journalism of attachment has not been without its critics, and we shall examine this debate separately in chapters 5 and 6.

The nature of truth and reality

Of all of the blows that have been dealt to journalistic objectivity, perhaps none is more fundamental than those concerning the notions of truth and reality it relies on. This criticism can be close to the bone for those journalists who see their role as truth-tellers or as holding up a mirror to reality. It includes criticism of the basic assumption to do with the separation of facts and values in journalism (see chapter 3).

This is partly a philosophical critique, as Carlin Romano notes:

In both philosophy and the sciences, the notion of a hardbound truth in the world that researchers 'find' or report has fallen on hard times. Ever since Kant argued in the *Critique of Pure Reason* that the nature of human thought makes it impossible to perceive things in themselves without shaping by the mind's categories, the idea that language or thought can mirror the world has been skeptically received. In the twentieth century, that doubt about 'naïve realism' seems to have gained the upper ground in every field except American journalism. (Romano 1986: 76)

Among a range of figures that have contributed to doubt over objectivity, Romano mentions Thomas Kuhn's critique of scientific knowledge; Paul Feyerabend's critique of scientific method; Hans-Georg Gadamer's theories of interpretation; Michel Foucault's work on power relations in society; and Richard Rorty's critique of capital T truth.

Alongside the philosophical critique, objecting to objectivity on grounds of truth and reality is also partly ideological, and draws on accusations of 'frame-blindness' and 'source dependence' examined above. Furthermore, sociologists of media have questioned the concept of external reality implied in journalistic objectivity as well as the suggestion that journalists just report reality. As Kevin Latham puts it, 'news works "as if" it refers, truthfully, to an external reality, whereas in effect any such reality is rather a product of the specific conditions, methods, systems and governing assumptions of news production, that is of its "regime of truth"' (2000: 636).

These regimes are supported by particular paradigms of media work, and organizational contexts. As Gaye Tuchman puts it, 'each newspaper story is a collection of "facts" assessed and structured by newsmen' (1972: 663). Tuchman puts forward a notion of the 'web of facticity' to describe an intermeshing of sources, facts and common understandings that underpins reporting. Facts are accumulated, validated, verified. The web of facticity 'both guides the search for news and perpetually reconstitutes itself as the frame for news' (1978: 103). It is difficult, from this perspective, to hold onto the view that the news mirrors society. News is instead made meaningful through processes of judgement, the transformation of facts, and application of frames. Yet, as Barbie Zelizer suggests,

> practicing reporters rarely admit their *usage of constructions of reality*, seen among critical observers as a common way of presenting the news. . . . They instead stress their adherence to notions of objectivity and balance, both of which are suggested by professional codes. . . . This raises questions about how and why journalists use professionalism as a way to conceal the constructed nature of their activities. (1993: 221)

'Objectivity is an attitude geared towards finding the truth' (ABC Editorial Policies 2008). This statement captures both a basic premise, and a broader framework. Truth-seeking is hotly debated in academic and professional circles, and the very paths of truth-seeking are changing. The issue of perspective and point of view, in particular, garners specific attention. In Milton's *Areopagitica* (1664) 'Truth' is depicted as a virgin woman of perfect shape. 'Then strait arose a wicked race of deceivers who ... hewd her lovely form into a thousand pieces, and scatter'd them to the four winds'. In this tradition, forming the truth is conceived in terms of gathering together pieces in order to reconstitute a perfect form (Hartley 1992: 149).

Contrast this with feminist and cultural studies approaches that critique the very dichotomy of the knower and the known, questioning the way objectivity works through *exnomination*, minimizing the impact of racial, class, gendered and ethnic ways of knowing. 'What counts as "truth" in a given instance is determined by who has the power to define reality' (Allan 2010: 149). As broadcaster John P. Santos argues, 'the long-hallowed cult of journalistic "objectivity" has too often been a veneer for what is essentially a predominating white male point of view in our news culture' (1997: 123; Allan 2010: 111).

Significantly, then, classical concepts of truth have been overtaken by contemporary analysis of knowledge and power (Foucault 1980). Today, collaborative on-line journalism collectivizes but also deconstructs this work. It also takes the search for truth beyond the newsroom, the specific view of gatekeepers, placing the emphasis on multiple perspectives emerging out of the interaction of a diverse community of users (Bruns 2005: 27).

At stake in this discussion is the very fate of an 'objective' picture of the world; but also the issue of what a post-objective (or post-truth) journalism looks like. Hartley uses the term 'post-truth society' to characterize a binary-oriented journalism in which 'reason and truth are not the guiding principles' but rather 'adversarial visions' that pit 'we' groups against 'they' groups (1992: 217). As described by Robert A. Hackett and Yuezhi Zhao, in post-truth journalism 'Truth-claims would be limited by and to their particular paradigm' (1998: 124). 'Any objectivity that was possible would operate on the basis of consensual standards shared within, but not across, the boundaries of discourse communities' (1998: 124). For David T. Z. Mindich, journalism as a 'post-objective' profession would focus on honest mediation rather than delivering 'reality' (1998: 141–2).

Others have also tackled 'post-truth-ness'. For Richard Rorty, there is '"nothing more" to truth and objectivity than justification and intersubjective agreement' (Ward 2004: 269). Intersubjectivity, or approaching objectivity through 'revealing and assessing our subjectivity and the subjectivity of others, knowing where "we" stand in relation to "them"' (Deverell 1996: 60), has become an important theme. Against this backdrop, Stephen J. A. Ward sees traditional objectivity as hopelessly one-dimensional: 'Objective reporters were *completely* detached; eliminated *all* of their opinion; reported *just* the facts' (2011: 224).

This state of affairs does not necessarily mean objectivity is irrelevant. As Gans suggests, 'It may exist as epistemologically impossible, but it can exist as journalistic intent' (1979: 315). Indeed, multiple perspectives, sources, make objectivity 'even more necessary': 'But objectivity would also attain a new meaning, for in the final reckoning, story selectors can be objective only by choosing news from several perspectives' (1979: 315).

For Stuart Allan, this post-truth paradigm, if operationalized in the correct way, would enable a critical examination of the link between objectivity and hegemony. Allan seeks to move beyond 'hard' versions of frame-blindness to explore more complex theorizations. Drawing on a postmodern critical framework, Allan seeks to push beyond a version of the hegemony thesis that relies on an unmasking of 'true' reality in order to tackle the indeterminacies and contradictions of the social order (Allan 1995: 130).

The view from nowhere

In a significant extension of the objections focused on truth and reality, critics of neutral and objective points of view raise the issue of 'the view from nowhere' (Iggers 1998: 96). While the phrase can be used to characterize objectivity in general, it has taken on a specific meaning in journalism studies. Promoted especially by Jay Rosen, the idea of the view from nowhere serves to highlight when reporters adopt a non-position. Here, balance becomes a shelter. In Rosen's version, because reporters can no longer be characterized as left or right, they evade accusations of bias. On the surface this looks (positively) like detachment. However, for Rosen, this can easily turn into a dark power, 'The daily gift of detachment keeps giving, until you're almost "above" anyone who tries to get too political with you, or at least in the middle with the microphone between warring factions. There's power in that; and where there's power, there's attraction' (2003). In other words, it leads to a (negative) commitment to politics and democracy. Detachment from any theorized political stance (a view from somewhere) has a particular aspect on political journalism, according to Rosen, because it becomes vulnerable to grandstanding, aggressive displays and politics as spectacle. Supported by concepts such as neutrality and objectivity, it evacuates the space of politics (Rosen 2004a).

Rosen does not dismiss all aspects of objectivity. The concept of the view from nowhere assists him to isolate the specific aspect of objectivity that is of most concern, which is that:

> In pro journalism, American style, the View from Nowhere is a bid for trust that advertises the viewlessness of the news producer. Frequently it places the journalist between polarized extremes, and calls that neither-nor position 'impartial.' Second, it's a means of defense against a style of criticism that is fully anticipated: charges of bias originating in partisan politics and the two-party system. Third: it's an attempt to secure a kind of universal legitimacy that is implicitly denied to those who stake out positions or betray a point of view. American journalists have almost a lust for the View from Nowhere because they think it has more authority than any other possible stance. (Rosen 2010b)

On all levels, the view from nowhere offers a false or unearned position of authority. Against the idea of a 'view from nowhere' dominating the press agenda, Rosen conceives of a pluralistic view in which the people who 'come from somewhere' co-exist with those who come from nowhere.

Let some in the press continue on with the mask of impartiality, which has advantages for cultivating sources and soothing advertisers. Let others experiment with transparency as the basis for trust. When you click on their by-line it takes you to a disclosure page where there is a bio, a kind of mission statement, and a creative attempt to say: here's where I'm coming from. (Rosen 2010b)

As Rosen acknowledges, the phrase 'view from nowhere' comes from Thomas Nagel, who published a book with that title in 1986. Like Rosen, Nagel is ambivalent on objectivity, offering both a defence and critique. Unlike Rosen, Nagel sets himself an over-arching problem, namely 'how to combine the perspective of a particular person inside the world with an objective view of that same world' (1986: 3). This attempt to fuse the two approaches, which Rosen treats as distinct, represents a fundamental philo-sophical challenge for Nagel. Nagel's approach is to 'juxtapose the internal and external or subjective and objective views at full strength' (1986: 4). Achieving or maximizing objectivity means stepping back from our initial view of the world to 'form a new conception that has that view and its relation to the world as object' (1986: 4). This is quite different from Rosen's posi-tion, and Nagel retains a strong commitment to detachment and transcendence of subjectivity.

Nagel does not rely on any straightforward separation theory of facts and values to secure his concept of objectivity. Rather, it is a question of standpoint and degree, and accommodating the subjec-tive in the objective, and vice versa. Subjectivity is crucial to appre-ciating the 'specific qualities' and incompleteness of the objective world (1986: 25). 'Reality is not just objective reality' (1986: 26). A standpoint becomes more objective when it is less grounded in the 'specifics of the individual's makeup' or their character (1986: 5). Objectivity is, for Nagel, the product of reflection,

> we can raise our understanding to a new level only if we examine that relation between the world and ourselves which is responsible for our prior understanding, and form a new conception that includes a more detached understanding of ourselves, of the world, and the interaction between them. (1986: 5)

Balancing this commitment to reflection is a principle of integra-tion: that we should endeavour to recognize and reconcile with subjective or less objective viewpoints (remembering that this may become an impossible task). Nagel is particularly conscious of the attempt to eliminate point of view and perspective from objectivity.

Nagel has little sympathy with a simplistic view that we must get outside ourselves and view the world from nowhere within it. Nor is his conception of objectivity based on an absolute 'god' position. His response is to re-work the idea of detachment, by appreciating a viewpoint of the world that 'includes us', and our conception of the world, in a way that 'is not tied to our particular point of view' (1986: 70). An 'objective advance' may eventually be turned into a mere appearance, which would prompt more self-understanding. Transcendence and re-integration are coupled in this sense.

Inspired by the work of Nagel, and Julian Baggini (2003), foreign correspondent David Loyn (2007) proposes objectivity as a means to truthfulness. In a 2007 response to Loyn, peace journalism researcher Jake Lynch focuses on Nagel's apparent use of objectivity to enforce epistemological 'correctness' which seems to focus on eliminating 'peculiarities': 'In pursuing objectivity we alter our relation to the world, increasing the correctness of certain of our representations of it by compensating for the peculiarities of our point of view (Nagel 1986: 91; Lynch 2007: 3). Lynch is not alone in casting suspicion on the idea of transcending our peculiarities (D'Agostino 1993). His critique is focused around the vague nature of this process of assessment, and its foundation. Indeed, Nagel is not clear on the standard of correctness that should be applied here; but this may be because his focus is not on correspondence theories of truth, but on the re-integration of standpoints. So it is still open to debate whether Nagel is a transcendentalist, reliant on objectivity as a view from some absolute, God-like position. As Nagel states, 'A view or form of thought is more objective than another if it relies less on the specifics of the individual's makeup and position in the world. A standpoint that is objective by comparison with the personal view of one individual may be subjective by comparison with a theoretical standpoint still farther out' (1986: 5). Here, Nagel, like other philosophers

(D'Agostino 1993) is turning to ideas such as conversation to underpin a renewed commitment to objectivity.

Conclusion

For some readers these objections to objectivity, and the issues raised by them, will have missed the mark. For others, they amount to a death blow. It is not hard to create doubt around the concept of objectivity. As Richard Sambrook of the BBC notes, 'These days it is fashionable to question whether there is any such thing as "truth". Whether facts actually prove anything; whether objectivity is worth striving for' (2004). But I want to suggest that there is more than fashion at stake, and a range of objections to objectivity need to be taken seriously, alongside defences of it, and new avenues of exploration associated with alternative philosophical perspectives. Issues related to relativism, framing, ideology, need to be carefully engaged with. As with any term that helps to structure our understanding of the media, it is important to debate it, to pick the issues apart, whether in meetings, pubs, in coffee shops, or in universities, in order that our media culture stays active and inquiring. For some practitioners this 'deconstruction' might bring feelings of fear or threat, but hopefully it leads to new ways of thinking about matters of importance.

3

Why is there so much dispute over 'the facts'?

At the core of objectivity in journalism is the concept of reporting the facts. Indeed, a reverence towards facts goes to the heart of objectivity itself. Facts sit at the centre of concerns of many of the objections to objectivity discussed in the last chapter, including selectivity and values, scientism, source dependence, and the very nature of truth and reality. Before considering some of the defences to objectivity in the next chapter, it will be useful to examine some of the disputes over facts – especially issues of the status of facts, and the separation of facts from values, which are the most contested aspects. We shall also discuss several different schools of philosophical thought. This is because terms such as 'realism', 'objectivity', 'positivism' and 'empiricism' are frequently used to categorize objectivity without a great deal of precision, leading to empty debating points, and a muddied view of objectivity. As we shall see, while many of the '-isms' we discuss below share a common base, they do signal quite different ways of setting out the relationship between the truth and the facts.

The uses and abuses of philosophy

A great deal of dispute over 'the facts' goes to debate over the philosophy of objectivity itself, one that affirms a world that exists independent of mind, that forms 'a coherent and accessible world of objective facts capable of being known through observation, understood with the use of reason, and accurately represented in thought, literature, and the arts' (Shi 1995: 4–5). For the objectivist faithful, this view of the world is entirely reasonable. Others might question parts, such as the possibility of 'accurate' representation in any kind of language. Nick Davies, declaring objectivity a classic 'flat earth tale', writes 'Reality exists objectively, but any attempt to record the truth about it . . . involves selection . . . In this sense, all news is artifice' (2008: 111). But other critics might go further to question any concept of 'independent' reality. They might suggest that '"reality" – or what we believe to be reality – emerges from the consciousness of the observer' (Hanitzsch 2004: 488). They might refuse the idea of 'telling it as it is', proposing instead that 'it is as you tell it' (Barkho 2010: 15). Others discredit objectivity as an epistemology, or way of knowing the world. For Jay Rosen 'journalism is the last refuge of objectivity as an epistemology': 'Not even in the hard sciences do they really see the pursuit of truth this way' (1993: 48). Rosen focuses on a key issue which is that this epistemology alienates or disconnects journalism from wider intellectual debate:

> [O]bjectivity as a theory of how to arrive at the truth is bankrupt intellectually. There isn't anybody else who believes in it and for good reason, because everything we've learned about the pursuit of truth tells us that in one way or another the knower is incorporated into the known. Objectivity has the further unfortunate effect of alienating the American journalist from intellectual debate and intellectual conversation, which is a very dangerous thing. (1993: 51)

Rosen argues that journalism's reliance on this theory of truth has serious implications for the role of journalism in society.

An important caveat should be raised at this point. It is tempting to explain and define objectivity purely on the philosophical level, as an expression of this or that philosophical movement. It is desirable to think that this is possible because one expects objectivity to be a well-thought-out and consistent form of theory and practice. While an understandable view, there are difficulties with a purely philosophical analysis. One difficulty is that philosophy is not the sole 'source' of objectivity. There is a growing argument, especially in the English case, that legal understandings of 'matters of fact' and impartiality are central to the development of a fact-oriented journalism in England (Shapiro 2000: 26). In the US, objectivity was filtered through political theory (Lippmann 1920). Furthermore, 'practice' can itself be a source. As we noted in the Introduction, it is possible to practice the procedures of objectivity without assuming the entire epistemology. As Jeremy Iggers observes, 'most defenders of objectivity are not troubled by such abstract and theoretical problems as defending the concept of objective analysis or explaining the possibility of a neutral point of view' (1998: 96). In other words, journalistic objectivity can be seen as a kind of hybrid or 'bitzer' of different ideas and approaches. Despite these issues, I want to suggest that an excursion into the philosophical side can be useful to tease out some aspects of the dispute around facts, and hopefully go beyond 'dispute' as a mode of discussion of objectivity in journalism.

Putting facts and truths together

One of the most troublesome aspects of the debates around objectivity and facts is the way that the concept of objectivity is given a dual role: that of a view of the world, but also a way of representing and communicating truths. This gesture treats the word 'objectivity' as short-hand for 'objective reality' as well as a mode or method of perception of this reality. This fusion of reality and perception narrows the space between facts and truths. It closes down a very important philosophical area that has been explored by many movements and theorists. Facts, truths and objective reality are thus merged or melded into constructs such as 'objective truth' (Windschuttle 1998: 8). But there is a distinction between facts and the truths derived from them, as well as an issue of the method used to approach truth and facticity, and present them in the form of news.

Walter Lippmann addresses this issue by being sceptical of the idea that the news presents objective truths. In a famous passage, he challenges the idea of treating the news and truth as two words for the same thing.

> The hypothesis, which seems to me the most fertile, is that news and truth are not the same thing, and must be clearly distinguished. The function of news is to signalize an event, the function of truth is to bring to light the hidden facts, to set them into relation with each other, and make a picture of reality on which men can act. Only at those points, where social conditions take recognizable and measurable shape, do the body of truth and the body of news coincide. (1922: 358)

Lippmann's idea that the function of truth is to set hidden facts into relation with each other usefully leads us into a discussion of ways of knowing or understanding facts and events. For Lippmann, objectivity plays a cardinal methodological role in anchoring facts in relation to truths. However, in many discussions of objectivity in journalism, truth and facts are treated (against Lippmann's advice) as close to identical. In this sense the discussion oscillates between a naïve empiricism and raw scientism: either the facts 'speak for themselves' or the reporter is close to some kind of camera, an apparatus. Significantly, there exists a number of ways to approach this issue of the relationship between truth and facts.

Correspondence and coherence

Donald McDonald defines objectivity as 'an essential correspondence between knowledge of a thing, and the thing itself' (1975 [1971]: 69). In doing so, McDonald draws upon one of the key theories of putting facts and truths together, namely a 'correspondence theory of truth'. Accusations of 'slant' and 'distortion' commonly draw on a correspondence theory.

The correspondence theory has to do with what Denis McQuail describes as 'the degree of correspondence between the version of events offered by the news and the "reality" of these events, and "good performance" of the news task has come to be equated with a high degree of correspondence and accuracy in this respect. The news media are expected to "tell it as it is"' (McQuail 1986:

2). Yet, as McQuail points out, the correspondence theory makes certain assumptions. 'Objectivity helps to sustain the belief that there is one given reality (i.e., that there is no alternative to the existing social order) and that news is a reliable account of it (i.e., that objectivity is possible)' (1986: 6).

The contrasting 'coherence theory of truth', as implied, does not determine truth through the correspondence of a representation with an object. It values a consistency of propositions: 'For coherence, a statement or proposition must be consistent with a suitably defined body of other propositions, and this body needs to be consistent within itself' (Dawson & Gregory 2009: 127).

One of the reasons why the coherence theory is not always favoured in discussions of objectivity in journalism is because it gives a limited role to experience: 'For a pure coherence theorist, experience is only relevant as the source of perceptual beliefs, which take their place as part of the coherent or incoherent set' (Blackburn 2008). That said, it could also be argued, such as when Schudson tells us that the ideal of objectivity developed because facts could not speak for themselves (see chapter 1), that objectivity is precisely a coherence theory, a form of perceptual belief that is not dependent on correspondence per se.

Under the correspondence theory, truth corresponds to an objective reality, which is both understandable or knowable and rational (Dawson & Gregory 2009: 127). It allows for concepts such as 'fidelity' or 'faithful' representation. The issue of the manner or nature of this correspondence is important, and it can be characterized in different ways. We shall examine some of these below in relation to problems of communication and facticity, but it is clear, as Iggers points out, that many journalists favour 'the vocabulary of objective and pictorial representation' (1989: 94), which accounts for a reliance on metaphors such as mirroring, reflecting, etc.

Empiricism

Empiricism is often invoked in discussions of objectivity and granted a dominant position. It also takes many different forms.

Broadly speaking it constitutes a philosophical position that says knowledge is derived from or dependent on the sense experience of the external world (Novack 1968: 8). It holds that experience rather than reason is the source of knowledge; although philosophers have differing views on the exact relation between our knowledge and sense experience and may focus on sensations, facts or phenomena. The focus on experience, observation and induction has an obvious attraction for many theories of journalistic reporting, especially those that assume the reporter to be a *tabula rasa* or blank slate of knowledge. The philosophy is usually linked to British Empiricists of the seventeenth and eighteenth centuries such as John Locke and David Hume. Stephen J. A. Ward provides a useful description of Locke's psychology when he writes, 'The mind is empty of ideas until external objects cause bodily sensations of colour, heat, shape, pain, and so on. The mind reflects on these sensations and produces the ideas . . . in the mind. It then combines these ideas into judgements, such as cause and effect. It can also reason, moving by inference, from ideas to other ideas' (Ward 2004: 68). This account highlights one of the key areas of controversy in empiricism; namely, the status of the observer who is 'constantly organizing sense data, according to some pregiven schema or pattern' (Hackett & Zhao 1998: 110).

Another key figure is Francis Bacon. A version of Bacon's 'common-sense' inductive method, based on the view that observations were sacred, characterized official academic philosophy in the US and England throughout the nineteenth century (Novick 1988: 34). Schiller tells us that 'Baconian observation and deduction were the American version of positivism' (1981: 83). James Gordon Bennett is recorded as declaring '"I have struck out the true Baconian path in commercial science, and it must succeed"' (Schudson 1978: 54; also Schiller 1981: 83).

It is perplexing that, for all of the talk of naïve empiricism, journalism scholars rarely discuss *non*-naïve or sophisticated forms of empiricism. But more complex forms of 'transcendental' empiricism exist, questioning the presuppositions and conditions upon which we understand our 'given' experience (see Deleuze 1991; Voloshinov 1973 [1929]). The decision to ignore complex forms of empiricism has been determining, however. Ward suggests that journalism had a choice to base its approach on active or passive varieties of empiricism, and regards the decision to go with the passive observer as a 'fatal conceptual error' (2004: 198). 'The theory of journalistic objectivity took on an epistemologically indefensible position and an inaccurate representation of the reporting process' (2004: 198).

Positivism

Many scholars have noted a link between positivism and journalism (Gans 1979: 184; Schiller 1981: 83–4; Hallin 1986: 65; Glasser 1992: 176; Hackett & Zhao 1998: 10). Positivism has been taken up by a range of figures, but is most frequently linked back to the French philosopher Auguste Comte, and also John Stuart Mill, who placed the testing of truth and falsity at the heart of his ideas of the liberty of the press (see Mill 1997 [1859]: 24).

Positivism as an approach is often associated with observable and retrievable facts. Ward aligns it with what he calls 'pure objectivity', 'narrower in concept and stricter in method', an 'attempt to inoculate science from bias' (2004: 78).

> Pure objectivity conceived of the scientist as a dispassionate observer of nature. It favoured procedures and new instruments that grasped the facts . . . Ontologically a fact was a hard nugget of data that no one could invent or manipulate. The truth of a factual statement followed from a direct correspondence of the sentence and the state of affairs it describes. Facts could be the objective, evidentiary basis of science only if science could draw a hard line between facts and values . . . 'Objectivity' was *not* being subjective, *not* interpreting. (Ward 2004: 78)

Drawing on empirical philosophy, positivism combines aspects of empiricism and rationalism in the spirit of modernity and progress (Hjørland 2005: 130), which gives rise to a concept of a uniform, objective world (Schiller 1981: 83). Positivism holds that science and facts are the only ground of valid knowledge. It dislikes speculation, focusing on the 'positively given' (Blackburn 2008). It seeks to go beyond theology and metaphysics (which is meaningless), and identify general principles that are common to all sciences. These principles are put forward as the basis of social organization and human conduct. On this basis, 'the accumulation of facts would lead to predictive laws of society that would guide political reform' (Ward 2004: 79).

Positivism impacts on discussions of journalistic objectivity because of the specific way it puts facts and truths together, usually focusing on quantifiable facts that can be 'counted, measured and weighed' (Shi 1995: 71). It informs the separation of facts and values associated with objective journalism, as well as its emphasis on verification and checking. Especially significant here is logical positivism, associated with the Vienna Circle of philosophers of the 1920s, which went furthest in laying out conditions for objective knowledge: namely, that it should be value-free, that claims should be expressed in elementary or clear language (Hjørland 2005: 139). As Ward notes, any experiences '*not* translatable into or verifiable by experience', were considered 'literally meaningless – they were neither true nor false. At best, they expressed subjective emotions or attitudes' (2004: 84). This is not dissimilar to the way in which absence of appropriate verifiable sources disqualifies certain kinds of facts in journalism.

Pragmatism

Sitting in the tradition of empiricism, but treated in quite a different way, pragmatism is often referred to in discussions of journalism (O'Donnell 2007). However, as we shall see, it can find different treatments. Iggers, for example, ties pragmatism directly to a 'rejection of journalistic objectivity' (1998: 136). James W. Carey suggests that 'Idealism and pragmatism have undermined the notions of objectivity and objective truth that ground the explanatory apparatus of such [behavioural and functional] sciences' (1989: 91). Ward, by contrast, turns to pragmatism to reinvigorate objectivity (2004).

Today, pragmatism (especially the form promoted in the work of John Dewey) is commonly linked with the liberal project of finding an alternative to traditional thinking on democracy and culture, and elitist constructions of democracy that exclude the public (see Iggers 1998: 129; also Schudson 2008). Jeremy Iggers outlines a positive pragmatist ethical theory for journalism:

> In the pragmatist view, reality is socially constructed, emerging out of the human activity of creating words and concepts as tools to meet human needs. ... As we transform our social reality through our productive activity, we continuously transform our language and concepts and categories through which we see the world. (1998: 134).

From this point of view the media is a kind of custodian of the common values that underpin social action.

As an attack on the 'brittle certainties and rigid determinism' of positivism (Shi 1995: 75), pragmatism certainly has a place in the discussion of a critique of objectivity. However, arguing against Carey and Iggers, I would suggest that the relationship between pragmatism and objectivity has been mis-cast as an opposition. In fact, going beyond both a correspondence and coherence theory of truth, pragmatism suggests that truth is not static, but becomes or is made true (Shi 1995: 76). It is tied to action, as the Greek word *'pragma'* suggests, and facts. A pragmatic theory of truth ties truth to utility and purpose, to the 'projects and purposes formed by its possessor' (Blackburn 2008). Distinct from both the correspondence and coherency theories of truth, pragmatism sees truth condition as linked to human and communal activity (see Iggers 1998: 135). Reality is thus, as William James argues, not ready-made; it is the product of creative activity: 'In our cognitive as well as in our active life we are creative. We *add*, both to the subject and to the predicate part of reality. The world stands really malleable, waiting to receive its final touches at our hands. Man *engenders* truths upon it' (James 1998 [1907]: 108). This leads to a dynamic conception of truth: 'The truth of an idea is not a stagnant property inherent in it. Truth *happens* to an idea. It *becomes* true, is *made* true by events. Its verity is in fact an event, a process: the process of its verifying itself, its veri-*fication*. Its validity is the process of its *valid*-ation' (James 1998 [1907]: 87).

In such statements there is the basis of a very flexible theory of truth that, through its practical and factual orientation, the focus on consequences, events and happenings, is complementary to journalistic ideas of 'the story' – and dare we say objectivity? James is no devotee of objective truth, and doubts it exists (1998 [1907]: 34). James and Dewey felt that 'mirroring a stable reality was an illusion' (Shi 1995: 78). But James was careful to clarify that this is not the same as saying truth does not exist nor that there are no objective standards (James 1998 [1907]: 99). Rather the pragmatist is guided by the truths of the past and the 'coercions' of the world ahead (James 1998 [1907]: 99). These form a kind of 'objective control'.

All of this could be regarded as somewhat academic, but for two reasons. The first is that while pragmatism may have challenged absolute truth, and may even appear to reject objectivity (Iggers 1998: 118, 136), the idea of a 'practical truth' is compatible with journalistic objectivity. Critics such as Ward have been at the forefront of exploring 'pragmatic objectivity' (see chapter 4). The second inter-related point is that one of the key figures of Schudson's ideal of objectivity, Walter Lippmann, can be considered a pragmatist (Iggers 1998: 66). Indeed, Lippmann characterized his own work, and that of others, as 'applied pragmatic realism' (Shi 1995: 295). The periodical *New Republic*, of which Lippmann was a co-founder, was the 'organ of applied pragmatic realism'. On this basis, the on-going characterization of objectivity in terms of naïve empiricism may indeed be inaccurate.

Realism and naturalism

Iggers argues that 'objectivity may have begun as a method of systemic doubt, but in practice, in its institutionalized form, it has become a sort of naïve realism' (1998: 66). More than the other approaches we have examined so far, realism is directly concerned with representation, or mimesis, the aesthetic work of reflecting and mirroring reality. In his examination of realist impulses in American culture 1850–1920, David E. Shi reminds us that the term 'realism' derives from '*res*', the Latin word for thing (1995:

89). As such realism invokes a world of physical objects and material desires that other 'isms' in their abstraction do not. Yet this material world is of keen interest to journalists, especially photojournalists. In literary culture, realist writers and artists were encouraged to relish the '"delights of the actual"' (Charles Leland quoted in Shi 1995: 67), and explore facts and the raw details of the world in a way that was not limited to any particular science. Literary realists made a claim to objectivity but put it to quite a different purpose:

> No matter how sincere their quest for truth, no matter how brassy their claims of objectivity, the realists were in fact quite diverse and complex in their representations of reality. Many of them promoted far more than documentary accuracy. They wanted to use realistic representations of contemporary life for a special purpose: to rein in the runaway aspects of a turbulent new society. (Shi 1995: 90)

Shi notes that the same spirit motivated many social scientists, who 'strove to find "realistic" ways to enhance social stability amid an increasingly turbulent society filled with labor unrest, ethnic diversity and racial tensions' (1995: 99). This goes far beyond any simplistic mirroring or documenting of society. Realism and objectivity became a 'vision of solidarity' (Shi 1995: 100), an expression of a social agenda as well as a literary aesthetic (1995: 116).

While a celebrated literary genre, realism for many theorists is something of a risky topic, since any construction of a static objectivity is deemed problematic, if not ideologically an expression of hegemonic understandings of social relations (Belsey 1980: 3). Realism has, since the revolutions of modern art and physics, been savaged; the 'mirror of representational realism' had been cracked (Shi 1995: 284). The meaning of the 'representational' has shifted from meaning the 'capturing' of reality to 'codes, conventions, and social schemata' (Tuchman 1978: 108).

Yet, in the mid to late nineteenth century, and therefore concurrent with the development of commercial news, realism was vital and diverse: realists were the radicals of their time, 'assaulting the positivistic assumption that people gain knowledge solely through the rational processing of sensory data' (Shi 1995: 279–80). There were genteel realists, sentimental realists, brutish realists, muck-raking realists, all tackling the issue of reality and representation in distinct ways (Shi 1995: 7). In the late nineteenth century in the US there was an acknowledgement that 'holding a mirror to a culture in motion produces a blurred image' (Shi 1995: 7). Only the immediacy and breadth of newspapers seemed adequate to the task (Shi 1995: 108).

Is it possible that journalism has not been objective enough, and that the informational model of objectivity cut journalism off from some vibrant influences? Read alongside realism, objectivity in journalism feels less constrained, less subservient to experience and proactive in engaging with the world. Realism is focused on facts, but promotes a 'situated' understanding of them; more than just pieces of information but embedded in social and cultural interactions.

Interestingly, while realism has become something of a pejorative term in theory debates, 'critical realism' has emerged as a new philosophical paradigm for journalistic objectivity, avoiding the perils of constructionism or conventionalism, and positivism.

> Unlike conventionalism, critical realism strongly affirms the existence of a real world, a world independent of the observer and his/her categories and concepts. . . . Moreover, critical realists maintain, the world is accessible and understandable. It is not a perpetually opaque and impenetrable 'thing in itself' that always eludes language and thought. Rather it can be meaningfully described and explained. . . . In opposition to positivism, critical realism acknowledges that such descriptions of the real unfold only through concepts that are themselves socially constructed. . . . Yet it rejects the conventionalist notion that the world can be reduced to concept or discourse. (Hackett & Zhao 1998: 129)

Critical realism is a response to both the excesses of positivism, and the excesses of constructionism/conventionalism. The attempt to balance the belief in a world independent of the observer while acknowledging conventionalism, the desire to negotiate correspondence and a postmodern conception of the truth, raises many questions, which are being taken up and addressed (see Lynch 2007: 6). It is impossible to adequately cover this area fully, as it extends into social movement theory, activist debates and theology (Wright 1992). Critical realism has taken on many meanings and 'is not a homogenous movement in social science' (Danermark et al. 2001: 1). However, one area of concern is that in terms of debates around journalistic objectivity, the 'critical' in critical realism is highly reactive and circumscribed by dualism. It is 'critical', in Hackett and Zhao's case, because it refutes positivism and 'conventionalism' (1998: 129). In this view, realism is too heavily identified with positivism. Furthermore, conventionalism is stereotyped as totally relativist and reductive. These are all contentious ideas (see Davis 1997).

Critical realism is also appearing in the discourse of media organizations. Mark Thompson, Director-General of the BBC, has taken up the term, but the concern is in these more professional versions that critical realism becomes a veneer for traditional ideas about reporting reality; and in this sense critical realism may be about providing a way to see past conventionalism and keep the mirror/mimetic conception of reporting intact.

If, as Michael Schudson argues (see chapter 1), an 'informational' mode of journalism took ascendance in objectivity debates from around the 1900s, realism (especially read through the work of Shi) provides a different perspective on 'story' journalism, one that goes 'beyond a concern for descriptive "accuracy" in order to convey a dramatic sense of truth"' (Shi 1995: 233).

An even more intriguing term is 'naturalism', an approach closely tied with realism and difficult to distinguish fully. Both seek an impression of life (Shi 1995: 220), but naturalism seeks specifically to go beyond the genteel drawing rooms to engage with the lower classes, and characters who engaged with 'violent, barbaric, lustful, and other criminal behavior', focusing on the 'commonplace and sensational' – much like some of the crime and sensationalist reporting of the era. If objective realists responded to science by seeking to become more rigorous and accurate in their delineation of facts from values, and to work towards progress in culture, objective naturalists take on board a Darwinian conception of survival of the fittest to explore characters who are not always rational or in control of their fate. As Shi puts it: 'Instead of acting as free agents, characters in naturalistic stories confront overpowering environmental and economic forces, inherit controlling hereditary tendencies, and succumb to unconscious drives and sexual urges' (1995: 221). Naturalism gives a rawer picture of events in the world than realism, which assumes an environment that is controllable, systemic, positivistic, consistent and viewable from all sides. For all of the discussion of naïve empiricism and an informational model of reporting, we can suggest that a strong naturalistic streak persists in many forms of journalism (muckraking, social pages, photojournalism), especially when scandal, infidelity or corruption are the focus, and the discussion turns to motives such as revenge and betrayal. Naturalism thus arguably forms a wellspring of objectivity in journalism that is not always sufficiently recognized.

Facticity and issues of communication

As noted above, a key issue in any correspondence theory of truth is how correspondence is imagined. As Carlin Romano notes, there is a risk of concealing a key distinction 'between language and the world'. '"[F]act" is a word that describes language *about* the world, and not the world itself' (1986: 63). Facts are 'not objects in the world' (Hacking 2000: 22). The idea that facts are not objects has significant implications for journalism. When objectivity is put forward as reporting facts as 'objective truths' that exist outside of any representations, there is a risk that we misconceive the nature of facts.

'Facticity' is the name we can give to this problem of drawing a distinction between facts and the world. Put simply, facticity describes a test, or set of conditions, through which experiences, information, statements, become facts. Many disciplines (law, science) have processes for establishing facts, usually through evidence. It is a key area of dispute in objective journalism, where it is resolved through 'separation theories' that seek to separate fact from opinion, or facts from values (see next section), modified by special organizational factors such as news deadlines. Thus, 'according to news convention', McQuail suggests that 'facts can be considered as self-contained units of information in any account which claims to report on actual events or situations. A "fact" is clearly different from a subjective opinion or a comment and it should, in principle, be verifiable by reference to reliable sources or to other independent accounts' (1992: 83).

However, McQuail downplays a key issue for facticity, which is that 'facts or data are not merely observed and collected; they are represented in language' (Bonney & Wilson 1983: 4). It should be noted that this is not the same as saying that there is no such entity as a fact; rather, that they are descriptions and statements, and of a unique kind. Indeed, one of the reasons citizens and readers appreciate facts is their supposed immutability, the way they form secure or stable points for rational debate and discussion (see White 1971: 80).

Gaye Tuchman's seminal text *Making News: A Study in the Construction of Reality* (1978) offers an extended discussion of facticity and objective journalism. The book teases out the power of the news media in shaping knowledge and information through language used and frames chosen. Facticity has several dimensions. In terms of the observational dimension of the news production process, it relates to the news chosen for publication or broadcast. This will determine the salience of different facts and how they are packaged. Some facts may be deemed not relevant or just not noticed (either because they are taken for granted, the reporter may be poorly trained, or they may be filtered out by a frame) (Tuchman 1978: 8–9).

What Tuchman calls the 'news net' refers to the spatial (where reporters go), organizational (which agencies they use) and social (who they talk to) field in which facts are developed, distributed or shared. It is a hybrid network, consisting of human beings (for example, translators and 'fixers') as well as technologically augmented elements (databases, for instance). But as the metaphor implies, some things travel through the net. 'Today's news net is intended for big fish' (Tuchman 1978: 21). It provides limited access to social movements (1978: 133–55). The news net is partly conceptual as well; it excludes some occurrences and orders work priorities according to set standards (1978: 37–8). Faced with a situation in which the news net 'produces more stories than can be processed' (1978: 45) the news net assigns different facts and stories newsworthiness. Typographies such as hard versus soft news, and spot versus developing news, help control the flow of work: 'newsworkers use typifications to transform the idiosyncratic occurrences of the everyday world into raw materials that can be subject to routine processing and dissemination' (1978: 58).

Tuchman's concept of the 'web of facticity' undermines the idea that facts are self-contained nuggets of information. It specifically relates to the way facts are handled in news organizations, preoccupied with news deadlines, but also threats of libel and their own credibility. Tuchman defines facts as 'pertinent information gathered by professionally validated methods specifying the relationship between what is known and how it is known' (1978: 82). As such, she is interested in professional practices directed towards sanctioning or legitimating facts.

> Facts must quickly be identified. But for newsworkers (as for scientists), having witnessed an occurrence is not sufficient to define one's observation as factual. In science, the problem of facticity is embedded in processes of verification and replication. In news, verification of facts is both a political and professional accomplishment. (1978: 82–3)

The intertwining of politics and professionalism here points to the complex web of sources, attributions, on and off the record statements that form the inner fabric of the news net. Verification of statements is central to facticity here, but Tuchman is careful to note that organizational needs and pragmatics can trump scientific accuracy (1978: 85). Tuchman sees the web of facticity as undergoing a gradual institutionalization: 'By stressing methods – gathering supplementary evidence, presenting conflicting truth-claims, imputing facts through familiarity with police procedures, and using quotation marks . . . – newsworkers produced a full-blown version of the web of facticity' (1978: 160).

Two aspects of the concept of web of facticity are worth highlighting specifically, both of them linked to communication. The first has to do with the relationship between facts and the construction of sense and meaning. For Tuchman, 'taken by itself, a fact has no meaning. Indeed, even "two and two equals four" is factual only within certain mathematical systems of theories. It is the imposition of a frame of other ordered facts that enables recognition of facticity and attribution of meaning' (1978: 88). The 'chain', 'web' or 'link' structure is thus crucial to the validity and recognition of facts.

The second point has to do with the demands facticity makes on language. Objectivity is embedded in 'particular discursive parameters' (Conboy 2010: 12). The inverted pyramid form, short paragraphs, headlines and specific use of tenses are obvious aspects. Tuchman also highlights newswriting as 'news-speak', 'full of awkward lengthy sentences, packed with nouns connoting facticity' (1978: 106). The 'language of news prose . . . frames and accomplishes discourse. It is perception and guides perception' (1978: 107). In other words, facticity has a strong discursive element. Broadcast journalism goes to special lengths to 'accomplish' its own discourse. 'By seeming *not* to arrange time and space, news film claims to present facts, not interpretations. That is, the web of facticity is embedded in a supposedly neutral synchronization of film with the rhythm of everyday life' (1978: 110). Rules around camera placement and composition support facticity, with breaches of the conventions leading to 'distortion'. 'Distortion is said to hamper the viewer's perception of the central figure or event, and hence the facticity of news' (1978: 113). These discursive demands show us that style is intertwined with our very sense of the facts, and indeed experience of objectivity. How to carry out the task of 'bearing witness' while resisting the temptation to 'whip up feelings' becomes harder than ever (Seaton 2005: 232–3).

Separation theories

The question of how the knower is connected to the known is fundamental to debates around objectivity, and the way one answers the question has a great deal to do with whether objectivity is seen in scientific, cultural or political terms. One of the more controversial areas of journalistic objectivity is a reliance on a separation of facts and values or opinions to underpin facticity (see Schudson 1978: 5–6). Broadly speaking, the separation is based on the idea that statements of fact can be regarded as value-free, and that description can be distinguished from evaluation (Blackburn 2008). In journalism, Jay Rosen describes the theory in this way: 'It states that if you separate facts from values, or information from opinion, or news from views, this will permit you to know the truth. These separations are central to American journalism's image of itself' (1993: 48). It should be noted that this separation is an evolution and codification of a long-standing distinction from the era of the penny press, namely that between news and editorial, or news and opinion (sometimes expressed as news versus views). The distinction has, therefore, taken on new layers and forms while retaining past understandings.

The main criticism launched against the separation is that 'the perception of anything as a "fact" may itself involve value-judgements, as may the selection of particular facts as the essential ones' (Blackburn 2008). Outlining a feminist argument, for example, Stuart Allan argues that 'facts cannot be separated out from their ideological and hence gendered, conditions of production' (2010: 149). The separation seemingly posits facts as beyond any kind of theorization or interpretation. Facts are said to come from direct experience and are thus in a sense 'uncontaminated' by values. The problem, then, is with what we might term an empirical attitude to facts in which facts *present themselves* to our senses. But, as Chin-Chuan Lee notes, 'facts do not speak for themselves; they must be interpreted within a framework' (Lee 1990: 19). As such any positivistic conception of the pure separation of facts and values is difficult. The genius of the separation theory and the way it is used in discussions of journalistic objectivity is precisely the way it makes discussion of facticity difficult, or at least counter-intuitive, and makes ideology a second-order consideration in professional practice. 'Most American journalists pride themselves on being professional, objective, neutral, and nonideological by segregating facts from opinion. But they are by no means ideologically free' (Lee 1990: 19). Traditionally, the separation of facts and values is a marker of professionalism, but the concept of the separation itself evades investigation.

Herein lies one area in which an over-use of positivist reference points to characterize objectivity in journalism creates a problem. In a positivist frame, facts are pure while values are impure. Arguably, pragmatism offers a different and more flexible version of the separation theory in which facts and values are considered intermixed, but through judgement are separated for the purposes of reporting. As Stephen J. Ward notes,

> in the past news objectivity was interpreted as a rigid separation of fact and judgement (or opinion). But this narrow interpretation is no longer a sufficient basis for journalism ethics. Nor is this interpretation a dominant force today as objective reporters provide context and interpretation for a daily blizzard of information. A richer, more flexible idea of objectivity is in play. (Ward 1998: 122)

Questioning a *tabula rasa* view of the reporter, Ward argues that 'the mind of an objective reporter is not a blank TV screen that receives impressions from the senses'. His alternative view is that 'What objectivity requires is an active mind that uses its mental powers in ways that reduce the distortion of reports caused by wishful thinking, bad reasoning, petty feelings and personal interests'.

'Postmodernism'

Postmodernism deserves specific mention in a chapter about disputing facts. It is a difficult term to define and is sometimes linked to the critique of objectivity. Conboy sees it as a 'series of crises in representation and rationality, both key terms for the press' (2002: 139). He links it to 'a crisis in representation and notions of truth, a collapse of meta-narratives such as class, nation and religion, globalizing forces, the erosion of the divide between popular and elite culture and the intrusions of margins upon the centres of established social and cultural life' (2002: 137). For some, it represents a kind of relativism (Romano 1986: 77). For others, it merges with a general crisis in the master-narrative of facts. 'Faith in facts has given way to an understanding that facts don't interpret themselves and to a distrust of all sources of authority, including newspapers and the experts whose authority they transmit' (Iggers 1998: 4).

Postmodernism is linked with a 'social construction of truth' argument that has become highly politicized (Meyer 1995; Hackett & Zhao 1998: 121–8). An extremist note has crept into discussions of social constructionism, and its thesis that reality is not simply a given but is socially constructed, and that social construction itself is important to study. It is worth noting that in *The Social Construction of Reality*, Peter L. Berger and Thomas Luckmann stress that the idea of society exists as both objective and subjective reality (1971: 149).

Stuart Allan sketches an outline of the controversy around postmodernism when he writes: 'Formulations of "reality" as an *empirical fact* to be located outside of the social relations of signification are often sharply counterpoised against those formulations of "reality" as a *cultural construction*. Angry charges of "unreconstructed positivism" are routinely met with accusations that "everything is being reduced to discourse"' (1995: 134). Allan observes that while postmodernism appears frequently in debates about journalism, often pejoratively, it 'is only rarely discussed in news media studies in a sustained or rigorous fashion' (1995: 130). Many journalists see themselves as truth-tellers. Postmodernism can be confronting to this viewpoint because it problematizes 'truth', situating it in dynamics of power and knowledge. It describes 'those modes of thought that deny the existence of an *objective* reality outside of the various *subjective* accounts of it being routinely manufactured by journalists' (Allan 1995: 130). It stresses the end of an Enlightenment project of continuous progress (McQuail 1992: 303). From this perspective, postmodernism might suggest that truth is never there just for the telling; that language speaks us, and that the public makes truth in chaotic ways. It is worth recalling here Schudson's argument that the ideal of objectivity was installed precisely to preserve a faith in facts and not to succumb to chaos and disorder of modernity (1978: 120). As such, objectivity is arguably 'anti-postmodern' in its DNA. But the corollary of this is that it creates a problem for any journalism grounded in objectivity for thinking about social change, unrest and the postmodern condition itself. As Conboy suggests, the technological and economic changes of the late twentieth century are leading to a significant 'epistemological shift'. Postmodernity is blurring the normal boundaries and complicating the 'myths of the Fourth Estate and objectivity' which are grounded in modernist grand narratives (2004: 211).

Some journalism educators dismiss and disagree with postmodernism as a form of nihilism, a philosophy of nothingness. While the counter-arguments are too numerous and complex to tease out here, my own discussion takes as a general working assumption (one that would need to be argued in relation to different theorists and arguments) that 'postmodernism' does not dismiss referents, reduce the world to concepts or discourse, nor deny the existence of truth. Interested in the way practices of many kinds constitute knowledge and sense, through regimes that act with force and power, 'postmodernism' is more positively viewed as a constructivist philosophy.

Nevertheless, a typical reaction from the media ethics literature suggests that 'Many academics believe truth claims are impossible after Jacques Derrida and Michel Foucault. In a world of sliding signifiers and normlessness, ethical principles seem to carry little resonance' (Christians et al. 2005: xii). Suffice to say that it is incorrect to suggest that the argument that meaning is culturally constructed means there is no truth. Mark Davis highlights a problem with this kind of argument: 'To argue that social convention makes truths true and falsehoods false isn't the same as saying there is no such thing as truth or falsehood, or that they are a matter of whim' (1997: 163). Truths, even those constructed within formations of power and knowledge that are in a sense relative, retain their force. As political philosopher Duncan Ivison notes: 'The relativity of norms, then, is relevant to moral judgements in all kinds of significant ways. But it doesn't follow, therefore, that moral judgements are *in general* relative, especially given our practice of critically evaluating those norms that shape our judgements about what is good or right or virtuous (a practice we find in human societies everywhere)' (2003: 35).

The dismissal of postmodernism in some discussions is unfortunate. Why? Because the positions and ideas often bundled together with postmodernism provide some very interesting ways to reinvigorate and reinvent objectivity (see Allan 1995). As Hackett and Zhao (with Nick Dyer-Witheford, their co-author in the chapter in question) note, in an otherwise critical account of postmodernism, 'critics and journalists influenced by postmodernism have brought radical new perspectives to the issues of media and reporting . . . They have reinforced the recognition, already emergent in structuralism, of the constitutive nature of language and discourse' (1998: 124).

4

What are the grounds on which journalistic objectivity has been · defended?

Reading the robust objections to journalistic objectivity discussed in chapter 2, it seems difficult to conceive of a defence of objectivity in journalism. Despite this, some critics argue that 'reports of the death of objectivity are greatly exaggerated' (Hackett & Zhao 1998: 8; also Hackett 1996). Michael Schudson argued that 'there is no new ideal in journalism to successfully challenge objectivity, but there is hope for something new, a simmering disaffection with objective reporting' (Schudson 1978: 193). In this context, appreciating the grounds on which critics and commentators defend objectivity becomes as important as understanding the main objections.

This chapter responds to the question 'What are the grounds on which objectivity has been defended?' In it, I discuss some of the key defences that have been offered. My purpose here is not to answer every criticism of objectivity in journalism, or summarize every defence. The aim is to identify the key grounds on which a defence of objectivity might be staked out.

Coherency grounds

One important defence of objectivity is to question the very coherency of the critique being made. It is a venerable defence, focused on rooting out confusion. As Julian Baggini writes, 'While it is true (rather than "true") that we have to reject certain naïve and simplistic understandings of what truth and objectivity are, both remain perfectly coherent ideas and for the journalist, proper ideals' (2003). Coherency can relate to confusion in definition, argumentation and categorization. Michael Ryan notes that, 'few observers base their critiques on precise definitions of objectivity' (2001: 3). Gilles Gauthier bemoans the 'lack of intellectual rigour' in modern critiques of journalism. 'Much of the time, the notion is criticized but not defined' (1993).

While at first glance 'coherency' is an obvious ground for defence (as it suggests the application of basic logic), it has been given specific form by Judith Lichtenberg as a way of tackling what she terms a 'compound assault' on objectivity. In her essay 'In Defense of Objectivity', Lichtenberg focuses on a particular confusion in critiques of objectivity: 'We are told by some that journalism *isn't* objective; by others that it *cannot* be objective; and by still others that it *shouldn't* be objective' (1991a: 216). Objectivity is thus impossible on the one hand, and undesirable on the other. Both propositions cannot be correct. For Lichtenberg, sociologists of knowledge and postmodernists conflate these different critiques into one another: the idea that objectivity in journalism cannot exist, and couldn't exist, is intermixed with the idea it should not exist. Lichtenberg's response is to resist the conflation of allegations and deal with each on its own terms. Separating out the different issues, Lichtenberg argues that the different 'values captured by the term "objectivity" vary greatly', thus the 'legitimacy of the complaints varies as well' (1991a: 218). From this basis, her work questions a number of key critiques of objectivity to do with bias, ideology and favouring official sources (1991a: 227).

The question of definition gains a special place in the debate over coherency, since the shifting nature of the term objectivity introduces difficulties for both critique and defence of the term. Richard Streckfuss, in his historical reassessment of the concept, argues that current critics are engaging with what is but 'a shadow of the original concept' (1990: 973). Streckfuss argues that objectivity should not simply be reduced to neutrality, and that we should begin to appreciate the context in which the concept was put forward. 'Objectivity was not founded on a naïve idea that humans could be objective, but on a realization that they could NOT. To compensate for this innate weakness, advocates in the 1920s proposed a journalistic system that subjected itself to the rigors of the scientific method' (1990: 974).

Gilles Gauthier pursues his own attack on incoherency by arguing that the criticism of objectivity in journalism is riddled by basic category errors. He writes: 'In my opinion, much scholarly writing criticizing objectivity in journalism is completely invalidated by the fact that it is based on a category mistake: it is based on the application of the concept of objectivity to an inappropriate aspect of reporting' (1993). To correct such category errors Gauthier introduces a series of five propositions designed to narrow the area of application of the concept. His propositions try to clarify how objectivity should be applied to journalism, specifically straight news reporting, not analysis or commentary. He responds specifically to the criticism that because selection is involved, objectivity is impossible. Gauthier argues that selection is a reality of all reporting and representation. The idea that an objective report fails to match reality or reproduce the whole truth is not for him a convincing critique because 'Objectivity does not come into play at the time of the original choice but during a later phase of reporting' (1993). Gauthier's critique rests firmly on coherency grounds, which is to provide a satisfactory definition of objectivity in journalism.

Interpretive grounds

Interpretation is a contentious issue in objectivity debates. For Daniel C. Hallin and Paolo Mancini, in a discussion of political broadcast journalism in the US and Italy, interpretation is a concern, firstly, because of the way it is made out to belong exclusively to political and journalistic elites, and, secondly, because of the way the conventions of reporting in the US embed interpretations in the events themselves, masking the interpretive work of the journalist (1984: 847). Notwithstanding this critique, interpretation has become an important ground for defending objectivity. Defences based on interpretation seek to restore to objectivity its interpretive powers. They question the way that objectivity has been made passive, and separated or distanced from more active understandings of interpretation. Schudson has argued that objectivity and interpretation were contiguous in the 1930s (1978: 144–7) and only later came to be treated as oppositional. From this interpretative perspective it is possible to make room for a conception of objectivity that is compatible with aggressive analysis and explanation (see Berry 2005), and radical questioning in the public interest (Bowman 2006). Ward (2004) makes interpretation central to his concept of pragmatic objectivity (see the discussion below). This re-assessment of the relationship between objectivity and interpretation is not restricted to journalism, and picks up on broader developments in literary theory (Putnam 1984).

Factual grounds

One of the key areas of dispute around objectivity in journalism has to do with the status of facts. Lichtenberg does not engage fully with the issues of facticity discussed in chapter 3, but does consider similar issues when she examines objectivity in relation to a continuum of subjects and statements news reporters investigate. These range from 'relatively straightforward and uncontroversial facts' to highly ambiguous situations. Lichtenberg concedes that 'for many of the complex goings-on between people, both at the "macro" political level and the "micro" interpersonal level, the language of truth and objectivity may be thin and inadequate' (1991a: 226). However, she makes two points: firstly, that the realm of the ambiguous and interpersonal is limited in journalism; and secondly, that a conclusion about ambiguity should be drawn reluctantly, and only after much consideration. 'We must, in other words, proceed on the assumption that there is objective truth' (1991a: 226).

In response to the dispute over facts and truth, Lichtenberg mounts a defence of objectivity as a commitment to the idea that 'some questions have determinate, right answers – and ... all questions have wrong answers'. Based on the idea of 'unassailable facts', she questions the repudiation of objectivity. In her counter-critique, Lichtenberg questions the extent to which social constructionism invalidates facts. She notes that 'the aspiration to objectivity can, paradoxically, contain biases of its own', but these tendencies are not 'insuperable' (1991b: 69). Using the example of the fact that 'George Bush is President' (a fact in 1991) she suggests that 'however constructed "George Bush is President" may be, it is no less true or credible for that' (1991a: 223). In other words, truth claims are not necessarily made less credible by the idea that such truths arise from social interaction or even particular theories (depending on how contested they are). 'Facts, then, may be theory-laden; but whether they therefore lack objectivity depends on the particular theories they carry as freight' (1991a: 224).

For Lichtenberg, matters of interpretation are indeed significant and point to radically different understandings, but these do not necessarily make facts irrelevant. Facts can constrain interpretations in significant ways. As she states, 'the insistence that an interpretation of the facts is beyond the reach of objective evaluation is simply overstated. . . . Some interpretations are better than others, and some are simply wrong' (1991a: 224–5). One of the key issues for a defence of objectivity on factual grounds is a separation theory that posits a clear division between facts and values. Lichtenberg does not address the role of separation theories, but the defence nevertheless highlights the importance of well-established theories and processes (and indeed consensus) in sifting through facts. The Western legal system, for instance, which is strongly reliant on evidence and facts, is an example of an institution where objectivity operates on the basis of established theories and processes.

Metaphysical grounds

One common area of objection in relation to objectivity has to do with first principles, the very concepts of understanding, communication and reality at play. When James W. Carey writes that 'communication is a symbolic process whereby reality is produced, maintained, repaired and transformed' (1989: 23), he is making inroads into metaphysics. Most significantly he is tackling the concept of a pre-existing reality and its place in what we can term the 'reality first, representation later' argument.

> Both our common sense and scientific realism attest to the fact that there is, first, a real world of objects, events, and processes that we observe. Second that there is language or symbols that name these events in the real world and create more or less adequate descriptions of them. There is reality and then, after the fact, our accounts of it. . . . While language often distorts, obfuscates, and confuses our perception of the external world, we rarely dispute this matter-of-fact realism. (1989: 25)

Declining to make metaphysical claims, Carey nevertheless gives voice to a core challenge to 'reality first, representation later' idea, and the realism that for many underpins journalistic objectivity. As he puts it, 'Under the sway of realism we ordinarily assume there is an order to existence that the human mind through some faculty may discover and describe (1989: 25–6). 'Reality is not given' or 'independent of language'. 'Reality is brought into existence, is produced, by communication' (1989: 25). The terms of this critique permeate many discussions of objectivity, especially those related to social constructionism, but also critical realism (discussed in chapter 3).

The metaphysical ground upon which this criticism can be defended can best be described through reference to the eighteenth-century German philosopher Immanuel Kant. Kant is a touchstone for critics as diverse as Lichtenberg (1991b) and Ward (2004: 27). Put simply, a critique such as Carey's, while raising relevant issues, remains curiously pre-Kantian in its structure because it ignores the challenge Kant made to the 'reality first, representation later' argument two centuries earlier. When Kant set out to define his approach to pure reason, he sought to enact a 'Copernican' revolution in our approach to knowledge. Rather than assume that 'all our cognition must conform to the objects', Kant explores how the objects of our senses 'must conform to our cognition' (Kant 1997 [1781]: 110). Kant's contention is that we can have a 'pure' or '*a priori*' understanding of objects, meaning an understanding prior to, or independent of, experience. Rejecting '*a posteriori*' understandings, or judgements coming from experience, Kant proposed a 'transcendental' approach that, in the words of his translators, 'does not deal directly with objects of empirical cognition' (Kant 1997 [1781]: 6).

Kant does not deny perception but sees it in a particular way. The object first appears as an empirical intuition through sensation (Kant 1997 [1781]: 155; Burnham & Young 2007: 38). 'Appearances' (a category which includes the thing-in-itself as well as mere appearances like a rainbow) emerge through (*a posteriori*) experiences into empirical intuitions. But they also take shape in our understanding through *a priori*, pure concepts. An example might be the way the experience of a journey takes place in a field of expectations about a trip or holiday. These 'make one able to say more about the objects that appear to the senses than mere experience would teach' (Kant 1997 [1781]: 128). For Kant, transcendental cognition 'is occupied not so much with objects but rather our *a priori* concepts of objects in general' (1997 [1781]: 133). This formulation implies a different realm of objectivity from that usually linked to realism and empiricism (what Kant would see as the realm of appearances).

Some critics have pointed out that Kantianism was not at the front line of thinking about scientific methodology in the early twentieth century. (Although it should be noted that Walter Lippmann had more than a passing familiarity with Kant's work.) Many journalists were inspired by 'scientific naturalism': 'a school of thought holding that there are no *a priori* truths, that attempts to explain the universe in metaphysical terms foster not understanding but ignorance and suspicion, and that only knowledge gained by scientific investigation is valid' (Streckfuss 1990: 975). This makes metaphysics a curious ground to defend objectivity.

Nevertheless, the significance of a Kantian perspective has to do with the fact that the realm of human concepts and their usage is a discursive domain. This opens up a link between Carey's argument about communication and Kant. Kant suggests that 'cognition of every, at least human, understanding is a cognition through concepts, not intuitive but discursive' (1997 [1781]: 205). As such, judgement always deals with questions of mediation through representations. Kant's attention here is not on how experience gives rise to cognitions, the sense of matter and form of an appearance. He seeks an approach independent of experience.

Placing objectivity in the realm of understanding rather than intuition or sensation, as articulated by Kant, provides an alternative metaphysical ground on which to contest ideas of objectivity based on a notion of 'reality first, representation later'. Kant would promote an emphasis on the discursive basis of reality. Where he would diverge from Carey is in the assumption that by critiquing realism objectivity is compromised. As Lichtenberg notes, understood through Kant, 'idealism poses no threat to objectivity' (1991a: 219).

Kant's philosophy provides support for the view that objectivity is active rather than passive, an act of judgement rather than mere intuition (see chapter 5). One legacy of Kant's work is the idea that thought should not seek to 'mirror' reality, but rather that it should regulate it. Reason, through understanding, orders and constitutes objects, gives unity to knowledge. 'In Kant's terms this means that the knowing subject is active – not a passive "viewer" of a moving, changing and active world – and understanding knowledge means understanding the constituting role of this activity' (Burnham & Young 2007: 21). Reason, considered regulatively, sets the goals and directions of our inquiry, and organizes knowledge (Kant 1997 [1781]: 18). While it cannot be said that Kant provides a fully-fledged account of objectivity, his philosophy remains influential for the way it gives a role to reason in establishing our very sense of what is objective. It also supports a focus on independent judgement, which has been seen as crucial to updating objectivity (Cunningham 2003: 31).

None of this is to suggest that Kant's metaphysics is beyond critique. Indeed, the idea of the 'I' as the 'fundamental psychological concept' (1997 [1781]: 613) which underpins the unity of Kant's system has been complicated by theories of language and discourse, and the idea that the 'I' and 'subject' is an effect of language. This, for some, undermines the universalism of Kant's critique and the basis of objectivity (see Lichtenberg 1991a: 219). Furthermore, post-colonial critiques question whether the unified 'I' of Kant's theory is an expression of a Eurocentric perspective (Lichtenberg 1991b: 59–60). Kant has, however, opened up a perspective on categories and concepts that endures in the Western philosophical tradition and persists beyond any dismissal of objectivity as naïve empiricism. As Lichtenberg suggests, 'we may deny that a particular account is objective – accurate, fair, or complete – but we need not deny that it is possible to tell an objective, or at least a more objective story' (1991b: 62). Of course, some critics do deny this possibility, but Lichtenberg invites us to reflect on the metaphysical grounds on which we do so. In other words, while we may debate the very categories and from different cultural standpoints, we do this upon architecture of categories and concepts. Our expectations for deeper understanding (Cunningham 2003: 26) and independent judgement thus come from somewhere.

Procedural grounds

While the ideal of journalistic objectivity was broadly inspired by developments in science, the actual methods used to ensure this objectivity focused on the separation of facts and values, the provision of differing perspectives, a focus on accuracy, and the use of predictable news formats. While the deadline-driven, personal and visceral nature of journalism seemingly mitigates any scientific method, a key ground for the defence of objectivity in journalism has come from those who seek to re-assert or re-invent the focus on objectivity as a method or procedure.

As Lichtenberg notes, 'objectivity must be "operationalized"' (1991a: 228). Today there is debate around how that happens, and a view that some of the pitfalls of a reliance on strict separation theories and an empty commitment to balance can be avoided. For example, while Lauren Kessler and Donald McDonald regard objectivity as a false and impossible ideal, they regard procedural values such as honesty, fairness, accuracy, completeness and complexity as attainable goals (1989: 28–9). For Stephen J. Berry, it is not so much the standard of objectivity that is the problem, but the operationalization of it, and a failure to challenge and verify information (2005). Similarly, Doug McGill affirms the 'uncorrupted ideal of objectivity' as 'indispensable in journalism', expressing his real concern with 'an omnipresent and abused pseudo-objectivity', a reporting-by-numbers approach to fairness and balance. McGill makes clear, 'when I compare the ideal of objectivity to the observed practice of it, I see a great gap' (2004).

Feminist critiques of objectivity draw on this procedural argument when they argue that failure to account for 'male norms, values and beliefs' can 'subjectively distort' reporting (Allan 2010: 148). This approach re-commits to concepts of truth and accuracy in the context of gendered, political, economic and social realities. One of the problematic aspects of objectivity is that it exnominates issues of ethnicity and gender that are deemed adjunct to a particular 'scientific' world view. A critical approach, attentive to issues of culture and identity, can offer, in this view, alternative ways to operationalize objectivity (see the discussion of 'Standpoint' below).

In a robust defence of objectivity in journalism, Ryan attempts to unpack the philosophical constructs that underpin both science and objective journalism: values such as accuracy, precision, scepticism, imagination and honesty, to mention a few (2001: 4). In proposing his list, Ryan is trying to turn objectivity into something more than a dogma by seeking a renewed link to scientific values. He does not deny that values exist, but wants to factor a commitment to science and knowledge among them, and feels a commitment to impartiality is in itself an act of integrity. Also, he wants journalists to be analytical, to engage in interpretation. Once properly defined, what Ryan argues is that it is the implementation of objectivity that is the problem not the idea itself (2001: 16). 'Objective journalists believe a real world exists and that one can produce a reasonably accurate description of that world. They do not guarantee that their descriptions are accurate in every respect, only that they have followed a process that allows them to produce a description that is more accurate than any other process allows' (2001: 5). Linking his procedural argument with one about coherency, Ryan questions whether critiques of objectivity based on the idea of it being a myth, or morally passive, lose sight of the importance of following proper procedures of accuracy.

In defending objectivity on procedural grounds Ryan follows others such as Everette E. Dennis who suggests that 'journalistic objectivity is possible if we adopt methods that lead to systematic decisions' (Dennis & Merrill 1984: 114). Dennis upholds objectivity by promoting a 'practical and practicable strategy that will make journalism better and more reliable' (1984: 114). 'Objectivity in journalism or science does not mean that all decisions do not have underlying values, only that within the "rules of the game" a systematic attempt is made to achieve an impartial report' (1984: 118).

'Standpoint'

Drawn primarily from feminist critiques of knowledge, so-called 'standpoint' epistemology has offered another ground upon which to defend objectivity (Durham 1998). Standpoint epistemologies turn some of the precepts of aperspectival objectivity on their head. Rather than transcend partial viewpoints, escape from perspective, and treat any intrusion of subjectivity as a 'distortion', 'contamination' or 'infection' (Machan 2004), standpoint epistemology embraces the social situatedness of knowledge.

Refusing to eliminate bias and ideology from view, standpoint epistemology begins from the assumption that knowledge is socially situated, and as such different marginal, oppressed or dominated groups have their own standpoints and truth-claims. Standpoint epistemology is thus explicitly counter-hegemonic, and as a consequence it asserts that the traditional observers and reflectors of society such as journalists and scientists should not be allowed to exclude themselves from the sphere of analysis. As Meenakshi Gigi Durham points out, 'Standpoint epistemology uses the socially situated nature of various knowledge claims as the basis for maximizing objectivity. This involves a reformulation of the term "objectivity," taking it away from any notion of eradicating bias and value neutrality toward a method of acknowledging and incorporating bias into the structure of the scientific method' (1998: 127).

Not all standpoint epistemologists see value in objectivity. Some question the concept altogether: for its universalizing assumptions, for denying the idea that knowledge is socially situated, promoting value-neutrality, excluding the question of politics from research, and failing to theorize the relations between subject and other (see Harding 1991: 138–9). For Sandra Harding, one of the key problems with traditional definitions of objectivity is that it actually provides a very weak standard for maximizing objectivity (1993: 71), as it fails to foster a critical examination of the historical contexts of research, or the origins and consequences of inquiry. Refusing to reject the term, Harding proposes that feminist standpoint epistemology 'requires strengthened standards of objectivity' (1991: 142).

Harding's 'strong objectivity' has numerous aspects: it refuses to perform the god-trick of erasing the traces of human involvement in research; it engages with issues of ethnocentrism (without placing one group at the centre of research) and relativism (without asserting that all views are equal). Rather than abandon objectivity, then, Harding seeks to challenge the (false) view that the only alternative to objectivism or absolutism is cultural relativism. Indeed, Harding suggests that 'relativism appears as a problematic intellectual possibility only for dominating groups at the point at where the hegemony of their views is being challenged' (1991: 153). Harding writes, 'a strong notion of objectivity requires a commitment to acknowledge the historical character of every belief or set of beliefs – a commitment to cultural, sociological, historical relativism. But it also requires that judgemental or epistemological relativism be rejected' (1991: 156).

For Durham, journalistic concepts of balance and fairness that do not engage with the political and ideological standpoint of different perspectives lock journalism into epistemic emptiness (1998: 126). Her alternative idea of objectivity leads to 'a praxis that recognizes and grapples with issues of ideological bias and the problems of alienation of socially marginalized groups from mainstream news coverage' (1998: 118). For Durham, standpoint epistemology is a means to address some key tensions in the theory of objectivity. For example, the tension created by a continuing commitment to 'value-free facticity', such that journalists are asked to commit to a separation of facts and values so rigid that it is 'the equivalent of erasure, the eradication of the reporter's positions from the reporting' (1998: 119). Another example is how one balances this erasure of the reporter's viewpoint and voice with the commitment to represent pluralism in a culture (through different viewpoints and voices). For Durham, these tensions have a crippling effect on journalists.

A journalism based on standpoint epistemology would, according to Durham, study society through a lens that foregrounds the social location of those who are part of the news. In practical terms, a standpoint journalism might look at the social situatedness of activities such as caring (questions arise such as Who is assigned the work of caring? Where? What is the status of caring relative to other forms of work?) (Harding 1993: 55). Ryan has voiced concerns over the practicalities of this: 'Who decides when the views of dominant insiders must be counterbalanced by the views of the marginalized? Also, who decides which views of which marginalized groups should be considered first?' (Ryan 2001: 15). But to some extent this misses a more central task of recognizing and legitimating knowledge claims, and a structural shift in the terms of who is allowed to speak and who is spoken for.

For Durham, such a journalism would be reflexive, taking a cue from anthropological and literary research which have found ways of taking the location of the observer into account. Essential here is to begin the research from the point of view of those most affected and 'most marginalized by dominant institutions and practices' and who find themselves 'looking inward' (Durham 1998: 131–2). 'Thus a journalist must strive to conceptualize him- or herself as the outsider, to become engaged in the consequences of the story from the point of view of those most disenfranchised by it, rather than in the simple aggregation of its parts' (1998:

133). Integral to reflexivity is an affirmation that 'social identities are complex and heterogeneous', and as such the 'standpoint' of the observer is always a product of social relations between the subject and 'the Other'. 'Incorporating standpoint epistemology into journalistic praxis would require, then . . . an examination of the social relationships between the knowers and the known, that is, between the journalist, journalistic institutions, the person who would experience marginalization in the context of the news story, and the knowledge claims at stake' (1998: 134).

'Pragmatic' grounds

The philosophical school known as pragmatism is an unlikely contender as a 'ground' for defending objectivity. It is a major source of scepticism about detachment, truth and objectivity. Pragmatist philosopher Richard Rorty questions any clear-cut definition of appearance and reality, as well as the correspondence theory of truth, and representationalist theory of language that hangs from it (Rorty 1998: 2–3). Nevertheless, he leaves room for a concept of progress as 'problem-solving' and a notion of objectivity as 'intersubjective agreement – agreement reached by free and open discussion of all available hypotheses and policies' (Rorty 1998: 7).

Pragmatism (discussed in chapter 3) prioritizes practice and action, and in that respect it has an affinity with journalistic endeavours. But it also represents some challenges for journalism. For if, as Rorty tells us, there are two main ways that reflective human beings try to give sense to life, either by solidarity or objectivity, journalism is caught uncomfortably and seemingly irrevocably between the two. Too much solidarity and one ceases to ask hard questions of the community. Too much objectivity and one finds oneself in the realm of 'nonhuman reality', transcending the world of the community, and readers (Rorty 1991: 21). Rorty's neat extension of this distinction is that realists seek to 'ground solidarity in objectivity', and pragmatists 'reduce objectivity to solidarity'. Pragmatism does not reject objectivity but does not accept it as a transcendent principle either. It focuses instead on cultural agreement and betterment. 'For pragmatists, the desire for objectivity is not to escape the limitations of one's community, but simply the desire for as much intersubjective agreement as possible, the desire to extend the reference to "us" as far as we can' (1991: 23).

While Jeremy Iggers sees pragmatism as a rejection of journalistic objectivity (1998: 136), the idea that we transform social reality through productive activity, and that truth can be established through human projects and purposes has proven attractive to other scholars. For Klaidman and Beauchamp, objectivity and seeking the truth remain important virtues in journalism. What they term a 'reasonable reader standard' allows for an orientation towards truth that places the reader's needs as a central concern for journalism. 'What the press has a duty to report is roughly correlated with what the public has a need to know' (1987: 32). In this framework, objectivity is not directed towards an abstract and absolute truth, but is a work of sifting through values. A commitment to accuracy rates highly in this context.

The most ambitious and comprehensive redefinition of objectivity in recent years has come from Stephen J. A. Ward in his book *The Invention of Journalism Ethics* (2004). The third part of his book defines a new ground for objectivity in the form of what he terms 'pragmatic objectivity'. Ward's reformulation of objectivity begins with a critique; namely that traditional news objectivity is a spent ethical force, and that it is 'built upon an indefensible epistemology and a false characterization of reporting as passively empirical' (2004: 261). 'The epistemology of traditional objectivity presupposes epistemic dualisms of fact/value and fact/interpretation that distort our understanding how we know, interpret and value. Traditional objectivity is flawed by the mistaken belief that objectivity requires claims to be based on absolute standards or facts, as ascertained by neutral, perspective-less agents' (2004: 262).

In proposing his progressive and practice-oriented model of objectivity Ward seeks inspiration from other practical domains such as law and public administration where objectivity operates as a fallible yet determining product of reasonable judgement (2004: 263). Seeking an empiricism that is not subject to a strict separation of fact and value, Ward aims 'to find a place for objectivity in a world where fact, value, theory, and practical interests intertwine inextricably' (2004: 263). The centrepiece of Ward's theory is a pragmatic view of inquiry, in which 'the inquirer understands phenomena holistically, against a background of pre-existing ideas that form the content of his or her conceptual schemes' (2004: 264).

On this model objectivity is not defined through opposition to subjectivity nor primarily through attachment to objective reality. Objectivity arises through an encounter between the world and conceptual schemes that provide criteria of knowledge and truth. It defines a work of understanding and evaluation, an imperfect testing of belief linked to both practical wisdom and theoretical exploration. Forgoing the idea that one can transcend all values beliefs, pragmatic inquiry strives for a more purposeful approach: 'What is possible is a partial transcendence of our current situation through well defined inquiry, questioning, imagination and interaction with other ways of thinking' (2004: 266).

What, it might be asked, defines this approach as objective? Ward suggests that pragmatic objectivity is the 'evaluation of inquiry by objective standards' (2004: 280). The mind reflexively turns on itself, monitoring and correcting activity according to standards of objectivity which lay down conditions for being rational. 'Objectivity is the epistemic evaluation of situated inquiry . . . a fallible, context-bound, holistic method of testing interpretations' (2004: 280). Furthermore, 'we judge an interpretation to be objective if it has good support, according to the best available standards of a conceptual scheme' (2004: 280). Objectivity arises out of the application of 'generic and specific standards' (2004: 288). For Ward, 'all good journalism, including reporting, is active inquiry. It consists of searching and interpreting, of verifying and testing, of balancing and judging, of describing and observing' (2004: 292). As Ward sees it, journalists are neither fabulators nor stenographers. 'They interpret their experiences against the background of their conceptual schemes' (2004: 297).

Conclusion

Andrew Calcutt and Philip Hammond suggest that 'The critique [of objectivity] has long since become the orthodoxy: not only is there consensus against objectivity among scholars of Journalism Studies, but journalists themselves have internalized the critique and often seem unwilling or unable to offer a robust defence of what was once a defining ethic of the profession' (2011: 98). However, surveying these grounds for defence of journalistic objectivity, several lines of resistance to criticisms of objectivity emerge. Aside from the fact that none of the grounds we have examined are based on objectivity as a 'view from nowhere', it becomes possible to say (in no particular order): that the critique is incoherent in important respects; that it misconceives objectivity as lacking interpretation; that it fails to grasp the significance and importance of facts; that the critique is based on mistaken metaphysical grounds; and that pragmatism and standpoint epistemology do not mean the end of objectivity, nor an objective commitment to truth. Even on the question of ideology and power there is a sense that consideration of speaking position or standpoint could make objectivity stronger, not weaker. Most certainly, the idea that any deviation from absolutism or objectivism ends up in relativism has been thoroughly questioned. The positions surveyed in this chapter raise questions about the linking of objectivity and neutrality (preferring instead to see objectivity as the result of an act of interpretation rather than the by-product of eliminating subjective values). Personal values need not be decoded as distortion or prejudice.

It is not my purpose here to measure the effectiveness of these responses against the specific objections raised in chapter 2. What is evident is that any simple dismissal of objectivity as impossible has been complicated. Objectivity need not be tied to an idea of a reality that exists independent of mind. The critique of objectivity as an epistemology has been heard; and naïve empiricism is no longer the sole model.

It seems clear that of all the aspects of journalistic objectivity the one that remains most problematic is a separation theory insisting on a strict separation of facts and values. Far from defending this aspect of objectivity, alternative ideas of objectivity as a regulatory ideal, an epistemic virtue and standard of judgement are emerging. Similarly problematic is a representational argument that suggests objectivity is a mirror on objective reality, or suggests that language is a mere vessel for communicating content. The 'invisible frame' that forms part of the language game of objectivity needs to be openly tackled as a frame, a feature of discourse, a stylistic convention, a mode of performance, rather than in relation to some empirical window on the world. Indeed, what constitutes an appropriate style for contemporary 'objective' journalism, and how the journalist moves along the 'subjectivity scale', which sees any interpretive or background writing as a move away from the objectivity ideal and 'straight news reporting' (Hulteng 1973: 7), is an important area of investigation at a time when the convergence of media and entertainment are placing pressures on the style of news (see Conboy 2004: 184–5).

Finally, it becomes important to consider the standpoint of the observer. Interestingly, the different defences demonstrate a willingness to write subjectivity back into objectivity, both in terms of the importance of autonomous judgement, but also in terms of the frailty of the human situation. As Berry writes, 'Those of us who value objectivity as an essential standard of journalism approach its use by first recognizing our humanness – our subjectivity. Precisely because we understand our frailties, we insist upon maintaining the pursuit of objectivity' (Berry 2005: 16). On this basis, human frailty and judgement are strong reasons for objectivity, not reasons to denounce it.

5

Is objectivity a passive or active process?

Out of our discussion of disputing facts in chapter 3, a very basic question arises: namely, is objectivity a passive or active process? How we answer this question has important ramifications for our view of objectivity. The question of passivity also takes us into debates in journalism history, especially around the treatment of ideas of interpretive reporting.

In light of our guiding question, what should we make of the view that 'a reporter should be as a mere machine to repeat, in spite of editorial suggestion or dictation' (Pray 1855: 472). Or that 'news coverage should recount events without the intrusion of value judgement, interpretation, and point of view' (White 2000: 390). As Stephen J. A. Ward notes, there is a tension between the idea of the reporter as 'active selector of materials' and 'a recording machine' (2004: 198). As Judith Lichtenberg stresses, 'objectivity does not mean passivity' (1991a: 228).

Passive and active are, of course, loaded terms. By 'passive' I mean a view that associates objectivity with a neutral, detached, disinterested outlook, implying that the observer is a bystander (Morrison & Tremawan 1992: 114–15). This is a controversial view. C. A. J. Coady argues that 'objectivity should not be viewed as a camera-like passivity in the face of unambiguous reality. A camera is a bad model of objectivity though it can be a useful instrument of it in the hands of an investigator. After all, a camera merely records events, it doesn't investigate, explore or discover facts; it cannot distinguish between the significant and the trivial'

(ABC Editorial Policies 2008: 2). By contrast, an active outlook on objectivity links it to judgement and interpretation. A critical reader might interject here and argue that disinterestedness and neutrality may not be passive but can be the product of a rigorous, active mind – a point that I would agree with. Nevertheless, a passivity thesis has become prominent in discussions of objectivity in journalism. As 'passive' agents 'Journalists are not supposed to make claims, engage in arguments, or make judgements between contending positions' (Hackett & Zhao 1998: 54). Harold Evans makes a distinction between a 'horizontal' school of journalism, waiting on events, rendering 'words into print along a straight assembly line', leaving 'scandal and injustice ... unremarked unless someone else discovers them', and an 'active' or 'vertical' school, setting its own agenda (1983: 340). To be passive is to accept contradictions and be objective. To be active is to question presuppositions and risk accusations of bias.

How we answer this question about passivity and activity goes to what we expect of objectivity. James W. Carey sets the scene here by insisting that the turn to objective reporting led to a 'conversion downwards' of journalism, a process whereby a reporting is 'de-intellectualized' and turned into a technical form of writing (1997 [1969]: 137). This is supported by a general view that 'objectivity strips reporters of their creativity and imagination, thereby transforming the journalist into a passive link between source and audience, or a worker more technical than intellectual' (Harless 1990: 229). Of course, even technical work is active in a sense, but the broader point goes to relationship between reporting and the mental work of interpretation.

Objectivity through 'subtraction'

The idea of objectivity as passive arises in some aspects from empiricist philosophy, where sensations and feelings form our experience, and things happen to us. The mind is a blank slate; characters and impressions furnish the mind. Observation of external sensible objects (as well as reflection) is said to supply understanding with the materials of thinking. Ideas enter through the senses, which are likened to windows, and objects of sensation are a primary source of ideas. All of this gives rise to a receptive role for the perceiver. Questioning the idea that innate principles, brought into the world with us, are stamped upon our minds, empiricism gives rise to the view that our experience is like white paper upon which knowledge is written. Objectivity is achieved by getting out of the way, subtracting the self, experience, interpretations. It arises from an 'absence of subjectivity or personal involvement' (McQuail 1992: 72).

Journalists have picked up on this view, and for Paul H. Weaver 'liberal journalism strives to be a kind of *tabula rasa* upon which unfolding events and emerging information inscribe themselves' (1975 [1974]: 91). It is possible to extend this analogy to other forms of technology, such as a 'mindless stenographic machine' (Harless 1990: 230; Carroll 1955: 27) or a camera:

> [E]very reporter is a camera on events of public interest, a camera to record what happens or is said, and to present it simply, briefly, directly, interestingly and impartially, ungarnished by opinion, accusation, speculation, sensation, or conclusion. (Barnes 1965: 72)

Notwithstanding Philip C. Rule's argument that the 'TV Camera . . . is no more objective than a writer's typewriter' (1971: 541), the analogy of the camera suggests that events register on the consciousness of the reporter like light and shade on celluloid. This process is seemingly independent from any subjective thought process. The idea seems to be to record and report without selection, reflection or even emotion – which in itself is a very extreme version of the separation of fact and values (see chapter 3).

This passive and subtractive understanding of journalistic objectivity receives a great deal of criticism. In simple terms, it is suggested that subjective elements cannot be subtracted, that all decisions and perceptions of a story are influenced by judgements and values. The argument has been put forward that the nervous system itself limits cognition, that

man's entire nervous system, in its interpreting, sensing, and trans-
mitting to the brain the information it receives, builds up through
the years total-response patterns which, as they stabilize, thenceforth
affect in a definite accept-reject manner the perceiving capacity of a
person. (Livingstone, quoted in McDonald 1975 [1971]: 70)

In other words, every story and signal passes through a sieve or
filter (see also Taflinger 1996).

'Additive' objectivity

It is possible to argue that this passive idea of empiricism is based
on a misreading of Locke's theory of understanding, and that
complex ideas arise out of the reflective operations of the mind
and are therefore, actually, active. A philosophical re-reading of
empiricism could show that our mind does not simply record what
is out there, but operates on the ideas given to it.

Placing less emphasis on the idea that the mind is initially empty,
that there is nothing in the mind prior to sensation or reflection,
pragmatism focuses on the idea that truth is made or moulded
through actions. This, for James D. Harless, forms a key middle
path through debates about objectivity in journalism. Shifting the
focus away from neutrality and passivity, he puts a positive frame
around the idea that objective reporting is subjective:

> The human being is the reporting agent; he or she assumes the respon-
> sibility of submerging his or her own personal values in the interest
> of attaining as objective a report as possible. In other words, this
> view suggests, each reporter must internalize the important value of
> objectivity and operate so as to honor and attain it. (1990: 231)

Regardless of whether the starting point is a neutral objective
reality or a subjective perception, Harless sees objectivity as an
additive or supplementary operational term linked to the exercise
of judgement. Submerging personal values may itself feel subtractive, but the broader goal is active. This understanding of objectivity as an active process links it to active processes of reflection.

Objectivity in this sense is a product of rational striving for objectivity. As Paul Taylor of Reuters suggests, '"Objectivity is not a state, is it, it's a goal, a process, a daily dialectic – and we're constantly debating it, as we should be, all of us"' (quoted in Lynch & Conflict and Peace Forums 2002: 12). To further illustrate this play between passive and active concepts of objectivity, we can draw on some important debates in journalism.

The journalism of attachment

The so-called 'journalism of attachment' represents an important moment at which passive and active concepts of objectivity meet in open debate. This movement, emanating from the writing of Martin Bell, is a product of its time, the mid-1990s and the conflict in Bosnia. For Bosnian journalist Kemal Kurspahic, objective fact-gathering was essential to moving governments into action in the face of genocidal atrocities (2003). David Loyn suggests that in this period 'the political establishment in America and Europe did not want to get involved, so they wrote it off as a Balkan tragedy where ancient ethnic hatreds had been awakened. . . . So the journalists became frustrated. Their reporting was not having any "effect". They wanted to be liberated from the yoke of objectivity' (2007: 5). Loyn is sceptical of the journalism of attachment and its desire 'to be allowed to "tell it as it is" – to take a position condemning the Serbs'. However, this should not overshadow the critique of the limits of objectivity put forward by advocates of the journalism of attachment.

Bell, a BBC reporter in Kosovo and later a Member of Parliament in the UK, witnessed events during the Bosnia conflict that forced him to reconsider some aspects of his journalistic ethics. Questioning the conventional valorization of detachment, Bell writes:

> I would describe objective journalism as a sort of bystanders' journalism, unequal to the challenges of the times. . . . In proposing an alternative journalism – one that is both balanced and principled – I

am not so much calling for a change as describing one that has already taken place. It had to. How else, for instance, were we to report on genocide? Were we to observe it from afar, pass by on the other side, and declare that it was none of our business? It was all our business, perhaps especially ours because we were the independent witnesses. And if genocide would not move us, nothing would move us, and what would that then say of us? (Bell 1998b: 102–3)

For Bell, the journalism of attachment is a journalism that 'cares as well as knows' (1998a: 16). Bell shifts his focus away from the 'circumstances of wars' (military tactics and personnel) and put emotions at the centrepiece of the way he wanted to bring people his stories. In a key point, Bell argues that there is 'nothing object-like about the relationship between the reporter and the event' (1998a: 18). Bell thus constructs objectivity as 'passive' on two levels, in terms of its positioning (as bystander) and also in its construction of reality (as merely 'object-like').

Stephen J. Ward's response to Bell questions the construction of objectivity as passive.

> According to Bell, dispassionate journalism means (1) a reporter cannot use his or her 'eyes and ears and mind and store of experience'; (2) a reporter is dispassionate in the sense of being devoid of passion and emotionally unmoved by events; . . . For Bell, dispassionate journalism is neutral in feeling, judgment and action. (Ward 1998: 121)

Ward disagrees with Bell's definition of news objectivity and argues that a rigid separation of fact and judgement (in which he also includes opinion) is narrow and no longer a dominant force. He sees objectivity as the product of an active mind and mental powers. 'A strict taboo on judgment' is no longer required. Ward rejects the idea that objective reporters can never offer an interpretation. He also suggests that neutrality arises from the application of judgement and public scrutiny to events.

In Ward's understanding, there is no contradiction in the idea that journalists can be objective and attached (that is, care). The reporter's judgement is what counts. Indeed, combining objectivity and attachment can lead to a better concept of objectivity. 'We need both the passion of attachment and the restraint of objectivity to work together to produce solid, yet engaging, reporting' (1998: 123). Clearly, competing ideas of journalistic objectivity are at play here: a passive conception put forward by Bell, and characterized by Ward as narrow and sterile; and a more active version (in Ward's eyes), seen as richer and more flexible. The ethical aspects of the controversy provoked by the journalism of attachment will be discussed in more detail in chapter 6.

Interpretive reporting

The 'conversion downwards' of journalism into objective reporting is seen by Carey as having several negative effects: the loss of independence of the journalist, the eclipse of traditional roles of advocacy and criticism, a diminution of the journalist as 'interpreter of events' (Carey 1997 [1969]: 137–8). This results in a shift in focus from intellectual to technical skills. Journalism defined broadly is distilled into what is termed 'straight reporting', which Richard L. Strout of the *Christian Science Monitor* and *New Republic* magazine described as taking the statement of one person, finding a reply from another, and putting them together in one story with a little colour (1950: 5). What we can call 'interpretive agency' (and its decline) often informs distinctions between passive and active ideas of objectivity.

Interpretive reporting has been debated by practitioners and theorists since at least the 1930s. It has attracted debate because of the different assumptions surrounding it. Interpretive reporting can be seen as a core but restricted component of objectivity, antithetical to objectivity, or a way to extend and improve it. One's starting point is central to how the judgement of passive and active gets made.

For instance, taking the case of interpretation as a restricted aspect of objectivity, working within the constraints of 'straight' reporting, journalists integrate interpretation into objectivity by attributing interpretations to sources. This puts strict limitations on the report. Thus a news worker reporting two competing claims over a document might report the positions rather than consult the document. As Robert A. Hackett and Yuezhi Zhao describe this situation, obtaining the document would have forced the reporter to make interpretations, and violate standards of judgement such as balance, neutrality and objectivity (1998: 45).

A different approach is to view interpretation as a way to improve objectivity. Arthur Hays Sulzberger, publisher of *The New York Times* insisted in 1952 that 'more background and clearer interpretation were needed today, with objectivity in presentation as a constant goal' (*The New York Times* 1952: 21). Lester Markel, writing in *The Bulletin of the American Society of Newspaper Editors* in 1953, insists that 'interpretation should not be separated from the allegedly factual story' and promotes what he calls 'objective interpretation' (Markel 1953: 2). Distinguishing interpretation from opinion, Markel defines interpretive reporting in terms of 'a deeper sense of the news. It places a particular event in the larger flow of events. It is the color, the atmosphere, the human elements that give meaning to a fact' (1953: 1). Putting forward a simple scheme, Markel suggests that to investigate and report is news, to explain is interpretation, and to remark and make overt judgements is opinion. Furthermore, interpretation is an objective judgement based on knowledge and appraisal of an event. Editorializing is subjective judgement.

Markel dismisses the argument that any departure from the facts or use of judgement leads to opinion. Instead of institutionalizing some notion of 'old style straight reporting' he contests the fallacy that 'the attainment of pure objectivity is possible' (1953: 2). His argument is based on the idea that all fact, and objectivity, is based on interpretation. Once the impossibility of pure objectivity is admitted – a notion that does not mean objectivity in journalism is a useless principle – objectivity and interpretive reporting are largely contiguous, 'and the kind of judgment required for the interpretation is no different from the kind of judgment involved in the selection of the facts for a so-called factual story and in the display of that story' (1953: 2).

A 1950 special Nieman Fellows report on 'Reporting "Background"' similarly asserted 'you can interpret and still retain objectivity'. The authors questioned a 'strictly factual' account of the news that offers no understanding – 'the reader is entitled to his objectivity served up in a form he can understand'. Rather than condemn objectivity, the authors encouraged critical reflection on it. The first obstacle to interpretive reporting is 'an unrealistic regard for objectivity'. 'Objectivity becomes unrealistic whenever it prevents the use of explanatory material in an array of facts and assertions that is confusing without it' (Nieman Fellows 1950: 29). The argument here is not with straight reporting treated as a synonym for objectivity, but 'slavish objectivity' which 'defeats its own purpose when it results in a slanted story' (1950: 30). The authors refer to 'straight-laced reporting' as a 'traditionally objective method' of handling some news matter, but also refer to news that provides background as 'real objectivity' that gives a true picture, distinct from 'false objectivity' (1950: 30).

Hackett and Zhao judge that 'while interpretive reporting has conceptually and practically refreshed the older ethos of objectivity, several considerations caution us not to exaggerate the extent to which it has changed old reporting conventions' (1998: 45). In their assessment, interpretive reporting constitutes a modest reform. While interpretive reporting 'has challenged the old-style straight reporting and opened the way for more contextualization. Given the power of tradition . . . the potential of interpretive reporting was very much limited' (1998: 46). The next section explores the relationship between this old-style straight reporting and objectivity in more detail.

Re-assessing interpretive reporting in the McCarthy era

Interpretive reporting stands at the centre of an on-going debate around objectivity as an active or passive process, and a set of fears that 'interpretive reporting, if allowed to become a cloak for propaganda, would take us back to the bad old days of unrestricted "qualified report"', which Frank Mott defines as reporting by rumour with little regard for the facts (Mott 1953: 83).

Interpretive reporting also came under intense debate during the McCarthy era in the US. This debate, I argue, has had an important impact on how objectivity is discussed and valued. There are many key episodes in US journalism (Vietnam, the Pentagon Papers, Watergate). Why, it might be asked, should we give the McCarthy era special attention here?

My justification is that this era set-up the discursive terms for what followed in a unique way. This is not to suggest that it was completely determining, however. Studies of Vietnam War coverage used concepts of straight reporting and interpretation received from the McCarthy era (see Hallin 1986: 73), and repurposed them into a tension between establishment and advocacy positions (1986: 67). While Vietnam brought the alignment of objectivity with official sources and dominant frames of understanding into clearer view (Hallin 1986; Gitlin 2003 [1980]), it further contributed to the construction of objectivity within an establishment versus advocacy narrative.

Watergate represents a slightly different course of events. Schudson suggests that 'Watergate overwhelms American journalism' (1995: 142), but in the backwash some repeated patterns are evident. Watergate focused the advocacy/adversarial position around ideas of investigative journalism (Zelizer 1993: 228–9). The idea of interpretive reporting as some kind of exceptional practice did not receive the same degree of attention as in the past. Indeed, as Schudson points out, the focus fell on investigative reporting 'as just plain reporting' (1978: 188). It could be argued that a dichotomy between objectivity and interpretation falls away here, but I would suggest it is still evident in the idea that 'the investigative tradition distinguishes its aggressiveness from objective reporting's passivity' (Schudson 1978: 189). Nevertheless, in the case of Watergate, the political conditions around the standard of objectivity assumed greater complexity. During the Nixon era, and in a speech on network censorship in 1969 by Vice-President Spiro T. Agnew, objectivity became central to a governmental discourse seeking to discipline the press (Agnew 1969; see Maras 2012). In this context, Schudson suggests Woodward and Bernstein 'make a case for a journalism true to an ideal of objectivity and false to counterfeit conventions justified in its name' (1978: 189). Schudson argues that, on the level of journalism education, this has an effect of a re-investment in the 'rituals of objective reporting' (1978: 192), which sets the scene for a repetition of the old tensions around objectivity.

Taken together, Schudson argues that 'in covering Vietnam and Watergate, journalists did not abandon "objectivity" so much as recognize what a poor shadow of objective reporting they had been allegiant to for a generation' (1995: 171). This is remarkable in light of the vigorous debate over interpretation in the 1930s and 1950s, part of what John L. Hulteng calls a 'long-continuing and multilabelled discussion' that extends from debate around interpretive reporting to the journalism of advocacy (1973: 133). My contention is that one of the sources of this 'poor shadow' of objectivity arose out of the post-McCarthy narratives about objectivity and interpretation. A conventional understanding of interpretive reporting sees it as a challenge to objectivity. In some respects, however, this narrative misconstrues the relationship between objective and interpretive reporting, primarily because it treats objectivity as synonymous with an entire tradition of 'old-style straight reporting' that leaves little room for interpretation.

The McCarthy era represents a significant period for any discussion of objectivity because of Senator Joseph R. McCarthy's 'devilishly clever manipulation of the dogmas of objective journalism of the sort we were taught at Columbia' (Boylan 1986: 31). In 1953 Ronald May argues that while 'no other principle is possible ... under pressure of McCarthy's methods, objective reporting serves simply as a transmission belt for outrageous falsehood' (1953: 11). Under time pressures 'Reporters wrote Mr. McCarthy's charges as fast as they were made and demanded more' (Strout 1950: 5). McCarthy himself understood the deep appeal of documentation and facts to the American public, and his rhetorical style was often based around evidence and proof of wrongdoing, documents and copies (Rosteck 1989: 293). To paraphrase Houston Waring from 1951, the 'God of objectivity' had fallen through the 'technique of the big lie' (quoted in May 1953: 11).

The impact of this manipulation was profound. For Barbie

Zelizer, McCarthyism represents a key juncture at which the objectivity ideal is re-evaluated and re-codified as a talking point for the profession and its responsibilities (see Zelizer 1993: 230–3). There is no question it revealed a weakness in approach (see Davies 2005). As Paul H. Weaver suggests, 'no demagogue can create . . . a movement without a sounding board in the press. By uncritically repeating and dramatically displaying the sensational charges made by a Senator – in keeping with the usages of objective journalism – the press provided Joe McCarthy with just such a sounding board' (Weaver 1975 [1974]: 96). This period in the history of journalism is marked by trauma and guilt. It has been described as a 'journalistic failure', with the press playing more of an accomplice than adversary role (Boylan 1986: 31; Zelizer 193: 230). Alan Barth, writing in the *Guild Reporter*, gives an early example of this response when he declares that

> the redoubtable fourth estate has been taken for a ride again – on the old, merry go round of reportorial objectivity . . . The plain fact is that members of Congress have stretched the tradition of objectivity until it has entirely lost its original shape. . . . And newspaper men who knew better than to take it seriously felt obliged to dish it out straight to a public that knew no better than to lap it up. (1951: 8)

Concerned, Barth finishes his report with an exasperated 'maybe we have a responsibility that goes beyond objectivity' (Barth 1951: 8).

While McCarthyism has given cause for a robust re-evaluation of objectivity, two misreadings have played a key role in casting objectivity as passive, or placing it in a negative position. As a consequence, the dynamic relationship between objectivity and interpretation has been distorted, and we have lost a strong sense of the way debates around interpretive reporting fed into attempts to reform objectivity itself.

The first misreading links interpretive reporting directly to McCarthy. J. Herbert Altschull provides an example of it when he notes, 'it was after McCarthy that a powerful demand arose for "interpretive reporting"' (1990: 315). Altschull creates a clear before and after narrative in relation to interpretation, with the turning point being McCarthy. Before McCarthy 'the comfortable code of objectivity was supreme' (1990: 314). After McCarthy, a 'widely expressed reaction among journalists against the code of objectivity' occurred, leading to new conceptualizations of the 'role and function of the American journalist' (Altschull 1990: 315).

This reading provides a misleading view of the origins of interpretive reporting, and its links to objectivity. Schudson dates the discussion of the two from the 1930s:

> In the 1930s there was a vogue for what contemporaries called 'interpretive journalism'. Leading journalists and journalism educators insisted that the world had grown increasingly complex and needed to be not only reported but explained. . . . Journalists insisted that their task was to help readers not only know but understand. They took it for granted by that point that understanding had nothing to do with party or partisan sentiment. (2001: 164)

In *Discovering the News*, Schudson shows how interpretive reporting and objectivity in the 1930s were not inconsistent with each other (Schudson 1978: 147). David R. Davies argues that from the 1940s the Associated Press actively debated the merits of interpretive reporting, and saw interpretation and objectivity as compatible (2005: 207–8).

The ideal of objectivity (see chapter 1) and the movement towards 'interpretive reporting' respond to the same sense of a growing complexity of the world following World War I, and concern over the methods of managing public opinion. Curtis D. MacDougall suggests this in the 1938 edition of his text *Interpretative Reporting*:

> changing social conditions, of which students of the principal media of public opinion have come increasingly aware during the past six years, are causing news gathering and disseminating agencies to change their methods of reporting and interpreting the news. The trend is unmistakably in the direction of combining the function of the interpreter with that of reporter after about a half century during which journalistic ethics called for a strict differentiation between narrator and commenter. (MacDougall 1938: v; Schudson 1978: 146)

In a section of his book on 'giving it substance' MacDougall summarizes criticisms of American newspaper handling of foreign news, and the failure of the Associated Press to provide background and interpretation of World War I (1938: 149). In his view it was both socially responsible and lucrative to provide interpretation. '[T]he trend unmistakably is in the direction of more interpretative reporting and writing of the news' (1938: 251). While he came to see it as a semantic debate, for MacDougall, interpretation was essential to objectivity, and objectivity without interpretation was 'impossible and, if possible, undesirable' (1947: 3)

For MacDougall, interpretive reporting sat alongside 'the ability to avoid emotionalism and to remain objective' (MacDougall 1938: 251). It rose to meet the challenges of making meaning out of complex social, economic and political trends. For Herbert Brucker, writing in his book *The Changing American Newspaper*, it sought to go beyond stunts and sensation, and to probe beneath the surface (1937: 4).

This is not to suggest that interpretive journalism and objectivity were exactly aligned or identical, and Brucker notes a 'widespread scepticism on the part of newspaper readers as to the objectivity of American journalism and news display' (1937: 28). But he sees interpretation as part of 'respect for the Fourth Estate's obligation of objectivity' (1937: 18). Schudson notes that the most visible difference was a striving for 'background and interpretation' evidenced in weekend and weekday news summaries, and the advanced specialization of reporting (Schudson 1978: 145; Brucker 1937: 7). Interested in greater background and explanation in reporting, Brucker saw himself in a broader debate over the journalistic formula of earlier editors such as Hearst and Ochs (1937: 12). For Brucker, a traditional prejudice against interpretation arose, in part, because of a desire 'to meet the needs of a simpler world', to facilitate the recitation of simple facts (1937: 11).

A second misreading has to do with the concept of straight reporting as the backdrop against which interpretation was positioned, and the way objectivity and interpretation are placed in a dichotomy. This dichotomy arises out of a tendency to view straight reporting as representing 'the tradition of journalistic objectivity' as a whole (Hackett & Zhao 1998: 46). It derives from a tendency in journalism history to see the divorce of editorial comment and the news in terms of the rise of 'straight reporting' (Mott 1953: 72). It is a leap in argument, however, to move from specific reporting practices to an entire code or tradition; and not all commentators of the 1950s took this leap, or confused the straight reporting of the 1950s with that of the 1840s. While commentators such as May were critical of the principle of objective reporting (1953: 11), his example was the copy flowing from the press service wire. This is salient because, as Douglass Cater makes it clear, not all reporting of the era operated under a single code:

> One of the frozen patterns that have hampered press coverage of the McCarthy charges is the distinction between the 'straight' reporting of the ordinary reporters and wire-service men, and the 'interpretive' or 'evaluative' reporting of the privileged few. A wire-service editor defined 'straight' reporting for me. 'The job of the straight reporter,' he said, 'is to take the place of the spectator who is unable to be present. Like the spectator, he does not delve into motives or other side issues except as they become a part of the public record.' (1950: 18)

Cater does not see the straight reporter as the only possible form of reporting available. Cater is scathing on the limits of straight reporting, but it is generally in quote marks. 'Faced with a phenomenon as complex as McCarthyism, the "straight" reporter has become a sort of straitjacketed reporter. His initiative is hog-tied so that he cannot fulfil his first duty, which is to bring clearer understanding to his reader. It results in a distortion of reality'. Cater does not confuse the straight reporter with objectivity.

As a consequence of both misreadings – the linking of interpretive reporting to the McCarthy era, and the confusion of straight reporting with the entire space of objectivity – it becomes easy to place interpretive and objective reporting in an antagonistic, conflictual relationship. As the writings of authors such as Markel, Cater and others illustrate, however, it is an oversimplification to frame the relationship between old-style straight reporting and interpretive reporting as a simple dichotomy. As a result, objectivity sits in a much more complex relationship to interpretive reporting than usually assumed.

Unfortunately, the 1950s debates between interpretive and straight reporting have been turned into a schism between interpretation and objectivity. As Elmer Davis puts it, a 'great gulf' had opened up in reporting.

> The good newspaper, the good broadcaster, must walk a tightrope between two great gulfs – on the one side the false objectivity that takes everything at face value and lets the public be imposed on by the charlatan with the most brazen front; on the other, the 'interpretive' reporting which fails to draw the line between objective and subjective, between a reasonably well-established fact and what the reporter or editor wishes were the fact. To say that is easy; to do is hard. No wonder that too many fall back on the incontrovertible objective fact that the Honorable John P. Hoozis said, colon quote – and never mind whether he was lying or not. (Davis 1952: 38)

Note, even here the gulf is between 'false objectivity' and 'interpretive' reporting; and Davis still holds to an objective rather than subjective standard of fact.

Edwin R. Bayley rightly warns us that treating the 'conflict between "objectivity" and "interpretation"' as a 'conflict of principle was somewhat misleading' (1981: 75). This treatment has the unfortunate effect of placing objectivity in a position of structured passivity. What risks being ignored is the way journalists engaged critically with the tradition of objectivity, particularly in the context of the straight reporting of the wire services, using interpretation, explanation, background and objectivity itself as key terms (see Bayley 1981: 77–81).

Bayley calls for a re-assessment (1981: 78). Jeremy Iggers likewise tries to shift the barricades and argue that the 'acceptance of interpretation did not mean an abandonment of objectivity, ether as an epistemological goal, or as a set of journalistic practices; rather, the concept of objectivity was expanded to include the problematic notion of objective interpretation' (1998: 95). Iggers suggests that 'In the wake of the McCarthy era, objectivity began to lose its tight hold on American newsrooms, as editors gave reporters more latitude to practice interpretive reporting. And objectivity continued to come under considerable attack by opponents of the journalistic establishment in the 1960s and 1970s' (1998: 69). But this continues the linking of interpretation to McCarthy, and the tendency to see interpretation at odds with objectivity. Davis, an advocate of interpretation, takes a longer-term view: 'we have been getting away from that dead-pan objectivity of late years – or were, till the rise of Senator McCarthy' (1952: 34). Bayley explores the practical ramifications of this. Editors called on the Associated Press to ensure safeguards against 'so-called interpretive writing' (Bayley 1981: 83). Politically, Bayley suggests 'all of the "fundamentalists" on objectivity were from newspapers that supported McCarthy editorially, and all of the editors who defended interpretive reporting were from newspapers that were critical of McCarthy' (1981: 85). At the same time, objectivity became harder to praise, more difficult to see as active. In the terms put by Wallace Carroll, it became a 'deadly virtue' (1955: 25). Objectivity found itself stuck in the frozen patterns.

Conclusion

Every norm or ideal operates in a wider field, both social and professional. In the case of objectivity this field included a pre-cast set of concerns, interpretation as 'opinion, prejudice, slanting, distortion, surmise, speculation, and advocacy' (McDonald 1975 [1971]: 81). As Donald McDonald notes, publishers reacted to this and

> developed what they thought was a splendid alternative, an objectivity so narrowly defined that what was eliminated was not only opinion-ated editorializing in the news columns but also any opportunity for the reporter to put what he was reporting into a context which would make it meaningful. This was thought to be the objectivity of the scientist in his laboratory, meticulously recording what his senses per-ceived, impersonal, unprejudiced, and, above all, humble before the demonstrable fact. Actually the scientist was doing much more than

138

this: his investigations led him to look for causes and relationships, and his intuitive and creative faculties were never idle. (1975 [1971]: 81)

This 'narrowly defined' objectivity was not universally promoted, as the debate around interpretive journalism shows. While it had the effect of limiting opinion, it also constrained reporting to what Davis called 'one-dimensional news', 'factually accurate so far as it goes, but very far indeed from the whole truth' (1952: 34). Davis echoes earlier concerns to go deeper than the surface, and expresses his own concern over the 'passivity' of objective journalism when he suggests that 'objectivity often leans over backward so far that it makes the news business merely a transmission belt for pretentious phonies' (Davis 1952: 32). Carroll similarly objects not to 'the ideal itself' but to a narrow, 'almost doctrinaire interpretation of objectivity', that borders on 'irresponsibility'. 'Too often our objectivity is simply the objectivity of the half truth' (1955: 25).

The fact that critiques of objectivity can be countered by an appeal to more active and interpretive forms of objective journalism suggests that objectivity is an adaptive norm, accommodating different perspectives. While a 'subtractive' reading of objectivity often takes the foreground, an 'additive' conception has contested the way objectivity is pigeonholed. Nevertheless, the idea that straight reporting (however that is defined) restricts interpretive reporting persists and feeds into implicit and structural judgements about the passivity, or otherwise, of objectivity. A gulf has developed between 'the bald and exact fact *versus* interpretation' (Mott 1953: 87), between those who report and those who interpret, criticize and advocate (see Janowitz 1977). This distinction became even more entrenched around the Vietnam War. As Julianne Schultz notes, 'the limits of neutrality and passive objectivity in journalism . . . became increasingly apparent during the social and political upheaval of the 1960s (1998: 43). Subjected to a strict (perhaps stricter) separation of news and editorial and opinion on the one hand, and a critical backlash on the other, the objectivity norm entered a period when it was both rejected and re-institutionalized, a source of bias as well as credibility (see chapter 1).

6

Can objectivity coexist with political or ethical commitment?

At first glance, the question posed by this chapter might seem like a non-question. The 'human element in the business of perceiving' has long been perceived as an issue (Myrick 2002: 50). Objectivity is so commonly associated with impartiality, detachment and value-free judgement that any sign of bias, favouritism or involvement is taken as an indicator of failure. In other words, objectivity cannot coexist with political and ethical commitments. However, this response is unsatisfactory, for it leaves unexamined the forms of practice, politics and ethics being discussed. The risk is that by neglecting questions of culture and context, and relying on the idea of objectivity as 'a view from nowhere' as a starting point, *any* kind of values commitment becomes suspect. However, if, as Thomas Nagel suggests, objectivity is related to standpoint, a view in the world from which 'the distinction between more subjective and more objective views is really a matter of degree, and ... covers a wide spectrum' (1986: 4–5; see chapter 2), then politics and ethics may re-enter the frame.

Taking the contrary approach, there is an alternative view of the association of objectivity with value-free judgement, which is that the idea that 'journalists committed to objectivity do not believe in anything except, perhaps, objectivity itself – is patent nonsense' (Knowlton 2005: 223). Here, journalism as a calling or vocation represents a values commitment in itself. Nevertheless, the idea that objectivity is exclusive of political and ethical commitment is common. Indeed, some media organizations demand that workers not be involved with political parties, unions or causes; or not write on them (Reese 1990; *The New York Times* Company 2005). These prohibitions are often linked with objectivity. When the (then) Australian Journalists' Association (AJA) debated whether or not to affiliate with the Australian Council of Trade Unions in 1984 the 'No' case related to objectivity: 'The AJA, it said, should not be aligned with any movement capable of compromising members' objectivity. "The journalist", it concluded, "must stand for objectivity, impartiality, and non-contamination"' (Dunlevy 1998: 132).

Theodore Glasser suggests: 'objective reporting has denied journalists their citizenship; as disinterested observers, as impartial reporters, journalists are expected to be morally disengaged and politically inactive' (1992: 181). Many critics agree with Glasser, and see objectivity as incommensurate with political and ethical commitment. His critique invites us, however, to explore the line between objectivity and moral engagement and disengagement carefully; and it is significant that, for Glasser, the focus is on *dis*-engagement and *in*activity not amorality or apolitical standpoints. Thus it could be argued there is another layer to Glasser's statement whereby the work of the journalist is always framed by moral and political concerns. For those who see objectivity as reconcilable with political and ethical commitment – or indeed a political and ethical commitment in itself – a more important issue arises of the purpose or goal of objectivity, and especially *how* it is achieved.

Any discussion of objectivity and political or ethical commitment faces a primary difficulty of pinning down the context. The context can give specific form to the way politics and ethics is treated. For example, industrial not personal politics comes into play in the US in 1930s, when 'publishers quoted the need for objectivity as grounds for refusing to negotiate with the Newspaper Guild, the journalist's union, which had taken political positions' (Iggers 1998: 67). Schudson highlights 'it was a term hurled back and forth in staff debates ... in the thirties (1978: 156–7). Publishers used it as a weapon against the newspaper guild. The objective observer emerges for the first, but not the last, time as an object of discipline and dispute.

The question of whether objectivity can coexist with political or ethical commitment cannot be tackled in a solely abstract manner. As a result, in this chapter, after a discussion of facts and values, I want to explore objectivity in relation to different forms of journalism or visions of the journalist. This will assist in exploring the limits of the separation of facts and values when it comes to dealing with the political and ethical commitments of journalists.

Facts, values and the world

Thinking about political and ethical commitment leads us to consider an important aspect of objectivity, which is the possibility of separating facts from values (examined in chapter 3). The norm of objective journalism is a highly circumscribed one, not simply in terms of the separation of facts and values, but in relation to a third term, 'the world'. Linked to a notion of an 'invisible frame' being placed around the events, this frame distances the journalist from the world, placing them in a particular role of reporter or on a particular stage (Schiller 1981: 1). Thus, even when speaking in the first person and providing an eye-witness account, this framing conditions the journalist's observations and experiences. Journalistic objectivity assumes a separation of reporter and event. So a description of the situation reporters might find themselves in might go:

Event to Reporter to World (as Audience or Receiver)

This helps make clear that the reporter's job is to report on events, which in turn is central to how journalists view knowledge and the world. Access to the event is seen as direct and unmediated. Reporting is conceived as transmission and correspondence. It rests on an assumption that 'presupposes a relationship between the facts and the report, the outside world, and the way it is represented, which is natural, obvious and transparent' (Lynch & McColdrick 2005: 212). This arrangement forms the basis of a unique relationship to knowledge and experience.

While providing expansive and 'direct' access to events, there are limits to this frame, specifically to do with imagining how the reporter fits into the 'world of events'. Is the job of the reporter to report events to the world? Certainly. But what of the reporter's position in the world? So we can rearrange our terms in this way:

World (of events) to Reporter to Event (as story)

Objectivity theory in its empiricist forms suggests that the event lives in an *external* reality, external to the reporter. But where does this leave the reporter's world? How do we think of the community the reporter lives in, the cafés, churches or clubs they go to? A strong view in the literature is that the reporter's world is something of an 'unthinkable', and the direct 'Event to Reporter' model untenable. As Annabel McGoldrick notes, it raises questions around 'what to do about the subjective aspects of the job' (2006: 2). For Robert A. Hackett and Yuezhi Zhao, 'objectivity offers few strategies for reconciling the personal and emotional with the political and the rational' (1998: 232). The problem is more than just a devaluing of subjectivity by objectivity, for with this bathwater goes the baby of identity, memory, attachment and connection – indeed a raft of experiences that can lead to greater sensitivity and insight in journalism. As Richard H. Reeb quips, 'reporters are not reporters for objective reasons' (1999: 119).

A lack of connection can be, and has been, celebrated. Walter Lippmann stresses that 'Emphatically he [the reporter] ought not to be serving a cause, no matter how good. In his professional activity it is no business of his to care whose ox is gored' (1920: 88). *New York Times* reporter and commentator James B. Reston notes that objectivity conjures an image of 'reporter devoid of any convictions about anything; a true cynic' (1945: 101). But he goes on to insist on the importance of 'human sympathy' and a 'sincere conviction about his obligation to the people to get to as near to the truth as possible', as the main way to 'attain that curious quality known as objectivity' (1945: 101). Similarly, Jackie Harrison argues 'accuracy' and 'sincerity' are good synonyms for objectivity and impartiality (2005: 146).

143

A common form of journalistic objectivity, then, gives rise to a way of thinking about the reporter as standing apart from the world. Or, put another way, it can make it difficult to think of the reporter or journalist as being in the world, as having values and political commitments, as being citizens in the fullest sense. The point here is not that the balance of personal lives with professional commitments is impossible to achieve, but rather that some theories of objectivity leave little room for it.

Objectivity as ethical and ideological commitment

There is one obvious criticism that can be made of Glasser's point that objectivity leaves journalists morally disengaged. It is that while journalistic objectivity implies a detached, scientific standpoint, the idea also defines an ethical approach. It is, as Michael Schudson describes it, a morally prescriptive norm (2001). A commitment to objectivity is often *in itself* an ethical commitment. Journalists have never pretended 'to be indifferent to the values, such as freedom of speech and press, on which their very craft is premised' (Hackett & Zhao 1998: 224). Journalistic objectivity implies values such as honesty, fairness and independence (the latter are headline values of the Australian Media, Entertainment & Arts Alliance 'Journalist Code of Ethics'). Even when 'objectivity' may not appear as a headline term in a code of ethics, these others often do. Indeed, they operationalize objectivity in more specific and practical ways. They may replace objectivity, but in some cases an implied 'objective' position remains in the substrate as it were. For example, one Australian journalism textbook explains that independence goes to integrity: 'Journalists should *operate freely and independently* of any influence that might affect objectivity' (Phillips & Lindgren 2006: 293).

For Stephen D. Reese this ethical commitment operates as a full professional ideology, and as such is part of a set of paradigmatic assumptions guiding the work of journalists. The 'journalistic paradigm has been developed, sustained, interpreted, and modified within this larger hegemonic context' (1990: 395). Values that do not fit with the paradigm are not explicitly suppressed but excluded through the maintenance of 'mainstream' boundaries. 'By accepting valueless reporting as the norm, the media accept and reinforce the boundaries, values, and ideological "rules of the game" established and interpreted by elite sources' (1990: 395). Examining the case of a socialist reporter at *The Wall Street Journal*, A. Kent MacDougall, Reese identifies a need for what he calls 'paradigm repair'. In the conventional view, any reporter holding socialistic values is a threat to, or 'violation' of, the ideals of objectivity. MacDougall outlines how he was able to promote some of his views through selection of sources and experts, and respecting factual accuracy. While the case provoked controversy it was also depicted as one where professionalism prevailed, and editorial checks and balances secured the necessary separation of facts and values.

Reporting the critical counter-culture

During the Cold War, the political field itself was in transformation. In the US, not only was a critical counter-culture placing new expectations around society, but following the 1960 U-2 incident and the 1961 Bay of Pigs Invasion, 'two *Presidents* had publically admitted lying and suppressing news' (Weaver 1975 [1974]: 96). The counter-culture of the 1960s is an unavoidable topic in any discussion of journalistic objectivity and political or ethical commitment.

On 7 October 1969, Managing Editor of *The New York Times*, A. M. Rosenthal wrote a memorandum to the staff. This document represents a robust re-affirmation of objectivity. It is part of a long-standing commitment to an informational model of journalism at the *Times* (see chapter 1). But it can also be seen as an address about the social unrest of the 1960s, and how journalism should (or shouldn't) respond. Rosenthal speaks of the paper's 'ability to mirror the world as it changes'. 'We've learnt too that a social movement . . . can be as real a fact as a speech or a parade'. Rosenthal frames this as a period of development and change in the *Times*, but at a deeper level, it is a response to the culture of the 1960s. This is acknowledged in the middle of the memorandum:

> the turmoil in the country is so widespread, voices and passion are at such a pitch that a newspaper that keeps cool and fair makes a positive, fundamental contribution without which the country would be infinitely poorer. The goal of objectivity is made more difficult – and becomes more important – as the stories we go after and the issues we cover become more and more complex. (Rosenthal 1969)

James Boylan, with a specific focus on the *Times*, characterizes this more dramatically as a period of 'newsroom mutiny': 'many reporters, witnessing the turbulence beyond the newsroom, found that their organizations were responding too slowly or not at all to the social and political crises of the Vietnam years; the magazines and the underground press seemed to get closer to the heart of things' (1986: 37).

There is, of course, a need to take care around terminology, as well as assumptions about the make-up of the counter-culture (generational or not, elitist or not), and its character (lawless, anarchistic, idealistic, hedonistic, etc.). This is not simply because, as activists learnt from that era, protesters can easily be transformed into agents of 'civil disturbance' rather than agents for 'peace and justice' (Gitlin 2003 [1980]: 6); but also because there is a risk of uncritically linking the 1960s to a critical culture without looking at particular issues or aspects of critical thought. For example, it is tempting to characterize the counter-culture in terms of a widespread if not total critique of objectivity in journalism. Following the work of J. Herbert Altschull (1990: 317–18), Hackett and Zhao identify nine movements in journalism that interact or work alongside critical or adversary journalism – including interpretive, investigative, adversary/critical, enterprise, precision and celebrity journalism. However, only three of them (advocacy journalism, underground journalism and new journalism) 'have unambiguously challenged the objectivity ethos' (1998: 52).

As Schudson notes, an 'adversary culture' (a term he borrows from Lionel Trilling) has been evident since the 1930s (1978: 177). By the 1960s growth in higher education gave adversary culture a new ground, leading to renewed interest in, and redefinition of, politics (1978: 178). Caution is advised, however, when it comes to drawing a link between this adversary culture and the profession of journalism. 'Journalists did not "impose" an adversary culture on their reporting of politics – they responded to a critical stance they found in their sources' (Schudson 1978: 180). Indeed, Paul H. Weaver suggests 'officialdom itself [Senators, committee chairmen, Washington lawyers, assistant secretaries] became sympathetic to the oppositional fashions of the decade' (1975 [1974]: 98).

From the perspective of those reported on, objectivity was experienced as an ideology. Drawing on the work of Stuart Hall, Todd Gitlin sees it derived from a 'profound myth in the liberal ideology: the absolute distinction between fact and value, the distinction which appears as a commonsense "rule" in newspaper practice as "the distinction between facts and interpretation": the empiricist illusion, the utopia of naturalism' (Gitlin 2003 [1980]: 48; also Hall 1973: 188). Objectivity became associated with hegemony, a view of how things are naturalized as common sense, masked as routine. Thus the 'taken-for-granted code of "objectivity" and "balance" pressures reporters to seek out scruffy-looking, chanting, "Viet Cong" flag-waving demonstrators and to counterpose them to reasonable-sounding, fact-brandishing authorities' (Gitlin 2003 [1980]: 4). Objectivity can lead to an over-emphasis on certified spokespersons (2003 [1980]: 149); or alternatively (despite the conventions around balance) leave New Left voices out of stories altogether (2003 [1980]: 80). Combined with a fear of being painted left-wing (a legacy of McCarthyism), Gitlin argues reporters had every reason to treat the counter-culture, specifically anti-Vietnam protests, unsympathetically (2003 [1980]: 74–7).

In line with the argument that objectivity is inflicted with something of a frame-blindness (see chapter 2), objectivity emerges as a manipulable value that falls victim to 'pack journalism' and can be used to support right-wing framings of protests at the expense of a broader understanding of the issues (Gitlin 2003 [1980]: 98–9). Like other scholars such as Gaye Tuchman (1972), Gitlin sees objectivity as closely intertwined with the routines of media work. But he suggests 'there are disruptive moments, critical times, when the routines no longer serve a coherent hegemonic interest'. At these moments 'political and economic elites (including owners and executives of media corporations) are more likely to intervene directly in journalistic routine, attempting to keep journalism within harness' (2003 [1980]: 12).

At this juncture, objectivity is very compatible with a commitment to politics, albeit one aligned with hegemonic interests. Caught between their own ties to the system and also their own need for autonomy, news organizations, Gitlin argues, are strained: if they ignore social unrest, they risk losing audience confidence. 'Even a news organization's methods for legitimizing the system as a whole, its code of objectivity and balance, pull it in different directions: at one moment towards the institutions of political and economic power, and at another towards alternative, and even, at times, oppositional movements, depending on the political circumstance' (2003 [1980]: 259). But media organizations have a strong motive to take the risk of engaging with oppositional movements. 'The network's claim to legitimacy, embodied in the professional ideology of objectivity, requires it . . . to take a certain risk of undermining the legitimacy of the social system as a whole. The network's strategy for managing this contradiction is . . . to tame, contain, the opposition that it dares not ignore' (2003 [1980]: 259).

Viewed from the perspective of those doing the reporting, young reporters of the era felt 'uncomfortable in their reportorial roles, almost as if they were agents of "straight" society spying on a subversive culture. They found themselves sympathetic to the ideas and values of the people they wrote about and increasingly sceptical, uneasy, or outraged at the transformation of their stories between copy desk and printed page' (Schudson 1978: 181). Resisting a simplistic generational argument Schudson suggests 'The movement affected younger journalists first and most profoundly, but this, in turn, influenced older and more powerful journalists' (1978: 181).

Inside news organizations, the counter-culture placed a new set of occupational stresses around the reporter and the news organization itself. This manifested itself in terms of a tension between autonomy and control. As Gitlin notes,

> To avoid a reputation for having an ax [sic] to grind, the top media managers endow their news operations with the appearance, and a considerable actuality, of autonomy; their forms of social control must be indirect, subtle, and not at all necessarily conscious. Their standards flow through the processes of recruitment and promotion, through policy, reward, and the sort of social osmosis that flows over-whelmingly in one direction: downward. The editors and reporters they hire are generally upper-middle-class in origin, and although their personal values may be liberal by the conventional nomenclature of American politics, they tend to share the *core* hegemonic assumptions of their class: that is, of their managers as well as their major sources. (Gitlin 2003 [1980]: 259–60)

In this passage, Gitlin teases out the complexities of a system in which hegemony is secured through the bounded autonomy of news workers. That journalists, newly empowered as autono-mous agents (admittedly with boundaries), would question this gilded cage is inevitable. As Boylan notes, 'Reporters, given new scope, were repeatedly able to test management oratory about press freedom, to place acute political questions before the press establishment, and gradually to change the ideology of press–government relations' (1986: 32). Boylan suggests that what occurred at this time was a questioning of objectivity as a standard of 'non-involvement' (1986: 38).

This dissidence, in the spirit of the era, informed the 'reporter-power' movement of the early 1970s (Boylan 1986: 38). Indeed, different models of professionalism emerged in this period, famously depicted by Morris Janowitz in a 1975 article as the 'gatekeeper' and the 'advocate'. Both set up a relationship to the world – only one in his view is compatible with objective jour-nalism. Objectivity tends to be the province of the gatekeeper, which is focused on a 'sharp separation of reporting fact from disseminating opinion' (1975: 618). '[T]his image of the journal-ist sought to apply the canons of the scientific method to increase his objectivity and enhance his effective performance. The model was reinforced in part by the increased prestige of the academic social researcher, and it assumed that, through the application of intellectually-based techniques, objective and valid results could be obtained' (1975: 618).

Replacing 'the scientific method with the concept of the journalist as critic and interpreter', advocacy journalists turn away from objectivity, and the static conception of reality, linked to the old gatekeeper norm. Janowitz describes this shift in attitude in terms of a feeling 'that there is a series of conflicting interests, each of which creates its own contribution to the definition of reality. Therefore the role of the journalist is to insure that all perspectives are adequately represented in the media ... The journalist must "participate" in the advocacy process. He must be an advocate for those who are denied powerful spokesmen' (1975: 619).

Writing in 1974, Weaver sees the institution of the press in a kind of limbo, occupying an 'ambiguous middle ground between its longstanding tradition of "objective" journalism and a new movement for an "adversary" journalism – no longer massively committed to the one but not yet certain, let alone unanimous, about the other' (1975 [1974]: 90). Giving a balanced perspective on the relation between objective and adversary journalism in this context is difficult, and Schudson seeks to go beyond any simple narrative of the old and the new or conflict:

> An adversary culture must be adversary *to* something. .... To the increasingly numerous and vocal critics, the rhetoric of objectivity seemed hypocritical or deceitful, or in Vietnam, criminal. The adversary culture's attack on objectivity conjured up a more unified and univocal Establishment culture than in fact existed. (Schudson 1978: 183–4)

The idea that the attack on objectivity needs more careful analysis gets support from Weaver, who, in a rebuttal of adversary journalism, identifies a certain romanticism that isolates 'a part of a tradition or doctrine and to treat the part as though it were the whole' (1975 [1974]: 95). For Weaver, values core to the adversary culture – autonomy, investigation – were also part of the liberal tradition that supported objective journalism. The extent to which mid-twentieth-century journalism 'has become enmired in a tradition trap' (Methvin 1975 [1970]: 202), and how that tradition has been cast, remains a topic of discussion and debate. While 'objective' journalism, was cast by some as 'the natural, proper, and undisputedly legitimate form of journalism' (Hackett & Zhao 1998: 52), for others, 'the upheavals of the 1960s and a reassessment of journalism's role in society, not to mention a journalistic revolution, shelved the concept [of objectivity] pretty dramatically' (Dennis 1989: 83).

The caring journalist

Journalistic objectivity understood as an ethical commitment operates within a set of structured values. This is especially significant to war correspondence, because it attempts to straddle issues of professionalism, public service, membership in a specific subculture of reporters, and social empathy (Tumber & Prentoulis 2003: 222). These values condition how the journalist is supposed to encounter external reality. The separation of subject (the knower) and object (the known) is thus coded through dualisms where, as Stuart Allan notes, supposedly 'masculine' attitudes toward reality ('held to be objective, rational, abstract, coherent, unitary and active') are 'discursively privileged' over 'feminine' attitudes ('posited as subjective, irrational, emotional, partial, fragmented and passive') (2010: 150). Any deviation from this structuring leaves journalism vulnerable to accusations of crusading and moralizing. The journalism of attachment, one that 'cares as well as knows' (discussed earlier in chapters 2 and 5), raises many issues around the shifting boundaries and values of war correspondence. Here, I want to focus on the ethical and political dimensions of Martin Bell's description of 'objective journalism as a sort of bystanders' journalism' (Bell 1998b: 102).

Looked at as a form of journalism with an explicit ethical commitment, the journalism of attachment has not been without its critics. Christopher Dunkley criticizes the emotionality of the journalism of attachment:

> Perhaps those who believe in the journalism of attachment would argue that the world would be a better place if only it were softer and more feminised; if only the Brits would abandon the stiff upper lip, embrace therapy culture, and let it all hang out. But to take that approach as the basis for a new style of news journalism sounds appallingly dangerous. (Dunkley 1997)

From a conventional perspective, the journalism of attachment is indeed dangerous. Not because it leads to unobjective journalism per se, but because attachment triggers values not always associated with de-sensitized war reporting: emotional, involved, 'softer', 'feminized'.

Within a heavily coded structural system that favours certain values, what is noteworthy about the journalism of attachment is that it raises issues of attachment and feeling, but mixes these in an unfamiliar fashion with forms of reporting valued for their distance, neutrality, and non-involvement; namely world affairs and war reporting. The 'danger' of the journalistic attachment is that it blurs the boundaries of war correspondence. This, I argue, explains the strong reaction evoked by Bell's attachment theory. Mick Hume writes, in a passage worth quoting at length:

> The new attitude demonstrated by some of the highest-flying foreign correspondents in the world signals a sea change in journalistic opinion. Of course, few war reporters have ever really been neutral. . . . In the past, however, major news organisations like Bell's BBC felt obliged at least to pay lip service to the image of the reporter as detached observer. . . . What is now being said openly is that it is not only impossible for a journalist to be a dispassionate bystander, but that it is *undesirable* anyway. . . . All of these reporters insist that the facts are still sacred and that, while they are not 'neutral', they do all they can to be 'objective'. . . . Yet, despite their denials, the evidence suggests that there is a clear contradiction between their formal commitment to objective reporting of the facts and their moral attachment . . . The stock-in-trade of today's top war reporters is moralism: the attempt to depict Bosnia or Rwanda as morality plays in which Good battles Evil. . . . These war reporters see fit to set themselves up as the Solomons of the cyberage, using their on-line laptops and satellite links to make instant yet final judgements as to who or what constitutes 'the original

sin and the unsullied virtue' in the world. But in going down that road they are entering a journalistic minefield. (Hume 1997: 7–8)

This passage illustrates how 'attachment' disturbs the inherited structures of journalistic objectivity in a very fundamental way; it threatens the dominant attitudes and sensibilities. Conventional approaches foster a very all-or-nothing approach. Either you are objective and dispassionate, or you are a moralist. There seems to be no in-between. This causes difficulties if one wishes to question the limits of objectivity.

Interestingly, Bell makes it clear that judgement is crucial, and that his vision of attachment is part of a 'principled journalism'. 'There is a time to be passionate and a time to be dispassionate – a time and a season for all things; and I would not report the slaying of innocent people in the same tone and manner that I would use for a State visit or a flower show or an exchange of parliamentary insults' (1998a: 18). Bell's heresy is to ponder the possibility that journalism is not a neutral and mechanical undertaking, but possibly a moral enterprise that should be informed by right or wrong – this opens up a debate about what kind of ethical and moral system should be applied. While he is critical of objectivity as a bystander approach, perhaps of greater significance is Bell's starting point, which is that 'we in the press . . . do not stand apart from the world. We are part of it'. The theory of journalistic objectivity is still coming to grips with this basic proposition due to the way it fails to situate the reporter *in* the world, and also because of the structure of judgement placed on attachment.

The engaged journalist and the public agenda

There exists a wide spectrum of examples of, for want of a better word, 'campaign' journalism, from the independent documentaries of John Pilger through to the sensationalist campaigning of proprietors such as William Randolph Hearst. Our focus, here, is on political journalism oriented towards social justice.

The suggestion that journalists should not just report the world, but seek to change it, is one that raises a concerned response from those interested in objectivity. The ideal of reporting from a detached and neutral position, in a fair, balanced or even-handed way, is threatened. More significantly, however, the concern is that the public agenda is hijacked by a personal, political partisan agenda. It will be helpful in this context to deepen our understanding of 'agenda'. Agenda-setting is a very large field of communications research that emerged in the 1960s (McCombs & Shaw 1972), with precursors back to the 1920s. It studies the relationship between the public agenda, media agenda and policy agenda. The interaction between a notion of objectivity and an agenda is therefore a large topic for discussion, beyond the scope of this study. For our present purposes we can note that any kind of agenda can have a distorting effect because an agenda lists and prioritizes particular items in social reality. Public agendas are said to be finite, capable of dealing with around four to six priority issues at a time. Almost by definition, things can be excluded (Dearing & Rogers 1996). An agenda is immediately an expression of both public and private interests. Indeed, a range of agents, from government to lobbyists and public relations professionals, seek to shape the agenda and the priority given to items on it.

Constructing crusading journalism as a threat to objectivity, and also a hijacking of the social agenda, is to miss a key distinction. The distinction has to do with how the agenda is formed and declared, and the way reporting is carried out, justified and legitimated. An engaged journalism can still be factual and fact-oriented, and write according to a declared agenda, which is different from an objectivity that is fact-oriented but de-emphasizes or doesn't declare the journalist's engagement with an agenda. So it can be said of George Orwell, for instance, whose starting point was 'a feeling of partisanship, a sense of injustice' (Orwell 1965 [1947]: 186), that he was fastidious in the accumulation of accurate data about wages, prices and rents, names and dates, and also made use of sources from trade unions and local authorities. For writers such as Orwell there is no contradiction between truthfulness and commitment to specific political principles (Hampton 2008: 483). Facts grounded his reporting in the everyday, and in an expositional mode. As Michael Bromley puts it: 'these elements provided an "objective" basis to which he added layers of subjective description, comment and analysis, contrast and hyperbole, and, finally, politics and ethics, in an attempt to achieve authenticity in the representation of ordinariness' (2003: 127).

While truthfulness and commitment to specific political principles need not be enemies, there is still strong debate around the limits of acceptable reporting, and the excesses of activism. For example, New Zealand freelance journalist Karl du Fresne, wishes to defend objectivity against activist journalism: 'The former is driven by a commitment to the public's right to know. The latter goes a step further: the information presented is shaped by the personal views of the journalist, who often desires a particular outcome' (2007). Here, the public's right to know, aligned with ideas of objectivity and disclosure of facts, is deemed acceptable, but an outright expression of change or revolution is not acceptable. If the information is shaped by personal views, then that is less preferred, supposedly, than a story shaped by ideas of neutrality and even-handedness. One is reportage that supports the public agenda, the other is a journalism that promotes an agenda.

The distinction or border between these two projects is not always clear-cut, however (see Hallin 1986: 117). Agendas are subject to revision and renegotiation; which is to say that different groups, of different political and policy persuasions, can have an influence from day to day. To turn the invisible frame of objectivity into a shield and suggest that the public agenda is not open to debate and dialogue is risky, in that it hides the political nature of agendas and the contested aspect of the public interest. That said, as we have learnt in our discussion of the history of objectivity and the way it was a response to propaganda and public relations, objectivity is attractive precisely because it offers an apparently 'agenda-less' perspective on the world (see chapter 1).

John Pilger is a figure who is often linked to a lack of objectivity, although it is doubtful this criticism would concern him since he openly advocates a critique of objectivity: 'For many, objectivity means not rocking the boat, presenting the Establishment point of view. In my opinion, journalism is about digressing from that view, having nothing to do with the government point of view, looking under rocks' (quoted in Dunlevy 1988: 133). As Maurice Dunlevy notes, this puts Pilger in a tradition of muck-raking that usually 'sees the ethos of objectivity as an inhibition' (1988: 133).

Pilger is left-leaning, and involved. As one editorial observes: 'Pilger is a critic of capitalism, a cynic about the new global economy and an ardent and often vicious opponent of Western, especially American, influence in world affairs. . . . Pilger mourns American hegemony, the arms race and the spread of trans-national capitalism to the Third World' (*Canberra Times*, 1998). His journalism is sometimes dismissed as the promotion of a par-ticular agenda. But we should think more carefully about where this dismissal comes from. If it comes from a view that deems the social agenda to be untouchable, beyond question, then clearly that very idea constrains debate.

Supporters of Pilger's work see him as keeping objectivity in check, of going deeper than the news media (Bowler 2006). And while his version of balance may be idiosyncratic, and he may be open in his bias, Pilger himself maintains a version of detach-ment in relation to power, in the sense that he regards himself as resisting propaganda and handling.

The idea that any engagement equates to bias is in many respects overly simplistic. It is important to go beyond the issue of individual engagement and bias to broaden out the equation to take into account different elements – such as the setting of the agenda – and different interests. As the *Canberra Times* puts it:

> Whether of the Right or the Left, engaged journalism can be produc-tive. It drives people to seek out what interests them, 'facts' and stories that would otherwise have not been discovered. . . . Engaged journal-ism, at its worst, can mean the crassness of parish-pump self-interest, tabloid banality, or the 'fixing' of foreign news to suit the national interest (or that of the proprietor).

Refusing to dismiss journalism with an overt agenda on the basis of facts, the paper continues: 'But engaged journalism is not the deliberate falsification of facts . . . Like objective journalism, the engaged variety may end in getting facts wrong, but it does not begin with error: that would be just bad journalism'.

Some commentators argue that despite conventions of impartiality, the version of events promoted by reporters often stays close to the official account or preferred reading of events (Taylor & Condit 1988: 293; also Gitlin 2003 [1980]). In other words, balance can lead to a skewing effect. Fairness can be manipulated. Voices can be silenced. So an engaged journalism perspective might argue that the fourth estate role of the media ties journalistic objectivity excessively to the rules of the political system (in which the media is a player), and the movements of established parties. The corporate nature of media outlets forms another 'filter' of information (Herman & Chomsky 1988). An analysis of power is, arguably, beyond the philosophical range of journalistic objectivity which is *dependent* on a separation of facts and values rather than a questioning of the terms of this separation. Journalistic objectivity can be seen as a form of engaging with the world, but it has tight rules around what is and is not appropriate. At its most critical, engaged journalism can see objectivity as a form of silencing or censorship (Pilger 2006), or indeed as a form of war journalism.

Objectivity as war journalism

For Annabel McGoldrick, peace journalism researcher and broadcaster, 'What journalists think of as "objective" reporting actually consists of a set of conventions which predispose news about conflict in favour of War Journalism' (2006: 2). The construct 'war journalism' has different aspects, but for Jake Lynch and McGoldrick, drawing on a model devised by Johan Galtung, it consists of four main elements. Firstly, it is war/violence oriented, focused on a '2 parties, 1 goal (win)' scenario. War journalism constructs conflict within an enclosed arena, it propagates an us/them journalism which casts the 'them' in a negative light. Secondly, it prefers secrecy over transparency and is propaganda-related.

Thirdly, war journalism is elite oriented, focused on the key figures, particular evil-doers. Fourthly, it is victory oriented, focused on a formula of 'peace = victory + ceasefire'. By contrast, peace journalism shifts the focus on conflict towards win–win situations, giving voice to all parties. It resists propaganda through the exposure of truth on all sides. Rather than being elite and victory oriented, it is 'people' and solution oriented, focusing on a 'formula' of 'peace = non-violence + creativity' (Lynch & McGoldick 2005: 6; McGoldrick 2006: 2).

Whereas, for Schudson, resisting propaganda and public relations were central concerns of the ideal of objectivity (see chapter 1), in peace journalism objectivity is *aligned with* propaganda and war journalism. Indeed, McGoldrick argues, the more objective you are, the more likely you are to report in a fashion biased 'in favour of war' (2006: 2). As Lynch and McGoldrick note:

> Three conventions of Objective reporting, in particular, are predisposed towards War Journalism. Their 'natural drift', as it were, is to lead us – or leaves us – to overvalue violent, reactive responses to conflict, and undervalue non-violent, developmental ones. The conventions are:
> a bias in favour of official sources
> a bias in favour of event over process
> a bias in favour of 'dualism' in reporting conflict (2005: 209)

The issue goes further than natural drift, however, as the authors suggest earlier that 'the trusty sword of Objectivity, forged in the Enlightenment and a choice weapon in later battles for commercial and political survival, has over time ensured the primacy in news of the "official agenda"' (Lynch & McGoldrick 2005: 204).

Peace journalism, like many other approaches that study news (such as propaganda analysis, framing and gatekeeper theory), regards news as convention-bound and constrained by routines. A form of interpretative reporting, it seeks greater context and background. With these perspectives, peace journalism shares the view that journalism is more than simply the reporting of facts, a notion that still functions 'as the guiding principle across a broad sweep of professional activity' (Lynch & McGoldrick 2005: 195).

Peace journalism is aligned with that theoretical apparatus that resists concepts of 'mirroring' reality in favour of ideas of constructing reality. Drawing on methods from conflict analysis, peace journalism goes beyond this view to serve as a reminder of the way peace can be excluded from the news agenda, and conflict framed in ways that narrow down options for peace. It provides a provocative approach to the issue of balance, raising the question of the over-valuing of violent, reactive responses to conflict as opposed to non-violent responses (Lynch & McGoldrick 2005: 197). It goes further to promote positive change (leaning towards non-violence and peace); and cultivate, support and give voice to 'change agents' that can intervene in cycles of violence.

However, it has proved a controversial approach, particularly around issues at the heart of objectivity to do with detachment versus participation (see Lynch 2007), and also whether the journalist should play the role of peace-keeper (Hanitzsch 2004). David Loyn for example, regards the peace approach as prescriptive, and a new orthodoxy (2007). He resists the opposition of war and peace journalism, and the casting of reporter as peace advocate:

> But the key point to be made here is that reporters need to preserve their position as observers not players. Galtung's demand that journalists should become active participants, playing a part in the complex 'cat's cradle' that makes a conflict, is wrong. By *searching* for peacemakers, reporters are immediately on the wrong side of the fence. Reporting and peacemaking are different roles, reporters who give undue prominence to passing peace plans, or search for peacemakers, distort their craft and do not serve their audience. (2007: 3)

Rather than dismiss the insights of peace journalism research entirely, however, Loyn argues many of the key insights of the latter are typical of good journalism not just peace journalism.

While peace journalism as a form of engaged journalism is critical of objectivity, it still embraces interpretation and reflexivity. 'It means that journalism needs some workable form of *reflexivity*, analysing and addressing its own role in shaping discussions and creating realities. Without this, it is fated to collude and conceal' (Lynch & McGoldrick 2005: xvi). Loyn resists the suggestion that this excludes objectivity.

> But surely the antidote to this is a fuller context in a reporting of events, not discarding objectivity. Both the reporter and the audience need to know that there is no other agenda than explaining what is going on – that what you read, see on the screen or hear on the radio is an honest attempt at objectivity; that reporters treat any and every event with an informed scepticism, rejecting any attempt to co-opt them into involvement. (Loyn 2007: 5)

Peace journalism could counter this claim by arguing that it is transparent in its goals and more critical in analysing and attempting to shift the agenda. It asks 'Is there such a thing as "non-agenda journalism"?' (Lynch & McGoldrick 2005: 211).

At the heart of this disagreement is, as Loyn acknowledges, an argument about perspective. On the surface Loyn seems to seek an objective, value-less position from which to report. 'A view from nowhere'. But he explictly rejects this, stating 'each reporter takes a "view from somewhere"' (2007: 4). He acknowledges that 'reporters live in a social context and share a language and certain assumptions with their audience' (2007: 4). Agreeing with Lynch and McGoldrick regarding the need for analysis and reflection, he promotes the idea of reinventing objectivity.

Despite a tendency in the literature to cast peace journalism and objectivity as mutually exclusive and theoretical rivals, there is a sense that objectivity is more than either a blind reporting of facts, or a function of war journalism. Recently, Lynch and Galtung have recast the meaning of objectivity: 'By objectivity we mean intersubjectively communicable and reproducible, that other journalists would have reported the same. No private fantasy' (2010: 52). 'Objectivity is not the issue. Selection is the issue, the criteria applied and the codes and contexts in which the event is placed and interpreted' (Lynch & Galtung 2010: 53). This 'working version' of objectivity resists being selective against peace.

Objectivity and the watchdog role

A watchdog role for the media over the public domain has captured the imagination of journalists and the public alike. Investigative journalism in this mould is regarded as some of the most noble, and can lead to real change. But is it consistent with ideals of journalistic objectivity?

For Glasser, this is at the core of his view that objectivity is an ideology: since 'objective reporting is biased against what the press typically defines as its role in a democracy – that of a Fourth Estate, the watchdog role, an adversary press' (1992: 176). However, consistent with our focus on context, we should be mindful of different ideas of the fourth estate, an ideal that operates differently in different media systems. For some, the idea goes beyond an adversary role. An integral social function of the media in Western democracies is to monitor the relationship *between* the Estates (the judiciary, legislature, and public service) (Pearson & Polden 2011: 11). Furthermore, not all nations provide constitutional protection for freedom of the press, which means the fourth estate operates via convention. In order to address Glasser's criticism, we should briefly examine the ideal, how the role itself can be interpreted in different ways, and whether it is incompatible with objectivity in all cases.

In Western democratic societies, there exists a belief that the media have a positive, independent role to play in the democratic process. That even though it has commercial aspects, and is not subject to election, it is an important political institution. 'This ideal is grounded in the notion that among the checks and balances that ensure that the powerful are held accountable, the media has an essential, and highly political, role to play' (Schultz 1998: 2).

The term 'Fourth Estate' can have a number of different meanings. Indeed, Henry Fielding puts forward a non-journalistic definition of the fourth estate as 'the Mob' in 1752 (see Fielding 1806: 83). While the idea of the press as having a watchdog role can have a very broad interpretation (from consumer rights to environmental politics), at the heart of the fourth estate concept is a role for the press as an independent broker of information, free from government control, but still active within the political process. The fourth estate idea is often traced back (through an unconfirmed attribution in an 1841 lecture by Thomas Carlyle) to Edmund Burke, a British parliamentarian, who allegedly stated in 1790 that 'There are three estates in Parliament but in the reporter's gallery yonder sits a fourth estate more important far than they all' (Ingelhart 1987: 143). There is some dispute around this quote, and essayist Thomas Macaulay is considered as the source of an alternative founding quote from 1828, 'The gallery in which the reporters sit has become a fourth estate of the realm'. Burke's three estates are said to reflect the British parliament at that time, The Lords Temporal, the Lords Spiritual, and the Lords Common. In most texts the estates take a more secular form, and the idea updated to mean that alongside the judiciary (the legal system), the parliament and the executive, the press has an independent role to further the public interest.

The fourth estate concept raises the issue of the media's place in the system of governance, but is not always specific in the limits of this role. Indeed, the fourth estate idea can be interpreted as a pejorative, casting a different meaning on the term. It has been seen as part of a quest for power on the part of the media. George Boyce views it as a 'political myth', ascribing to the press the key role of 'indispensable link between public opinion and the governing institutions of the country' (1978: 21). Julianne Schultz, noting the real organizational constraints that exist around concepts of objectivity and autonomy, suggests 'the extent to which journalists claim professional standing – and responsibility for a revived Fourth Estate – may simply mask a quest for power' (Schultz 1998: 135). Hackett and Zhao offer a more direct critique: 'media organizations use the watchdog ethic selectively, to justify a stance of general hostility to government or to launch vendettas or crusades that serve their own commercial or political interests' (1998: 138). They question the worthiness of the ideal insofar as it fails to provide comprehensive public philosophy for journalism, and is 'rooted in an outdated classical liberal view of government as the primary potential threat to individual freedom' (1998: 183).

Returning to Glasser's criticism of objectivity as biased: in those countries where freedom of the press is not guaranteed by the constitution as it is in the US, the fourth estate is not assumed as a pre-given function, but operates as an ideal alongside others such as objectivity. In such contexts, objectivity is not always considered incompatible with the fourth estate role. In a 'Media and Democracy' project survey administered in June/July 1992, Australian media researcher Julianne Schultz asked 600 news and investigative journalists about the fourth estate and objectivity, with 80 per cent of the sample responding. 'About 90% of the news and investigative journalists maintained an optimistic personal faith in the ideal of the Fourth Estate', while 39 per cent felt the actual situation fell short of the ideal and the media were more like a business (Schultz 1998: 120, 257). At the same time, in response to the question 'In your view, how important is it that a journalist try to be as objective as possible?', 88 per cent suggested it was very important, and 12 per cent somewhat important.

The survey addressed issues of politics. As objectivity can take different forms, the survey asked journalists to indicate which of five statements about good reporting were closest to their understanding of the term 'objectivity': 33 per cent nominated reporting that 'expresses fairly the position of each side in a political dispute', 23 per cent nominated reporting that 'does not allow the journalist's own political beliefs to affect the presentation of the subject, 22 per cent nominated reporting that 'goes beyond the statements of the contending sides to the hard facts of a political dispute', 21 per cent nominated an 'equally thorough questioning of the position of each side in a political dispute', and only 2 per cent felt making clear 'which side in a political dispute has the better position' reflected their sense of objectivity. Investigative journalists preferred fair expression of position (38 per cent), but also demonstrated strong affinity with the idea of going beyond the statements to get at hard facts (32 per cent) (Schultz 1998: 251–2). This survey casts the relationship between objectivity and politics in a much more complex light than Glasser suggests.

Historical factors can also impinge on perceptions of the role of fourth estate. James Curran argues that in Britain in the early twentieth century the fourth estate or watchdog role describes not so much press independence, but the willingness of press magnates to use their papers and instruments against the political parties (Curran & Seaton 2003: 45, 347–8).

In the US, between 1950 and 1970, the ideal underwent a significant reworking with the interpretation of the media as the 'fourth branch of government'. In 1959, Douglass Cater noted

> The American Fourth Estate operates as a *de facto*, quasi-official fourth branch of government, its institutions no less important because they have been developed informally and, indeed, haphazardly. Twelve hundred or so members of the Washington press corps, bearing no authority other than accreditation by a newspaper, wire service, or network are part of the privileged officialdom in the nation's capital. (1959: 13)

Taken together with Cater's view that government more than ever depended on publicity, resulting in 'government by publicity', this view of the press as a branch of government extends, I would argue, the very concept of the fourth estate and the relation of the press to power. Others have dwelt on this new governmental role. As James Boylan points out in regard to the Pentagon Papers and Watergate: 'This was truly the work of journalism as a Fourth Branch, devoted less to reporting on society as a whole than on the misdeeds of the Executive' (Boylan 1986: 40).

This issue of proximity to government (and the accompanying responsibilities) is important to any concept of the fourth estate. It has been since a London *Times* editorial of 6 February 1852 tackled the issue of responsibilities of government and the press. The editorial distances *The Times* from the labours of statesmanship, and focuses on the concept of disclosure: 'The first duty of the press is to obtain the earliest and most correct intelligence of the events of the time, and instantly, by disclosing them, to make them the common property of the nation' (*The Times* [London] 1852: 4). Given its focus on disclosure, *The Times* would have been nervous thinking about the press as an actual fourth branch of government.

If the belief is that a healthy representative democracy relies on the fourth estate, the press, to question acts of government and question the terms of debate, it is important to know that it can be interpreted in different ways. Objectivity can be reconciled with fourth estate roles such as clear and accurate reporting of disclosures; policing the separation of powers, and the other estates; also watching over civil liberties. This is not to suggest that grey areas do not exist (such as around 'off the record' comments), and that there can be conflicts between the estates in allowing disclosure (the courts prohibiting publication on certain matters, for example) but the roles are reasonably well understood.

Things become more complex with a purely political watchdog role, where the language of objective journalism begins to be seen as a leash that restrains the press. As Gordon Campbell, delivering the 2004 Bruce Jesson Memorial Lecture in New Zealand, puts it:

> In the name of objectivity, journalism largely shrinks from countering the spin machines of government and corporate public relations. There is a strong conservative ideology in journalism that says the format of news and current affairs should resemble a blank slate – on which the forces of the left and the right are invited to write, under equal fire from the host. I strongly disagree. I think the media outlet should be encouraged to reach conclusions based on its own prior evaluation of the evidence, and to subject the politicians to strong and persistent questioning to pursue the truth. (Campbell 2006)

In this view, objective journalism is linked to sanitized language, a censoring influence on the provision of context and background, an aversion to make judgement calls on contentious issues, and 'regularly leads it into putting the aggressor and the victim onto the same, morally neutral footing' (Campbell 2006). Watchdog journalism, especially in an investigative mode, needs to go for hidden facts, make judgements about right and wrong, air allegations. For Jay Rosen, the notion of journalist as watchdog 'just doesn't fit well with notions of objectivity because a watchdog is far more assertive than objective' (1993: 51).

Public or civic journalism

Another significant area of political commitment to consider is that of public or civic journalism, which is premised on the ideal of re-engaging citizens in public life, as well as the realization that 'journalism cannot remain valuable unless public life remains viable' (Merritt & Rosen 1998: 46). Jay Rosen, one of its principle theorists, sees it in fourfold terms: an argument about the task of the press; a set of practices and experiments; a movement of people and institutions; and a controversy, all focused around deliberation and democracy. Public journalism promotes the idea of journalists working more closely with the community, helping them (and covering their efforts) to solve civic problems. It works at the juncture of a range of debates around democracy, deliberation, participation, advocacy, campaigning and interpretation, as well as declining circulation.

Jay Rosen provides one of the more succinct definitions of the movement when he writes:

> Public journalism is an approach to the daily business of the craft that calls on journalists to: (1) address people as citizens, potential participants in public affairs, rather than victims or spectators; (2) help the political community act upon, rather than just learn about, its problems; (3) improve the climate of public discussion, rather than simply watch it deteriorate; and (4) help make public life go well, so that it earns its claim on our attention. (quoted in Iggers 1998: 143)

The 'movement' emerged on the scene in the early 1990s, with early experiments dating from after the 1988 US presidential campaign, described as a 'campaign of phony charges and counter-charges with only minimal attention to important issues' (Rosen 1994: 374). Examples of public journalism activities include: moving away from conflict-oriented news values and balance for the sake of balance; turning editorial pages over to readers; citizen- and issues-focused election coverage that emphasizes the voices of citizens (as opposed to numbers and poll driven or 'horse race' coverage); sponsoring neighbourhood roundtables; convening town hall meetings, think-tanks or special expert panels; collaborating with other news outlets and universities; co-creating community agendas; taking a public-policy role on issues such as violence, race-relations, urban planning and unemployment.

Treated very often as a movement, it is not always acknowledged that the concept is historically and discursively situated. Some key pivot points for the theory include: the 1988 presidential election; a theoretical debate between Walter Lippmann and John Dewey which gives rise to a view of objectivity as an official doctrine that 'tells us to worry about things like accuracy, balance, and fairness' rather than public engagement (Merritt & Rosen 1998: 51; see Schudson 2008); a view that objectivity after Vietnam and Watergate 'made less and less sense' (Merritt & Rosen 1998: 52).

Public journalism has been a contentious idea in journalism circles mainly for its call to go beyond reporting, and to get involved in communities by participating in programmes, holding public forums, creating new agendas, connecting citizens (see Richards 2005: 113–15). The idea is to give expression to community voices and for outlets to listen. For some, the idea is to 'create a learning community, one that discusses issues, not just on the basis of emotion but on facts about how things work' (Meyer 1995).

Public journalists have called for a re-assessment of journalistic values such as conflict, balance and neutrality, all with a view to making 'public life go well' (Merritt & Rosen 1998: 44) – although critics have suggested good reporting always does this. Perhaps the area of greatest controversy, aside from challenging the very role of reporter in modern journalism, is the crossing of the invisible frame of objective reporting that public journalism seems to promote by encouraging participation. This leads to questions around alliances with sources, community interests and forces of marketization, as well as issues to do with challenging or shifting public opinion (Richards 2005: 116). Certainly it offends traditional conceptions of the reporter as holding up a mirror to society, but also raises issues of disclosure and conflicting interests when news organizations report the same projects they campaign on. As one critic notes: 'Some – including me – have long argued that journalists can't march in the parade and watch it at the same time, that journalists should only be observers, not participants. To participate in the events we are reporting about was to provide the perception of conflict, even if there was no actual conflict, and hence to lose credibility with readers' (Russell 1995: 17; Shepard 1994: 33–4). In response, it is argued that 'public journalists do not equate their breaking away from detachment with the breaking away from neutrality. Indeed, Rosen readily states that the pledge of neutrality is vital to public journalism because "it separates 'doing journalism' from 'doing politics'"' (Holbert & Zubric 2000: 57).

Public journalism can be linked with quite strong negative claims about objectivity. In the task of creating 'an alliance between journalism and the public', one of the 'greatest obstacles . . . is journalists' traditional stance of detachment' (Iggers 1998: 141). Part of this has to do with objectivity's 'non-political' status which, it is argued, amounts to de-politicisation, a preoccupation with the flow of events and celebrities rather than policies' (Blumler & Gurevitch 1995: 213). Although Davis Merritt does not mention objectivity explicitly, he expresses strong negative views about detachment, which sets the journalist apart from the consequences of their work, and leads the reporter to ignore or demean criticism (Merritt & Rosen 1998: 42).

Objectivity in this negative view is not focused on the needs of citizens. On this basis, for Jeremy Iggers, 'objectivity, both as a procedural norm and as epistemological objective, must be rejected' (1998: 138), although he is careful to preserve values such as accuracy and fairness. Objectivity is linked to the exclusion of citizens from public debate (Iggers 1998: 140). Indeed, Iggers argues that the 'rise of objective journalism has been paralleled by a decline in citizen participation in public life' (1998: 125). Others echo the criticism. Despite the fact that the traditional press claims to act on behalf of the people, and that objectivity itself was egalitarian in its commitment to the free exchange of ideas, 'it was not the people themselves, but a privileged group, namely the major media and their sources, that came to define the terms of public discourse and be (in Schiller's phrase) the "lord of the facts"' (Hackett & Zhao 1998: 35). In short, the judgement is that 'objective journalism has contributed to the decline of communities and the public sphere' by focusing on the management of news by an elite, specialized class (Iggers 1998: 121).

Many of these debating points regarding elites and the public interest centre on the significant issue of credibility. For example, Jay Rosen suggests that objectivity is damaging to credibility because it deflects criticism of the work of reporting. But he goes further to posit a link between objectivity and different approaches to credibility. 'In the old theory, credibility follows from detachment and distance. You're credible because you're not involved. You're not interested, you have no stake. Under the new theory of credibility, credibility follows because you're concerned, because you care, because it matters to you what happens in the community' (Rosen 1993). Rosen would not mourn the loss of objectivity. Yet other supporters of public journalism seek to rescue it. Philip Meyer distinguishes between two definitions of objectivity, an 'objectivity of result', 'laying out of facts in a sterile, noncommittal manner, and then standing back to "let the reader decide" which view is true', and an objectivity of method, a 'scientific method applied to the practice of journalism'. 'Abandoning the traditional stance of journalistic objectivity to practice public journalism need not be a bad thing if we can substitute objectivity of journalistic method. It's a better standard anyway, and it can keep us honest' (Meyer 1995).

News has long been criticized for focusing on issues only when they become 'events', exceptional happenings, with the effect that 'significant phenomena that are not events (e.g. situations, trends, conditions) go largely unreported' (McDonald 1975 [1971]: 73). Public journalism provides a different lens through which to report the news, emphasizing longer attention spans, a need for deeper discussion, a preference for substance over tactics (Meyer 1995), understanding over conflict.

A response to corporatism in journalism, technological change, and a decline in civic engagement, this school is linked to a return to civic and democratic basics, to get involved with communities, to improve the life of citizens, and the quality of deliberative democracy. To do so, public journalists argue they need to go beyond the 'artificial constraints' journalism has imposed on itself. This puts objectivity in an awkward position. Objectivity can be seen as a 'lifeless doctrine' (Rosen 1994: 373), a passive response to a more urgent problem of people in communities growing divided.

Addressing this problem raises a by now familiar issue: namely, the way that objectivity gives rise to an idea that the reporter must stand apart from the community so that, as Philip Meyer puts it, 'you see all events and all viewpoints as equally distant and important – or unimportant'. From a public journalism point of view, this noncommittal, detached approach leaves unanswered many questions to do with the links between journalism and the community in which journalists work. While some journalists argue they have always been engaged with the community, others are concerned about how public journalism remains responsible. Marvin Kalb notes, 'When the journalist literally organizes the change and then covers it, I'm uncertain about such traditional qualities as detachment, objectivity, toughness ... The whole point of American journalism has always been detachment from authority so that critical analysis is possible' (quoted in Shepard 1994: 34). Drawing on Schudson's work, Holbert and Zubric argue that public journalism risks idealizing particular ideas of conversation and deliberation: 'public dialogue does not ensure a healthy democratic process. . . . The ability of the public to generate a quality debate should not be taken as a gospel' (2000: 62).

Another important criticism has to do with the autonomy and independence of journalists, and who sets the news agenda. The concern is that the media becomes a 'player' rather than a 'chronicler'. Public journalism can, without clear principles, become cause journalism. Any move away from objectivity risks falling in step with a community agenda that may be excellent, but could be misguided and could lead to a kind of censorship or filtering of news and critical opposition.

Public journalism has been linked to a reinvention of journalism. However, while it represents a broader commitment to deliberation and democracy, not just loyalty to a particular community, it has been controversial, for it means re-evaluating the basis on which the news outlet is a stakeholder in the community at a time when special interests abound. While serving the public interest has been a long-standing aspect of the media, public journalism opens up new issues around what the public thinks and what is best for the public. It can be viewed very cynically as a tactic to bolster circulation. For others, its definition is unclear. As Ian Richards points out, there is uncertainty and ambiguity surrounding the term. 'Public journalism's supporters use words such as "public" and "community" as if they were clear and well-defined concepts, rather than hotly contested notions' (2005: 113), although some of the best writing on the topic does explore these issues and recognizes the need for greater deliberation of them.

In terms of objectivity, public journalism has made an important contribution to the debate on journalism insofar as taking a public lens means re-examining the role of the press in reporting all kinds of issues, especially political ones. It has forced, as Rosen puts it, a kind of acknowledgement that following even the most traditional values of objectivity involves practising 'a kind of politics simply by viewing the political scene in a particular way' (Rosen 1994: 376). It gives rise to a different idea of the newspaper as 'fair-minded participant' rather than watchdog or judge (an antidote to the excesses of the fourth estate). Assessing public journalism and objectivity, borrowing a line from James Carey, it is as though objectivity 'took the public out of politics and politics out of public life' (quoted in Schudson 2008: 1033). With it, the public conversation is said to have withered. Focusing specifically on objectivity, perhaps because of the dominant position of objectivity as a way of thinking about journalism, it is inevitable that public journalism has had to define itself in relation to the norm. In doing so it has made astute observations about objectivity (see Rosen 1993). But critiquing objectivity has its own history, and public journalism can be seen as one episode in a long-standing debate about the status of objectivity that, I would argue, also needs to be taken into account in order to tease out the layers of discussion around interpretation, advocacy and democratic drift.

Conclusion

Considering the question of whether objectivity can co-exist with political and ethical commitment, we have seen that any answer is dependent on the form of politics, ethics and journalism being promoted. This chapter could easily be extended to encompass religion, for instance (see Rosen 2004b), concepts of biblical objectivity (see Olasky 1996, 2006; Beckerman 2004: 32), or existential objectivity (Stoker 1995). The question prompts reflection on some fundamental aspects of reporting, its place in the world and its mediating role. It also raises important questions of the position of the reporter.

The argument that any political or ethical commitment somehow 'invalidates' objectivity lacks cultural specificity. The debate over whether objectivity is compatible with fourth estate ideals is a case in point, as there are not only a variety of ways of conceiving this concept, but different ways of implementing it. Objectivity cannot be deemed exclusive from political and ethical commitment, partly because some writers have refuted this idea, but also because a category shift allows objectivity itself to be considered a form of political or ethical commitment.

7

Is objectivity changing in an era of 24/7 news and on-line journalism?

On 12 January 2012, Arthur S. Brisbane, Reader's Representative of *The New York Times*, sought 'reader input on whether and when New York Times news reporters should challenge "facts" that are asserted by newsmakers they write about' (Brisbane 2012a). Writing on his 'Public Editor's blog', Brisbane wondered, 'And if so, how can The Times do this in a way that is objective and fair? Is it possible to be objective and fair when the reporter is choosing to correct one fact over another?' Brisbane's posting raised a practical issue of how to handle falsehoods, but drew a wave of criticism from readers for the way it seemed to assume that facts should not be challenged by news reporters. In their comments to his post, readers expressed incredulity at the very posing of the question, and the way it reduced reporting to 'stenography', or a mouthpiece role. Brisbane felt that Op-Ed columnists have the freedom to call out what they think are lies, but his question was 'should news reporters do the same?' Critical reaction from the readers again queried the basis of the question, and the assumption news reporting should not contest facts put forward by newsmakers.

Going against the grain of dominant reaction, one minority response drew on a rigid distinction between news and analysis: that 'If a candidate for US president says something – anything – I would like to know what he or she said. That's reporting, and that's "the truth" in reporting: a presentation of the facts, as objectively as possible. Whether a candidate was coy about something, exaggerating something else, using misleading language, leaving something out of his or her public statements . . . all of these things are analysis'. This statement echoes a common idea in broadcasting, which is to report the facts and let readers decide on the truth (Albota 1991: 225). However, the majority of readers contested the separation of report and analysis. Readers made it clear that their standards for objectivity were different from the 'false objectivity' put forward as normal practice by Brisbane, and that the notion of fairness risked pandering to politicians.

The Internet figured in many comments. One commenter remarked: 'The New York Times public editor just asked the Internet whether the paper's reporters should call lies lies'. Commenters noted that this lack of testing facts may account for readers 'flocking' to the Internet; and also that the Internet makes testing facts crucial, since it takes untested facts and circulates them widely. The response from readers echoed a renewed interest in 'fact checking' found in other areas of the US media landscape (Spivak 2010).

This example captures many of the themes of this chapter: enhanced feedback, transparency in deliberation, the problematic nature of consistent and total objectivity (Sargent 2012), the fact-orientation of US media of the late nineteenth century now turbo-charged by new technology in the twenty-first. All this on the public record, hosted by *The New York Times*, about *The New York Times*, complete with a dissenting response to Brisbane's post from the Executive Editor of the newspaper, Jill Abramson (Brisbane 2012b).

It is a commonplace in discussions of the media to treat developments around digital technology and the Internet in a before and after fashion, with technology as the determining driver of change. An example is the decline of circulation of newspapers, a phenomenon attributed to the Internet but which in fact pre-dates it (see Tiffen 2010). The problem with this approach is that it often fails to offer a critical perspective on how media practice is situated historically and culturally. This becomes a crucial issue when looking at objectivity in journalism in the era of 24/7 news and on-line journalism.

The example from *The New York Times* illustrates the need for a historical perspective, for this episode links to well-established debates around reporting the truth. Do journalists report the truth as they *see* it, or as they *find* it by the application of scientific method? (Hulteng 1973: 137). This question represents a specific dilemma for the reporter as 'professional communicator' (Carey 1997 [1969]) to do with a commitment to what is factual versus what is truthful. Is it enough to simply relay statements made by officials, for instance, or should facts be contested at the point of assertion? Is there an obligation to dig deeper, past the handouts (Mott 1953: 79)?

It also relates to another debate which has gained renewed life in the era of the Internet, which relates to how to capture the complexity of social relations. Andrew Calcutt and Philip Hammond see this as a tension between two roles or activities of journalism: an 'investigative activity that addresses social reality in its lively contradictions, and mediating activity, which also forms part of social reality but which addresses such contradictions in order to deactivate them' (Calcutt & Hammond 2011: 126). Calcutt and Hammond suggest 'Newspaper journalism . . . undertook both of these tasks, but the second has tended to override the first' (2011: 126).

The collaborative nature of many (but not all) web and mobile platforms (part of a rapidly developing area of digital technology) allows new possibilities for participation in the process of producing and consuming news, and transparency in relation to the exercise of judgements and values. On-line collaboration opens up a way, furthermore, of reconciling the two perspectives above, of mediating in a way that affirms social reality in its lively contradictions. In other words, it forces journalism ethics to confront questions of pluralism, dialogue, collaboration and transparency. It also forces media studies to consider seriously questions of media use, by both readers and producers.

The Australian news and current affairs site Webdiary, founded by Australian journalist Margot Kingston in 2000 as a column on Federal politics for the *Sydney Morning Herald*, but now independent, serves as an example. Framed as a political diary, and conceived as a 'conversation' with readers, Kingston found that the web platform, and users themselves, forced her to open the site to other contributors and re-think transparency, accountability and ethics. In her description of developing an ethics for Webdiary, an act itself prompted by users, Kingston speaks of throwing off the stylistic 'shackles of the myth of objectivity, which is really an excuse to hide the truth from readers, not expose it. It also falsely sets the journalist up as observer/judge; not participant' (Kingston 2003: 161–2). Her code of ethics emphasizes trust, independence and honesty rather than objectivity.

Notions of objectivity have always been shaped by media workers' encounters with new technology. As we see below, in the era of 24/7 news and on-line journalism the concept of objectivity in journalism is being dismissed, challenged and modified, but also defended and reinvented. Attitudes of distance and detachment may be highly valued, but perhaps not in all cases (Tait 2007). The way journalists, citizens and media organizations use new platforms are revealing tensions around our historical connection to objectivity and concepts of professionalism, truth-seeking, authority and reputation, that are part of the dominant paradigm of news work; but which are also being renegotiated in their own right.

Cables, satellites and the challenges of change

The Ancient Greek word *pharmakon* signifies both poison and cure. Technological change in relation to the news can be summarized under something of this (double) heading. As Jackie Harrison points out, technological change brings opportunities and expansion, allowing one to 'bypass or improve upon mainstream reporting processes' (2005: 148). At the same time, Harrison notes some mainstream broadcast media see technology solely in terms of competition or erosion of what they currently do. On the level of work, technology can lead to both greater and lesser journalistic autonomy, depending on the system in place. Desktop video and smaller gear can lead to greater mobility. It can lead to greater possibilities for cross-media storytelling. Databases offer unprecedented access to checking. But all of this can also contribute to an intensification of work. While journalists are embracing new ways of working 'their employers are asking them to do more with less and, in many cases, to learn a whole new set of tools and techniques, while maintaining (or in most cases, increasing) their output' (Media Alliance 2010: 18).

Considered both a poison and a cure at different times, cable and satellite news, and other new media, have changed our sense of news and current affairs (Wark 1994). Cable News Network (CNN), SkyNews and FoxNews are now household and global brands. News production has been transformed by digital technologies allowing for frequent updates in multiple media forms, making news more perishable than ever. In 1955, Wallace Carroll warned that speed leads to inaccuracies and forms the basis of shallow reporting. 'Speed is one of the factors that have put us in the straitjacket of objectivity' (1955: 27). The impact of speed on reflection continues to be a concern. Mark Thompson, Director-General of the BBC observes, 'Twenty-four hour news services mean that the public can get their news pretty much when and where they like, but they can put a terrible strain on the time needed for reflection and judgement' (2005). As Brent Cunningham notes, 'the nonstop news cycle leaves reporters less time to dig, and encourages reliance on official sources who can provide the information quickly and succinctly. . . . This lack of time makes a simpleminded and lazy version of objectivity all the more tempting' (2003: 27). In broadcast journalism, the drive to put to air live footage from a breaking story is strong. Twitter feeds operating across multiple time zones are complicating how reporting happens in a 'cloud' of information that may be out of date, or moving too fast to capture or verify. These situations lead to stresses on the practices closely tied to objectivity such as moderation or editing, verification and providing context.

Alan Rusbridger, editor of the London *Guardian*, observed that

> The greater the speed required of us in the digital world – and speed does matter, but never at the expense of accuracy or fairness or

anything which would imperil trust – the more we should be honest about the tentative nature of what is possible. . . . Journalism becomes a never ending organic business of placing material in the public domain, of adding to it, clarifying it, correcting it, adding something here, subtracting something there, editing, contextualising, analysing, responding. Everything we do will be more contestable, more open to challenge and alternative interpretation. (2007)

On-line platforms represent a potential liberation here; specifically, freedom from the material constraints of the news hole associated with print news, and broadcast journalism. On-line, the space or time allocated for publication potentially expands. Furthermore, the on-line domain allows for corrections, comment, contextualization, analysis, background, response and interpretation, sometimes at the same time. This creates new challenges for editing and moderation, to ensure the coherency and relevance of the publication.

As a result of the proliferation of channels and views (not always accompanied unfortunately by less concentration in the media), the tenor of news has changed. The detached voice is not the loudest. 'Impartiality and objectivity are becoming rarer qualities in mainstream journalism' (Thompson 2005). For Rupert Murdoch, the diversity of news channels means a new diversity of voices which requires policy changes: 'the time will come when there will be no further need for impartiality rules for any of the media' (quoted in Hargreaves 2005; see also Curran & Seaton 2003: 394) – although that assumption is open to question (Dwyer & Martin 2010). Others highlight a return of the opinionated partisan press (Sambrook 2004), or populist forms of 'moral entrepreneurship', represented by those community-based figures who orchestrate populist moral panics – the latter embodied in the figure of the aggressive talk show host (Jones 2011: 8).

There are different ways of responding to these changes. For some, it will mean reapplying and coaxing more out of the objectivity norm, reaffirming the necessity of reflection and judgement, defending it in a changing world of journalism where accountability is an important problem (see the discussion of the BBC below). For others, as in the case of Al-Jazeera, it involves adapting objectivity to new perspectives. Finally, blogging and citizen journalism represent a challenge to the very conditions of the norm.

The foxification of news

Since its establishment in 1996, the Fox News Channel (FNC) has provoked controversy around its claims to objective journalism, embodied in its slogans 'fair and balanced', and 'we report, you decide'. Set up specifically to appeal to conservative viewers, it has created a successful business model, with *The Economist* reporting in 2010 its profits were more than its rivals CNN and MSNBC put together (*The Economist* 2011).

While FNC has been interpreted in terms of the media malaise thesis (which links the popular media to a decline in political culture; Jones 2011: 9), two trends make the foxification of news especially significant. Firstly, it is formed within a discourse about (liberal) bias in the news, thus addressing its audience in explicitly partisan terms. Without discussing the merits of this claim (see Bagdikian 1972), it represents a turning of the circle back to some of the conditions of the partisan US media of the 1800s, prior to the advent of the ideal of objectivity. The second trend is the proliferation of media channels, via cable, satellite, on-line and mobile phone. Advertisers have responded to this proliferation of channels by shifting expenditure away from established media. In this context, FNC has reacted by moving beyond strict impartiality and objectivity to generate greater identification with their audiences. While remaining fact-minded, and promoting the vestiges of objectivity as a branding strategy, this approach involves embracing opinion and commentary, with a questionable separation of news and editorial.

In some respects, FNC can be considered to have thrown down a gauntlet before other broadcasters. Some, such as the BBC, stick to their guns. Thus Mark Thompson, Director-General of the BBC, believes that although 'the case for polemical, opinionated news channels was "persuasive", ... the BBC's own news coverage would remain impartial' (Sherwin 2010). Others, such as Jay Rosen, respond to the FNC challenge by returning to essentials: accuracy, fairness and intellectual honesty (*The Economist* 2011). Another strategy is to replace objectivity altogether, which has happened with the suggestion that 'transparency is the new objectivity' (Weinberger 2009). This is a potentially attractive proposition given that hypertext-based media offer an unprecedented opportunity to link to raw materials and supplementary documents; although the Brisbane/*New York Times* case forms an interesting case example of how complex transparency can be. Nevertheless, transparency in this argument becomes a new condition of reliability:

> What we used to believe because we thought the author was objective we now believe because we can see through the author's writings to the sources and values that brought her to that position. Transparency gives the reader information by which she can undo some of the unintended effects of the ever-present biases. Transparency brings us to reliability the way objectivity used to. (Weinberger 2009; see also Lasica 2005)

A final strategy is, for want of a better term, 'emulation', and this, according to Ted Koppel (and with some controversy), is the approach of MSNBC. As Koppel writes 'We live now in a cable news universe that celebrates the opinions of Olbermann, Rachel Maddow, Chris Matthews, Glenn Beck, Sean Hannity and Bill O'Reilly – individuals who hold up the twin pillars of political partisanship and who are encouraged to do so by their parent organizations because their brand of analysis and commentary is highly profitable' (2010). Koppel continues, 'And so, among the many benefits we have come to believe the founding fathers intended for us, the latest is news we can choose. Beginning, perhaps, from the reasonable perspective that absolute objectivity is unattainable, Fox News and MSNBC no longer even attempt it. They show us the world not as it is, but as partisans (and loyal viewers) at either end of the political spectrum would like it to be' (2010).

In a special comment on Koppel's report, Keith Olbermann refutes the emulation argument, along with the suggestion that MNBC followed FNC. He also focuses on the issue of objectivity, and its improper idealization as a form of sanitized uninvolved reporting when in fact most instances of the good old days were guided by strongly held (even partisan) values:

> The great change about which Mr. Koppel wrings his hands is not partisanship nor tone nor analysis. The great change was the creation of the sanitized image of what men like Cronkite and Murrow ... and Koppel did. These were not glorified stenographers. These were not neutral men. These were men who did in their day what the best journalists still try to do in this one: Evaluate, analyze, unscramble, assess. Put together a coherent picture or a challenging question using only the facts as they can be best discerned, plus their own honesty and conscience. (Olbermann 2010)

But Olbermann goes further in declaring objectivity a false god, a failed project: 'the kind of journalism he [Koppel] eulogizes, failed this country because when truth was needed, all we got were facts, most of which were lies anyway'.

While defending his own practice as 'organic', Olbermann offers a distinct critique of the FNC model, and the transformation of an empty conception of objectivity into a brand, when it is (quoted from the transcript) 'no more than two men screaming at each other as a musical duet. But as long as there are two men, as long as they are fair and balanced, is not the news consumer entranced by the screaming and the fact that his man eventually and always outscreams the other? Is he not convinced he's seen true balance, true objectivity?' (Olbermann 2010).

Reinventing objectivity at the BBC

The BBC has had a long association with concepts of objectivity (explored in the next chapter). Jean Seaton argues that through World War II 'the BBC's claim to accuracy and objectivity was, in itself, a propaganda weapon – a demonstration of the superiority of democracy over totalitarianism' (Curran & Seaton 2003: 139). Despite being an unfashionable touchstone for media ethics, objectivity continues to be a key topic for the BBC. Indeed, far from moving away from it, there are signs that the organization is trying to reinvigorate the concept, and redefine it in relation to the on-line space. Speeches regularly use objectivity as a starting point to raise pertinent issues. Mark Thompson, the Director-General, notes: 'Some academics too doubt whether the classic claims for objective, dispassionate journalism can be sustained. Beneath the apparent "facts" lurk hidden assumptions, narratives or ideologies'. This prompts a redefinition of objectivity as a kind of 'critical realism':

> 'critical' because we accept that the facts come to us mediated through complex narratives and assumptions and that each of us needs to use both sophisticated analysis and individual judgement to make sense of them, but 'realists' because we believe that it is still possible – indeed it is our duty – to get to the facts and to form as objective and accurate view of the world as possible. (Thompson 2006)

Critical realism was discussed in chapter 3. Objectivity has been reinvented in response not just to academic arguments, but to specific challenges faced by the BBC. Among these are the rise of cable news channels such as FNC, but also more specifically issues around the investigation carried out by Lord Hutton in 2003 into the circumstances surrounding the death of Dr David Kelly – who played a key role in BBC reports into the 'sexing' up of the 'Iraq Dossier' on weapons of mass destruction. As Richard Sambrook notes, 'but it's only through an objective approach – facts, evidence, verification – that we can be sure of getting it right' (2004). The BBC has even been responsive to more 'epochal' issues such as the Information Society, which represents its own complexities. As Mark Byford, at the time Acting Director-General of the BBC, defiantly notes:

> This may be an information age but information itself isn't enough. It's the veracity, accuracy, objectivity and diversity of views which matter as we search for answers in an uncertain world and audiences search for trust and reliability. (Byford 2004)

But, we may ask, given our interest in the social and historical conditions of norms, how different is this uncertain world from the state of drift and doubt expressed by Walter Lippmann in 1914, and seen as a key factor in the development of the ideal of objectivity by Michael Schudson (1978)? (see chapter 1).

For the BBC, a distinct strategy of 'holding onto objectivity' is evident (Sambrook 2004). New measures are put in place, as outlined by Mark Thompson.

> Impartiality and objectivity are becoming rarer qualities in mainstream journalism. . . . In the aftermath of the Gilligan–Kelly–Hutton affair, we've strengthened many of our internal journalistic safeguards. We've put literally thousands of our journalists through new training courses in which issues of fair-mindedness and our absolute duty to give those against whom we make serious allegations the right to reply take centre stage. (2005)

Establishing a College of Journalism and clarifying editorial guidelines thus form one kind of response to a changing media environment, helping to reinforce a sense of 'our responsibility always to try to offer audiences objectivity and context'.

Al-Jazeera

Since its establishment in 1996, Al-Jazeera (Arabic for 'the island' or 'the peninsula'), the Qatar-based twenty-four hour news channel has been subject to intense academic and public questioning of its objectivity.

Following Muhammad I. Ayish, it is important to situate Al-Jazeera in the context of developments in Middle East broadcasting. Since the first broadcasts in the 1950s, roughly three approaches to broadcasting can be identified. The first is traditional government-controlled television, the second government-owned reformist television, and finally liberal commercial television (2002: 139). Sitting in the final category, Al-Jazeera fuses an Arabic obsession with politics; a commitment to 'new professional journalism values and norms unprecedented in government-operated television' (2002: 142); 'critical and pluralistic views of society' (2002: 143); and a CNN aesthetic focused on live interviews with prominent persons, and up-to-the-minute footage of clashes (2002: 149).

Al-Jazeera's regional identification has given it a unique place in the global mediasphere. Because of its interest in regional issues, in 2001 it was allowed to stay in Afghanistan when the Taliban forced others to leave. As a result, it was able to broadcast war footage from Kabul, and was the recipient and broadcaster of tapes of Osama bin Laden denouncing the US. The bombing of its Kabul offices by the US in November 2001 was seen as an ominous development. As was the bombing of its Baghdad offices in April 2003, in which senior correspondent Tarek Ayoub died. In 2004, the network was accused of cooperating with insurgents in Iraq. Some of its correspondents were expelled from Iraq by the interim government (El-Nawawy 2004: 14). It frustrated the US by broadcasting images of civilian casualties and also of US prisoners of war and dead soldiers (El-Nawawy 2004: 13), in the context of other broadcasters who offered sanitized coverage, 'free of bloodshed, dissent, and diplomacy but full of exciting weaponry, splashy graphics, and heroic soldiers' (Aday et al. 2005: 18).

Bearing witness to events in the Middle East from a non-Western perspective has proved controversial, leading to accusations that the network is unreliable and irresponsible (El-Nawawy & Iskandar 2003: 203). Commentators have raised a specific concern regarding Al-Jazeera's spare reporting of its host country, and of 'issues directly involving senior Arab officials, let alone ministers or head of states' (Moussa 2007). Especially controversial has been its invocation of Western norms such as objectivity. Many of its first editorial staff joined the organization from the BBC's Arabic TV Service, after the termination of its contract in 1996 (El-Nawawy 2004: 11). Reporters continue to be trained in Western techniques. It is regarded as following a BBC/CNN model; although some question the sincerity of this commitment. For critics such as Fouad Ajami, professor of Middle Eastern studies at Johns Hopkins University, the station is adept at 'mimicking Western norms of journalistic fairness while pandering to pan-Arabic sentiments' (Ajami 2001).

Melding Western norms with Arabic perspectives, and dealing

with the inherent contradiction in 'attaining objectivity in news coverage and appealing to a specific audience' (El-Nawawy & Iskandar 2003: 209), can be difficult. Al-Jazeera performs a balancing act between providing Arab news from an Arab perspective and responding to criticisms of bias through journalistic ideas of balance. Ayish notes that the

> TV broadcasters' handling of events and issues seems to be contingent on the type of issue and players at hand. When it comes to issues enjoying pan-Arab consensus, objectivity in the sense of balanced reporting of conflicting views seems to be virtually nonexistent. The coverage of the Palestinian uprising is a case in point. All broadcasters used the term 'martyr' to refer to Palestinians killed by Israeli fire in the violent clashes. The Israelis, on the other hand, were referred to as aggressors. In issues relating to Egyptian elections or the situation in Sudan, all broadcasters were reporting government and opposition group stands on the different issues. (2002: 150)

What Ayish points to is an interpretive approach to objectivity, working alongside what is deemed to be a consensus in Arabic opinion. But where that consensus doesn't exist, impartiality seems to prevail. That said, it has been argued that Al-Jazeera reflects its cultural tradition no differently from CNN approaching stories from a Western perspective (Aday et al. 2005: 16).

The station certainly can demonstrate balance, insofar as it broadcasts US spokespeople as well as Arabic sources, Palestinian alongside Israeli. As Thomas Johnson and Shahira Fahmy note:

> Al-Jazeera doesn't deny that it focuses on news of interest to an Arab audience and presents it from an Arabic perspective. However the network argues that it embodies its motto *The opinion and the other opinion* [or, as it is sometimes put, 'the view, and the other point of view'] because its news shows present the audience with all viewpoints with objectivity, integrity and balance to allow its audience to form its own views. (2006: 8)

Acknowledging the difficulty of separating facts from values altogether, and eliminating cultural bias, Mohammed El-Nawawy and Adel Iskandar devise the term 'contextual objectivity' to account for 'the pattern of covering an issue objectively and thoroughly, but coloring it with the innate perspective of the reporting medium' (2003: 209). (The term is not used publically by Al-Jazeera as far as can be determined.) This 'innate perspective' comes from the broadcaster's reading of their audience, region and cultural attitudes. 'While the term appears to be an oxymoron, it is not' (2003: 209). They insist that the term is about bridging principles of impartiality with local sensibilities.

Through the idea of contextual objectivity El-Nawawy and Iskandar work through what they see as some key dilemmas of professional broadcast news. That is, firstly, that reports should be comprehensive but are by necessity selective, and secondly, that news aspires to objectivity, but also to be meaningful to audiences (2003: 209). These different demands and commitments can be difficult to reconcile.

The term contextual objectivity can spark concern at the way it contradictorily grounds the idea of objectivity in context and perspective (as such it goes against the traditional empirical and positivistic basis of the ideal) (see Irvine 2011). However, as we saw in chapter 4, this is not the first time objectivity has been linked to an epistemological standpoint or perspective. In the case of Al-Jazeera the term raises interesting issues of how the media serve their publics and audiences, and how cultural viewpoints impact on journalism. If objectivity has to do with reflecting reality, the question is whose reality? Contextual objectivity describes the pursuit of objectivity within a particular orientation, reflecting all sides of any story while retaining the sentiments of the target audience. For El-Nawawy and Iskandar, contextual objectivity is to be found in broadcasting in the Arab World, as well as the US.

The subtleties of this position can easily be lost, and Al-Jazeera has been accused of adopting a rhetoric of objectivity to move between 'democratic transparency' and the 'propaganda of authoritarianism' (Awad 2005: 82). When Al-Jazeera Washington bureau chief Abderrahim Foukara was asked by *Time* magazine, 'How does that lens compare to the idea much vaunted in the US of journalistic objectivity?', he answered:

To be honest, I don't know what objective journalism means. The environment in which you broadcast obviously colors your coverage. If you are an American network broadcasting from the US, you will be broadcasting with a sensibility which may not look necessarily objective to an audience in another part of the world. And the same is true if you're a network like Al-Jazeera Arabic, broadcasting out of the Middle East. But we have to go beyond that. We should agree on the necessity to provide information in a timely manner. We cannot live in a world where a story like Egypt – which has consequences for the whole world – is unfolding and your audience doesn't know anything about it or enough about it. (Tharoor 2011)

This illustrates Denis McQuail's point that what is 'fair and reasonable in the way of objectivity may vary from one society to another and even from one theme or issue to another (1992: 203). Indeed, as Marc Lynch notes, in Kuwait, Al-Jazeera was criticized for its lack of objectivity (2006: 162). A 2002 Gallup Poll, surveying Saudi Arabia, Morocco, Kuwait, Jordan and Lebanon, found that 'objectivity is perceived as Al-Jazeera's weakest area, with less than half of respondents in some countries and barely a majority in others associating this virtue with the station's coverage' (Saad 2002). Even read relative to other Arab broadcasters, with the exception of Jordan, Al-Jazeera was not singled out as being more objective than other broadcasters.

For El-Nawawy and Iskandar, contextual objectivity is about the deep cultural orientations that permeate Arab and Western contexts. This orientation is agonistic: Facts arise out of the clash of opinions and views (El-Nawawy & Iskandar 2003: 200). 'Part of the Arab tradition is to argue and discuss issues passionately' (El-Nawawy & Iskandar 2003: 66). Hugh Miles sees Al-Jazeera as a 'model of professionalism and objectivity' (2005: 359). But he also sees a link between cultural difference, bias and commercial considerations:

Al-Jazeera operates the same stringent editorial processes as the Western media in covering the same events and ends up with a different product. This is because there are deep cultural differences between the people making the editorial choices and, like any commercial station, Al-Jazeera is pitching itself at its viewership. Bias is a natural consequence of the commercial process. Al-Jazeera treats its audience exactly as the mainstream cable networks and FM radio stations in the US treat their domestic audience. It caters to public opinion because . . . it wants to get audience share and it wants to sell advertising. (Miles 2005: 359)

Regardless of whether the bias is ideological or commercial, the proposition here is that cultural bias can stand alongside objectivity, part of a deep commitment to audiences. This is similar to the way that, in the US, objectivity was grafted on to commercial media and made part of a commercial strategy.

Al-Jazeera's code of ethics (2010) does not itself mention objectivity. Although the 'About us' web pages for the International English news service declared: 'Al-Jazeera English will balance the information flow from South to North, providing accurate, impartial and objective news for a global audience from a grass roots level, giving voice to different perspectives from under-reported regions around the world' (Al-Jazeera Press Office 2007), the code of ethics itself affirms values of 'honesty, courage, fairness, balance, independence, credibility and diversity, giving no priority to commercial or political over professional consideration', and commits to accuracy as well as a distinction between 'news material, opinion and analysis to avoid the snares of speculation and propaganda'. These are familiar terms linked closely to the objectivity norm.

Although not often declared, debates over objectivity often take on a strong national character, following the contours of the local political system, as well as a tightly controlled media landscape (especially in broadcasting) that limits new entrants. The Al-Jazeera example illustrates how, as the mediasphere becomes regional and global rather than national, and technology allows new participants to broadcast, the operation of objectivity as a transnational journalistic norm can lead to controversy. This can provoke a range of different reactions depending on the traditional media perspectives involved. It also serves as a case study of contextual objectivity, an attempt to deal with some of the key dilemmas of current professional news broadcasting.

News blogs and citizen journalism

The emergence of relatively low cost, 'open' publishing platforms on which to discuss current affairs, offer specialist or expert commentary, and indeed publish news and disclose leaks, has led to the rise of blogging and citizen journalism, which has further complicated the worlds of 24/7 news and online journalism. The nature of the technologies involved mean that often material on these platforms are multimedia in nature (combining video, audio and text), and frequently collaborative, ranging from the provision to make comments through to the capacity to edit and revise material written by others. While sometimes the content is hyper-local in focus, due to the fact that the citizen reporter is on the ground, the reach of these platforms is often global. These practices and technologies are transforming the way we create and receive the media, and our very understanding of the media.

Axel Bruns suggests that a key reason for the 'overall disillusionment with present day commercial journalism' is a sense that 'journalists do not accurately and objectively cover news events, and instead are governed by other agendas' (2005: 15). Indeed, in current affairs oriented blogging and citizen journalism circles, objectivity is not always actively promoted as an articulated norm, and indeed subjectivity and opinion is celebrated (Allan 2006: 85). John Pavlik sees objectivity as a 'romantic but unachievable goal' (2001: 24), noting that a 'single perspective' provides a limited view of the reality of events. Objectivity is an 'ideology' and a 'cloak'. On-line journalism, by contrast, allows readers to 'triangulate on the truth in a way that traditional journalism cannot, because of its objectivity ideology' (2001: 93). For Bernhard Debatin, truth in blogging arises as the result 'of a discursive process, an interaction of ideas that circulate and compete in the blogosphere' (2011: 838). 'While objectivity can be called a basic norm of professional journalism, journalistic blogging instead seems to follow a combination of three main norms, mainly transparency, accuracy and advocacy' (2011: 838)

The South Korean collaborative citizen journalism website, OhmyNews (launched in February 2000), which boasted upwards of 40,000 contributors in 2005 (Min 2005: 17), proudly shuns an overt commitment to objectivity in favour of affirming the idea – one with a long history in the radical presses of England and the US – that every citizen can be a reporter. An affront to the traditionally conservative South Korean press, this site has been characterized as 'editor-assisted open news' (Bruns 2005: 129). It has in place an extensive screening and copy-editing process to ensure factual accuracy that begins with persuading 'frontline copyeditors', usually professional journalists, that the material is newsworthy (Min 2005: 18). Citizen journalists are given 'Journalism 101' classes, which increases the possibility of the reproduction of established journalistic norms.

With a critical eye cast on mainstream news outlets, social media producers and commentators were already attuned to the abuses of objectivity by commercial agendas (Bruns 2005: 215). Building on a sensibility informed by debates around community media, underground and activist media, libertarian Internet discourses, as well as advocacy journalism, their critique of traditional media goes further, typified by a shift from a traditional model of 'gatekeeping' (Janowitz 1975) to 'gatewatching' (Bruns 2005). The term 'gatewatching' applies mainly to a section of the blogging community that watches the mainstream media (Rettberg 2008: 86). It suggests that digital media provides unprecedented means to monitor the performance of the media in the world. As Bruns puts it, news audiences 'have begun to reclaim their place in the news cycle' (2005: 9). But as he also observes, 'the first and most significant casualty of such broad collaborative and open approaches to the production of news, then, is the idea of journalistic objectivity' (2005: 308). The concept serves as a 'pretence' for quality journalism at a time when social media is opening up new possibilities for collaborative news creation (2005: 310).

News blogging and citizen media have prompted intense reflection on the pitfalls and possibilities of publishing and the key actors involved, and arguably shifted our understanding of the political economy of news. Objectivity is associated with a unitary, monolithic alignment of news values with a single (usually corporate) news source. From this perspective Trish Bolton celebrates a 'dramatic shift in news production and dissemination' which 'rejects notions of truth, objectivity, credibility and distance from its audience' using platforms 'that foster dialogue rather than monologue . . . [allowing] unmediated narratives that emerge from the lived existence of its audience' (2006). What was formerly seen as a problem for objectivity, namely the presence of values and 'subjectivising' (Dennis & Merrill 1984: 106) becomes a positive rather than a negative, a marker of authenticity. This has opened up a complex field of collaboration and dialogue, but also contested interpretations. In some respects, the space of blogging and collaborative news sites has fulfilled Herbert Gans' prescient view that the news media will be 'multiperspectival' both in its values, and the way it services audiences (1979: 314–15).

One of the difficulties of addressing the guiding question of this chapter, 'Is objectivity changing in an era of 24/7 news and on-line journalism?' is the sheer range of practices involved, and also the rapidly changing technological situation which regularly invokes a world without reporters, with news composed in a perfectly objective fashion through algorithms (Allan 2006: 176–7). Because the ground is always shifting, as it were, I want to propose three theses, each thesis requiring further research and contestation.

The first thesis is that on-line and citizen journalism may not in itself represent a challenge to objectivity, that new techniques of reporting and platforms for publishing can (and are being) incorporated into established news models, which are themselves adapting to a 24-hour news cycle. Thus, mobile phone vision or amateur video of a weather event, or a disaster, may find itself in traditional media, and subject (ideally) to all the standard checks and balances. Allan notes an early tendency in mainstream media to treat on-line sites as 'inherently untrustworthy – and lacking in the objectivity, professionalism, and independence members of the public expected' (2010: 221), but it rapidly became apparent that readers were turning to the Internet for breaking news, prompting a re-think. Jill Walker Rettberg points to a symbiosis here between blogs empowering 'ordinary citizens' and also serving the purposes of the mainstream media (2008: 108). This is not to suggest this is a zone without issues, and media organizations are faced with new decisions around working with citizen journalists and online communities, using amateur footage, managing consumer expectations, and using content from platforms such as Facebook. Of course, a different but no less serious set of reputational issues arise from staff reporters using social media such as Twitter, which demands a style of writing and opinion very different from that encountered in most news articles. In addition, there are wider issues to do with relations between blogging and journalism, and how to define journalism itself.

A second thesis is that these media are providing new channels for 'monitory democracy', whereby 'many hundreds and thousands of monitory institutions are now in the business of publicly scrutinising power ... to the point where monitory democracy and computerised media networks function as fused systems' (Keane 2011).

What has become known as 'Rathergate' or 'memogate', arising from a 2004 *60 Minutes Wednesday* programme on President George W. Bush's National Guard service, can be seen as a concrete example of monitoring on a micro level. The programme relied on four memos to justify its position. Discussants on a web-based discussion forum, Free Republic, questioned the authority of the documents released by CBS. Citizen journalists, drawing on specialist knowledge of 1970s typewriters, cast doubt on the authenticity of the documents, exposing serious deficiencies in fact checking, and pointing to a biased agenda against Bush. This gave solace to conservatives looking for bias in the (liberal) media, but also demonstrated the active role bloggers could play in gatewatching.

However, monitory democracy also suggests more macro-level developments whereby new and established actors utilize new media to amplify their democratizing efforts across previously unimagined cross-border communities and global publics. The discourse around communicative democracy is shifting from concepts of 'representation' to 'direct' democracy (Hartley 2000). For journalists and editors who once saw themselves as unelected representatives, this is a new world; one which they are responding to with concepts of transparency and accountability (Rusbridger 2007).

For Stephen D. Reese, the possibility of reinventing the objectivity norm through a re-alignment of a 'vertical' perspective, aligned with the nation-state and a 'horizontal' global outlook is upon us (2008: 243). Reese imagines what he terms 'aggregate' objectivity aligned with a cross-national global public:

> Old criticism of news 'bias' will be superseded by new issues brought about by the growth of global news, where a distributed access to events from multiple cross-referencing sources provides a new form of aggregate 'objectivity.' In the pooled results of this system, slanted or false reports are now more rapidly challenged or augmented – not only by other news organizations but also by thousands of readers and viewers who circulate, compare, and challenge reports via newsgroups and other on-line communities. (2008: 242–3)

For Reese, the 'compressed global cultural arena' and a 'levelling' of news practices and routines across different national contexts, 'brings new importance to traditional journalism concepts such as objectivity' (2008: 245).

A third thesis in relation to the admittedly very broad area of blogging and citizen media is that it is challenging and changing the very informational foundation of objectivity as a method for knowing and presenting reality. This shift has been met enthusiastically in some quarters: 'Something interesting and hopeful is happening as mainstream journalists find themselves suddenly outside of newsrooms' (McGill 2008). Doug McGill sees it as an opportunity to reinvent the journalist–citizen relationship, and for citizens to start teaching journalists about ethics. 'For nearly a century, thanks to the ideal of "objectivity," journalists have steadfastly refused to talk about ethics – these *real* ethics – in newsrooms' (2008). The promise of dialogue and interaction excites many scholars and commentators, and properly so.

However, given the extent to which objectivity in journalism is embedded in a particular vision of the information landscape dominated by propaganda and public relations, and also the extent of changes to the information landscape, a close analysis of this communication situation is called for. As Stuart Allan and Donald Matheson observe, 'The tacit, largely unspoken epistemological basis of newswork is being thrown into sharp relief' (2004: 82). It pays to explore, for example, 'how converging processes of integration, interactivity, hypermedia, and narrativity will re-inflect more traditional journalistic conceptions of truth, fact and objectivity' (2004: 82).

Drawing on Gaye Tuchman's terminology, I want to suggest the 'news net' is being radically reconfigured (see the discussion of Tuchman's concept in chapter 3). This, however, does not give us some 'news net 2.0'. While Tuchman's method of analysis and lines of questioning remain crucial, the very paradigm underpinning the news net is being re-worked in different ways. This is evident in changes in news procedure, the way facts are treated, new intra-organizational relationships, new forms and methods of criticism of performance, and shifting expectations around objective journalism. The assumption that 'if every reporter gathers and structures "facts" in a detached, unbiased, impersonal manner, deadlines will be met and libel suits avoided' may still hold in some quarters (Tuchman 1972: 664). However, the relevance of this formulation is being severely tested by the open, collaborative, distributed and personalized aspects of news platforms where facts are challenged and commented upon repeatedly. Objectivity is not the get out of jail card it once was.

In the classic view, objectivity as an epistemology forms an important part of the news net. New media forms are, however, changing our very conception of 'the real'. Viewed through an empirical and positivist lens, reality is deemed independent to the observer, and knowable. Objectivity is the method through which this reality is simply described and presented in its value-free form. Melissa Wall describes this as a 'modernist' conception of the news: 'a sense that reality could be observed and documented from an objective viewpoint, an emphasis on constant change and timeliness, and a belief in being able to represent reality accurately' (2005: 154).

Wall argues that 'some forms of on-line news such as blogs have moved away from traditional journalism's modernist approach to embody a form of post-modern journalism'. What she means is that 'reality is not fixed nor knowable outside of the self. Instead, we create reality through language and interactions or perform-ances' (2005: 158). This also transforms ideas about truth-seeking in journalism. Truth is not denied, but approached with a different 'will to facticity' to use Allan's phrase (1995), often linked to involvement and participation rather than distance and detachment. As Geert Lovink notes, 'There is a quest for truth in Blogging, but it is truth with a question mark. Truth here has become an amateur project, not an absolute value, sanctioned by higher authorities' (Lovink 2007: 13).

In Wall's study of war-time blogs, narrative style (point of view, detachment), relationship to audience (as participants and contributors), and the presence or absence of story formulas (such as the inverted pyramid), are all areas in which postmodernist tendencies are in evidence (2005: 162). While it can be argued that these postmodern features could also be present in other, so-called 'traditional' forms of media, I would contend that there is something unique happening in the on-line environment where the very conditions of representation underpinning objectivity have changed. We are in a post-positivistic space where the medium is the message, where the real is constituted from, and within, links and discursive fragments. Here, mirroring and reflection from a single point of view has given way to a process and performance of mediation and re-mediation (Bolter & Grusin 1999). With this change to our sense of the real, and also our capacity to know the real, objectivity then is being reworked through databases and digital media as one 'information technology' among many.

If, in a version of the invisible frame idea, objective journalism can idealistically be conceived as a channel that simply carries reality to the audience without transforming the material being transported – a classic 'transmission' view of communication in Carey's terms (1989: 14–15) – then perhaps we are in a situation where we are now in the belly of the whale looking at the channel from the inside. Bloggers (especially in war time) can give us a first-hand and real-time view of an unfolding event, one that is usually only partially known or known within a particular per-spective, and out of the reach of standard broadcast journalists (an example being the use of camera phone images on the front page of newspapers during the 2005 London Tube bombings; see Allan 2007). Rettberg discusses the work of Salam Pax in these terms (2008: 95; Pax 2003). Mainstream news outlets are laying bare their raw material, interviews and research documents, news lists, in unprecedented moves towards transparency of editorial judgement.

An important area in which the informational foundation of objectivity as a method for knowing and presenting reality is changing is detachment. As Rettberg notes, 'A journalist is presumed to be outside of the action, and to observe impartially and objectively' (2008: 99). Bloggers by contrast are very often participants in what they blog about. Commenting on the blogging of Salam Pax, Lieutenant Smash, and ntcoolfool, Rettberg argues, 'As participants, they made no attempt to be objective. The traditional journalistic creeds of credibility and fact-checking were of no relevance to them. Their strength was instead their authenticity – but it is a different kind of authenticity from the promise that "this is true", given by the mainstream media. This authenticity is evidenced by the immediacy of the bloggers' (2008: 101).

Consistent with the idea that we are looking at the communication channel from the inside, on collaborative news sites editorial processes are now frequently laid bare, externalized, open, and then automated. This can involve devolving editorial power to either a selective group of moderators or to users themselves, as well as drawing on ratings systems and recommendations to feed comments back into the (now distributed) editorial filtering system. Distributed news models place a premium on comments, but also a strain on moderation practices. Thus, to cite one example, *Slashdot* 'will only display those comments in a discussion which are ranked above a certain threshold value' (Bruns 2005: 42). Good users accumulate 'karma' and gain a louder 'voice', bad posters are slowly muted. Users with high karma are offered the opportunity to moderate.

John Hartley has used the term 'redactional' society to describe a current period of expansion in journalism which is 'rethought in terms of editing not writing' (2000: 43–6). Concurrent with this, however, is a re-location of editorial processes onto new collaborative, open and transparent platforms. The ramifications of this shift are enormous, not simply on the input, output and response stages of traditional news production (see Bruns 2005: 12), but more specifically on the very machinery underpinning objectivity as a strategic ritual.

Tuchman's concept of strategic ritual relies implicitly on a discrete newsroom model, built around company staff and formal news services and agencies for input. Objectivity works within a set of routine editorial practices. This habitus worked to ensure authority and control in the newsroom, but also to leave a space for independence and autonomy. This autonomy is justified through objectivity, in a bargain that 'allows journalists to reach conclusions and to state opinions' (Gans 1979: 183). As Stephen D. Reese notes, newsgathering is validated through consensus (1990: 393). Furthermore, as Leon V. Sigal notes, the forming of consensus takes place within routines. 'So long as the newsmen follow the same routines, espousing the same professional values and using each other as their standards of comparison, newsmaking will tend to be insular and self-reinforcing' (1973: 180–1). This insularity, and the environment of routine and consensus supporting it, is crucial to the 'ritual' aspect of the strategic ritual. This dimension of objectivity is now in transformation.

The consequences of the decline of this 'paradigm' are wide-ranging. How a norm is proposed and maintained in this environment is still being worked out. An illustration here is Wikinews, which rejects the idea of 'a single unbiased, "objective" point of view' (Thorsen 2008: 939). The site promotes a neutral point of view policy (NPOV). 'NPOV is absolute and non-negotiable', according to the policy website.

The **neutral point of view policy** states that one should write articles without bias, representing all views fairly.
Neutral point of view means that an article should *fairly represent* all sides in a news story, and not make an article state, imply, or insinuate that any one side is correct. (Of course, there are limits to which points of view are worth mentioning, and this can be an area of conflict.) (Wikinews 2010)

Interestingly, this policy does not detail the limits to which points of view are to be represented. In the advice for dealing with biased contributors, or egregious cases, the policy calls for drawing attention to the problem publically.

Wikinews is noteworthy for two further reasons: firstly, for its translation of the objectivity norm into a NPOV policy. As Einar Thorsen notes, 'The contributors strive to retain familiar notions of "truth" and "accuracy" associated with traditional journalistic objectivity – rationalized through their own conceptualization of neutrality' (2008: 936). The site has actively promoted the inverted pyramid form, and currently encourages all opinions to be attributed to someone. The policy document acknowledges this amounts to an illusion of sorts: 'We realize that this does not ACTUALLY convert that opinion TO a fact, it just says it is a FACT that: "this person holds that opinion"'. This translation has drawn criticism:

> *Wikinews* could be said to suffer from something of an inferiority complex which seems to lead to a dogged pursuit of traditional journalistic ideals of objectivity and neutrality even though these ideals themselves may stem from an outdated worldview ... A truly multiperspectival approach to news, by contrast, acknowledges that virtually all 'facts' are subject to interpretation, and unlike *Wikinews'* attempt to synthesise them, simply presents these interpretations and offers a space for a dialogic engagement between them. (Bruns 2006)

The NPOV enacts a complex balancing act between a concept of neutrality justified on public benefit grounds, while trusting readers' competence to form their own opinions themselves. It balances its Anglo-American ideology with the demands of ideologues whose views aren't neutral. The original statement of NPOV reads: '*The neutral point of view attempts to present ideas and facts in such a fashion that both supporters and opponents can agree*'. As such, it ties neutrality to agreement and consensus. As Thorsen notes, neutrality has its limits and the attempt to resolve disputes through consensus and common sense do not remove bias per se (2008: 940).

Secondly, Wikinews is noteworthy for its attempt to

operationalize this policy/norm within a collaborative citizen news production model. This is important, especially in a post-objectivity environment, because norms will still need to be operationalized. Just as consensus was crucial to the operation of objectivity in Tuchman's newsroom, it becomes a key issue on the propagation of any new norm. Distributed news models represent a particular challenge for communicating norms, where often they are proposed and policed in an editable on-line environment where the full identity of participants may not be known. In this context, it is important to note that the neutral point of view policy is what Thorsen calls a 'fixed principle', a non-negotiable policy of the Wikimedia foundation. In this sense, it operates at a level of code of practice. It seeks to install this policy as a norm, but under conditions very different from that of the traditional newsroom. While the bargain underpinning the traditional objectivity norm was closely tied to the autonomy and independence of the reporter, the NPOV edict is tied to the independence of the consumer: 'Namely, when it is clear to readers that we do not expect them to adopt any particular opinion, this leaves them free to make up their minds for themselves, and thus to encourage in them *intellectual independence*'. While setting out guidelines for publication, the policy falls short of protecting the independence and autonomy of the reporter, proposing instead a norm of publication.

Conclusion

Objectivity is changing in the era of 24/7 news and on-line journalism in numerous ways, leading to restatements of the concept (in the case of the BBC), disputes around the concept (in the case of Fox News and MSNBC), and new articulations of the concept (in the case of Al-Jazeera). Meanwhile, news blogs and citizen journalism are prompting a re-evaluation of objectivity as a method for handling information, and as a theory of truth, in a shifting environment of usage and consumption. These developments are revealing tensions around our historical conceptions of objectivity and result in changing paradigms and patterns of media practice. These developments raise important questions of media power and media ethics; questions which go to basic issues to do with how judgement is exercised, but also how judgement is *seen to be* exercised; and furthermore, how accessible the relevant information is for users to form their own judgements. This is leading to a new set of demands around transparency, participation and involvement that are beginning to be incorporated into user expectations around media performance, and indeed new attitudes around information and core values such as truth and trust (see Fray 2011). It will be exciting to see how the attempt to 'take journalism out of the alienated objectivity associated with monetised, centralised and bureaucratised' news organizations develops (Calcutt & Hammond 2011: 128–9).

8

Is objectivity a universal journalistic norm?

While journalistic objectivity has its roots in Western enlightenment traditions of liberal philosophy and scientific investigation, it has been seen as a specifically American creation (Donsbach & Klett 1993: 54), and at a stretch 'fostered only by Americans and Britons, together with certain others like the Swedes, Dutch and Swiss' (White & Leigh 1946: 85). Moves away from objectivity towards a 'more politically active and aggressive' reporting are constructed in the US as 'European' (Donsbach 1995: 20; Weaver 1975 [1974]: 106). Conversely, moves towards objectivity in European contexts have been described as Americanization (Chalaby 1996: 309). Objectivity, for some, is treated as almost synonymous with an 'American model' of journalism, tied in with the use of a lead, the five w's plus h, the inverted pyramid, a neutral style (Sánchez-Aranda & Barrera 2003: 497–8).

This leads to the question posed by this chapter, is objectivity a universal journalistic norm? It is a question with a particular *analytic* focus, to do with how norms operate in a culture and across cultures, and whether they are projected as 'universal', and how. Western news agencies have been seen as allied with western imperial interests and universalized 'western values' (Righter 1978: 13). At the same time, as we shall see, critics sometimes appeal to universal values as a way to achieve goals of greater development or to reach out across cultural boundaries. The question of 'universality' relates not just to the presence of the objectivity norm in different journalistic cultures, but its degree of articulation (whether it defines a model, or standard, or a more informal construct) and wider discursive context.

The question guiding this chapter also has an important *empirical* dimension. A full study in this area would grapple with how media and political structures interact with social systems, across different 'media system models' (Hallin & Mancini 2004: 11). For our purposes, the initial evidence is intriguing. Studies have found that 99 per cent of Spanish journalists view objectivity as important but prefer a version of objectivity that goes beyond presenting facts (Canel & Piqué 1998: 316). This fits with Daniel C. Hallin and Paolo Mancini's argument that in Southern Europe journalists express allegiance to objectivity as a global ideal but practise it in a way at odds with US and British concepts of neutrality (2004: 261). In Finland, by contrast, there is a shift from polemical forms of writing towards 'Anglo-Saxon' practices (Hallin & Mancini 2004: 252).

Taking the focus away from the US, UK and Europe, it is significant to note that objectivity is a key professional norm for Pacific Island journalists (Layton 1998: 134). In South America, objectivity has been adapted and contested in Brazil (de Albuquerque 2005: 487), perhaps in light of the fact that 'dispassion and neutrality was contrary to the political turbulence of the region' (Waisbord 2000: 45). In post-World War II Japan, journalists have invoked objectivity in political reporting to mitigate the influence of press clubs with pre-arranged access to sources, and close relations to politicians, and political party papers (Sugiyama 2000: 196–7, 201) but, at the same time, objective reporting can discourage reporters from taking a critical view of political discourse (Hayashi 2011: 534–5). Scholars have begun to explore the objectivity in the People's Republic of China (Li 1994; Zhao 2012: 165). Section 5 of the 1994 'Norms of Professional Ethics of Chinese Journalists' is called 'Upholding the Principle of Objectivity and Fairness'. It states: 'Journalists should uphold dialectical and historical materialistic viewpoints, proceed from the people's fundamental interests, reflect things as they are and ensure objectivity and fairness' (Xinhua News Agency 1994).

Finally, the question guiding this chapter has a *post-colonial* aspect, focusing on the normative and prescriptive nature of objectivity. In his discussion of the transfer of the ideology of media professionalism to the third world, Peter Golding notes a tension between localized understandings of 'development news' and the Western professional ideal of objectivity, which assumes an institutional separation of broadcasting and the state which does not exist in every country. The situation in the third world does not always suit the assumption that 'objective and unbiased reporting of events is possible and desirable' (1977: 300). In Nigeria, for example, 'a natural inclination to see journalism as socially purposive is given a guilt complex by training in the creed and practice of objective reporting as preached and conducted in European and American media' (1997: 303). Questioning the prescriptive nature of norms is tied to a wider project of de-westernizing media studies, which raises questions about the status of objectivity in a post-colonial world (see Curran & Park 2000). There is a strong trend towards comparative research in journalism to serve as an antidote to solely western perspectives (Hallin & Mancini 2012).

While this empirical and post-colonial aspect is important, my primary goal in this chapter is to consider carefully the analytical issue of the cultural limits of the norm and the fact that objectivity does not define every media system or journalistic culture. Taking up what Schudson calls 'the comparative question' (2001: 166), my aim in this chapter is not to map every articulation of journalistic objectivity across the globe. Nevertheless, some degree of mapping must inform any discussion of a trans-national norm, and as part of this task I address an important supplementary question to do with the extent to which objectivity has been adopted outside of the US.

Objectivity as a norm

Michael Schudson's essay 'The Objectivity Norm in American Journalism' (2001) extends his work on the ideal of objectivity in *Discovering the News* (1978). Schudson works within an understanding of norms as 'moral prescriptions for social behaviour' (2001: 151). They can refer to existing patterns of behaviours but Schudson wants to focus on more than what is simply 'normal'. He is seeking to capture 'morally potent prescriptions about what should be prevalent behavior', as he suggests that many habits have no moral prescription at all.

Focusing specifically on this issue of the prescriptiveness of norms, norms can be distinguished according to different dimensions. Who they apply to is an obvious dimension (everyone, a class of people, a profession, children?). Their degree of formalization or codification (in rules or laws) is another. Some norms blur into laws, others co-exist with laws. What we can call the 'domain' of the norm, the area it applies to (economic, technological, scientific) is another dimension. Indeed, this is an important issue for objectivity in journalism since it can be viewed in relation to the domain of reporting facts, the managerial world of the publisher, the democratic world of the reader – or indeed, a combination of the above. As Schudson notes, 'analytical fairness had no secure place until journalists as an occupational group developed loyalties more to their audiences and to themselves as an occupational community than to their publishers or their favoured political parties' (2001: 161).

Schudson's focus on prescriptiveness underpins his core question in the essay 'What causes the norm to be articulated' (2001: 150). This is a question that underpins his focus on the actual use of the term 'objectivity' in the 1920s onwards in *Discovering the News* (1978), which is quite distinct from a more general discussion of fact-mindedness. Schudson teases out four conditions that encourage the articulation, 'rhetorical formalization' or codification of norms (2001: 152).

1. Ritual solidarity, with events providing 'occasions for speech in which speakers are often called upon to state explicitly, and as moral rules, the ways of the group' (2001: 152).
2. Inter-cultural contact and conflict between groups can 'provoke the articulation of norms inside the group'.
3. Socialization or induction in large institutions (such as schools

or companies) where informal inter-personal contact would be inadequate.
4. The control of subordinates in a complex organization.

The last two conditions are particularly relevant to the complex work environments of journalism from the nineteenth century onwards (2001: 162).

Norms can operate as effective standards for ethical behaviour, laying down conditions of virtue and also shame. In this respect, Schudson's norm thesis does not conflict with his earlier work on the ideal of objectivity, rather the 1920s mark a period when 'the objectivity norm became a fully formulated occupational ideal, part of a professional project or mission . . ., objectivity was finally a moral code' (2001: 163).

Here, a question arises to do with articulation. Namely, does the fact that the term 'objectivity' is today infrequently used impact on the power of the norm, or mean that its power is on the wane? Answering this question requires us to be clear about how norms work and become meaningful. We can approach this issue from (at least) two directions.

The first direction is that we can follow Dan Schiller and suggest that 'mention' of the norm has a more complex relationship to codification and institutionalization than one might assume. Schiller, in a remarkable observation, states, 'Objectivity, which comprised the very basis of the journalistic profession, simultaneously obstructed its own further independent development' (1979: 53). In other words, there may be something implicit in the norm of objectivity that retarded or 'impeded' its articulation: 'for explicit codification was problematic so long as news people claimed merely to mirror an ever-changing world in their news reporting practices' (1979: 52). Schiller's insight explains why it is sometimes difficult to read norms off statements made by journalists, who are reluctant to talk about norms on the one hand, or may repeat or parrot norms – in the form of mantras about the fourth estate, for example – as part of same strategic ritual of defusing (the possibility of) criticism that underpins Tuchman's discussion of objectivity (1972). Schiller suggests, provocatively, that rather than being the product of professionalization, the objectivity norm constitutes a barrier to professionalism and articulation of the norm (1979: 53). In Schudson's terms, this could point to the effectiveness of the norm at maintaining ritual solidarity and group identity against forces of control in the newsroom.

The second direction we can follow in regard to the issue of the relationship between use or mention and effect of the norm is to say that, even though objectivity may no longer be fully institutionalized and codified in codes of ethics and practice, the on-going, broader, professional and academic debate around the concept can fulfil the essential task of re-evaluating the norm. Schudson suggests at least four ways of identifying the presence of objectivity, such as: professional discussion of the term; observations of occupational routines; content analyses that measure impersonality and non-partisanship in news stories; and resistance when the norm is challenged (2001: 149–50). Debate and discussion falls under the first and fourth categories. Admittedly, this argument opens up a potential point of tension with other scholars who may have a different view of the norm (for an example, see Chalaby 1998: 130). On the one hand, this may constitute healthy debate around the norm; on the other, it represents a further development of it.

Trans-nationalism, norms and social conditions

How, then, does one tackle the problem of studying the objectivity norm across cultures? Objectivity can be compared, surveyed and tracked across nations and cultures in different ways. But the devil is in the detail, and how this is done is significant. As Katrin Voltmer notes, terms such as 'objectivity' do not have a fixed meaning and are remarkably 'elastic' (2012: 233). While my goal in this chapter is not to create a comprehensive map of objectivity in journalism across the globe, it is interesting to consider different attempts to look at objectivity from an international perspective, not just to focus on norms in terms of difference, but in terms of their normative or universal value.

Of note here is the work of Thomas Hanitzsch, which tries to clarify what we mean when we use terms such as 'journalistic' or 'professional cultures'. Indeed, Hanitzsch deconstructs the very idea of a 'journalistic culture' (2007). Hanitzsch's work is a useful response to imperial forms of media study which seek to provide a transcendental view of culture because of the way it suggests that professional ideologies take up different positions in different societies.

In Hanitzsch's theory, objectivity is a sub-component of a three-part framework that teases out the institutional roles, epistemologies and ethical ideologies of each culture. Objectivity stands as a sub-section of epistemology. Hanitzsch clarifies that objectivism here relates to the 'question of how truth can be attained', a 'philosophical or absolute sense of objectivity rather than with a procedural sense of objectivity as method' (2007: 376). However, he also notes that objectivism and subjectivism can be seen in a circuit, with objectivity arising from, or out of competition between 'a potentially infinite number of subjective accounts' (2007: 376). Noting that 'Truth, and its pursuit' cannot always be 'separated from context and human subjectivity', this trend toward separation may indeed 'explain the reluctance of many Asian journalists to implement any Western-style objective journalism' (2007: 376).

Any definition of objectivity itself risks a kind of philosophical bias. Perhaps in response to this, a different approach has developed in some surveys, which is to suggest to respondents a range of statements about good reporting, and then ask which is closest to their idea of objectivity. This is the approach of different researchers working under a 1990s 'Media and Democracy' project. For example, Wolfgang Donsbach and Bettina Klett (looking at Germany, Italy, the UK and the US) ask respondents to first indicate their criteria for 'good news reporting', then ask which of these criteria comes closest to their understanding of the term 'objectivity' (1993: 63). From such studies we gain a picture of a global profession with strongly shared norms, but also strong variations. These surveys asked journalists to associate objectivity with ideas such as no subjectivity, fair representation, fair scepticism, hard facts and value judgements. Julianne Schultz posed the same questions, with additional questions on the fourth estate, to Australian journalists (1998). Most US and Australian journalists surveyed saw 'fair representation' (expressing fairly the position of each side) as coming close to their understanding of objectivity. German journalists valued 'hard facts' (going beyond contending statements to the facts). That said, a very high percentage (80 per cent or greater) of journalists across five countries responded to a question about how important it was for a journalist to try to be as objective as possible, with 91 per cent of US respondents indicating it was 'very important', with Australian (88 per cent), UK (84 per cent), German (81 per cent) and Italian (81 per cent) journalists not far behind.

Surveys such as these provide an indicator of variations in attitude and belief. However, from the perspective of norms, Schudson reminds us that an awareness of social conditions is crucial.

> Journalists work in Germany or China or Cuba or Argentina with norms that differ from the objectivity norm. To understand the emergence of a norm historically, it is necessary to understand not only the general social conditions that provide incentives for groups to adopt 'some' norms but the specific cultural circumstances that lead them to adopt the specific norm they do. (2001: 165)

Schudson examines strategic conditions and organizational factors to do with control and socialization; but he also draws attention to the 'cultural environment the group can draw on, the set of ideas, concepts, values that they have access to, find attractive, and can convey convincingly to themselves and others' (2001: 166).

The specificity of these social conditions raises questions about the character and development of objectivity in other countries. Any construction of what we might call a 'model' out of a norm involves making ideological decisions about the 'essence' of that norm. Beate Josephi calls this model norm a 'representative specimen' (2007: 302). Josephi questions whether the American model can be representative, but also links objectivity in with this questioning.

The American model of objectivity is by far the best known professional model worldwide, yet it has too many flaws to be used as an
object of imitation. The ideal of objectivity, central to the model,
has been incisively critiqued . . . and so has the possibility of value
neutrality . . . Across the Atlantic, the objectivity norm has not taken
root and journalists preferred championing favoured values and ideas.
(2007: 302)

The issue of where and why the objectivity norm takes root,
and where it doesn't, becomes a key question, complicating any
concept of universalism that might be in play. Thus, for instance,
Kai Hafez points to a number of explicit commitments by the
Federation of Arab Journalists and Egyptian and Pakistan journalists to the concept of objectivity (2002: 229). Meanwhile, Renate
Köcher notes 'it conflicts with the German journalists' view of
their role and is thus rejected by them' (1986: 50).

Building on Schudson's insight that 'all journalism is ethnocentric' (2001: 164), Josephi celebrates difference, but going against
the grain she sees value in a 'normative' model of some kind to
which professionals everywhere can aspire to. In other words, she
remains committed to a 'normatively infused journalistic professional model that is based on the ideal of freedom of expression
and which upholds a journalism practised without fear or favour,
reporting factually and independently' (2007: 304). A focus on
normative imperatives accounts for some robust universalizing
statements about the global mediasphere on the part of some other
critics. Commenting on the Russian media in the 1990s, Brian
McNair notes that 'journalistic objectivity has not yet emerged as
the dominant professional ethic in Russia, which it will have to do
if television is to contribute in the long run to the consolidation
of liberal democratic norms in post-Soviet society' (McNair 2000:
91; see also Akhterov 2011: 698). Kai Hafez also goes against
the grain of the new deconstruction of journalistic culture to
focus on 'universalization': 'Despite existing differences between
Western and Middle Eastern/Islamic journalism ethics and in
contrast to the overall neoconservative (Islamist) trends in societal
norms, formal journalism ethics has been a sphere of growing

universalization throughout the last decades' (2002: 225). Thus, while universalization is a problematic in the way it can handle differences between cultures, some writers see value in a strategic use of the term.

To *what extent has the objectivity norm been adopted outside of the US?*

In the Introduction to this book I discussed some of the issues of approaching objectivity as a trans-national norm, and suggested that while a comparative analysis of the development of objectivity in multiple countries might be desirable, we lack some groundwork for such a project and noted that there are conceptual problems with it, especially to do with how we study norms and their articulation. Analytically, this raises the issue of not just whether the norm exists in a particular context, but how it exists, with what 'purchase', strength or force. These involve questions to do with culture, relationship to government, organizational processes and discourse. Hallin and Mancini highlight the fraught nature of comparative research, which can be highly ethnocentric and invest too heavily in false generalizations (2004: 3). In terms of objectivity in journalism, the groundwork for this kind of analysis has arguably been more fully worked out in the US than anywhere else. Needless to say, it is a very large research area, and is beyond the scope of this book. While my primary goal in this chapter is to examine the analytical issues linked with looking at objectivity as a universal norm, it will be useful to explore the extent to which the objectivity norm has been adopted outside of the US. The answers will help inform our analytical perspective. In this section, I focus on some of the key regions that have arisen in objectivity research in English.

Objectivity and 'European' journalism

Schudson begins his essay on the objectivity norm with a declaration that ' "objectivity" is the chief occupational value of American journalism and the norm that historically and still today distinguishes US journalism from the dominant model of continental European journalism' (2001: 149). The rest of his essay explores the basis of this claim. This establishes Europe as a key region for comparative research into the objectivity norm.

Objectivity in European journalism has been the subject of wide-ranging research, with a number of different countries or regions forming the focus: including Spain (Sánchez-Aranda & Barrera 2003; Berganza-Conde et al. 2010), Scandinavia (Westerhåhl 1983; Hemánus 1976), Switzerland (Berganza-Conde et al. 2010), and Britain (Smith 1978; Hampton 2008). A number of multi-country studies also contribute here (Donsbach & Klett 1993; Donsbach 1995 looking at Germany, Great Britain, Italy, Sweden and the United States; and Köcher 1986; Esser 1998 looking at Germany and Britain).

For Frank Esser, the regional focus of German newspapers, combined with a newsroom structure that refused a separation of reporting and editing, and a philosophical inclination towards idealism and abstraction, meant that objectivity could not develop as a reporter ethic (1998: 384). In their early 1990s study, Donsbach and Klett highlight how, in Germany, the expression of public opinion and *Weltanschauung* (or individual world-view) is privileged over objectivity. The commercial conditions that supported the rise of objectivity in the US also did not exist in Germany because of state monopolies on advertisement: 'this source of revenues was barred from the newspaper business until the second half of the nineteenth century'. Furthermore, in Germany (as in Italy), literary writing and writers were influential on journalism (Donsbach 1995: 19). Donsbach notes that the party press emerged later and persisted longer in Germany. And also that, unlike US newsrooms, German newspapers did not always distinguish between reporting, editor and editorial writer or commentator as distinct jobs, and the roles overlapped (thus a reporter might write a commentary on the same issue) (also Esser 1998). These are just some of the differences which can play a role in thinking about objectivity. 'Generally, continental European journalists take reporting the news for granted and believe that the journalist's primary job is to interpret and evaluate the news' (Donsbach 1995: 23). Donsbach also suggests that in Germany (as in Italy) journalists are more likely to 'champion particular values and ideas' than US journalists.

In his overview of Italian journalism Paolo Mancini suggests that, while neutrality and objectivity are central terms in the liberal professional model based on the separation of news and commentary, it has an 'uncomfortable abode in Italy' (Mancini 2000: 272). Once one goes beyond a two-party parliamentary system (as in the case of Italy) impartiality and bias become complicated: 'objectivity is almost impossible' (2000: 273). In his discussion of the Italian case, Mancini outlines how objectivity has a place in the dominant professional model, but is seen as inherently weak and biased at the same time. It is an 'empty commonplace' with an ambiguous role in public debates about Italian media.

France is a significant case to consider following Jean K. Chalaby's work. He argues that not only is journalism a nineteenth-century invention, but that it was an Anglo-American one. This argument challenges notions of journalistic invention celebrating the French revolution, for instance (see Hartley 1996). In a 1996 essay, Chalaby found the French press of the 1800s less informational and factually oriented than the British press. Resources were restricted, and Anglo-American papers focused more heavily on news and information in a number of different areas (parliament, court reporting, the provinces, foreign correspondents). The occupation of journalist and reporter also gained legitimacy later in France, in the interwar period (1918–39). Chronicle, opinion, commentary, political partisanship, polemical debate and literary form (rather than the telegraphic style) were, according to Chalaby, more typical of French journalism.

In his 1998 book, Chalaby argues that a discursive norm of objectivity did not operate in eighteenth-century France (1998: 9). This supplements his earlier argument that one of the key 'fact-centred discursive practices' related to objectivity, the dissociation of facts and opinion, was not a key facet of French journalism around the turn of the twentieth century. This had an impact on the style of journalism. 'The Anglo-American news report may also be differentiated from the classic French journal article by the way it is written. News reports, notably because they place the most newsworthy fact first, are constructed "around facts" and not around "ideas and chronologies". In French newspapers, the organizing principle of many articles was the mediating subjectivity of the journalist' (Chalaby 1996: 312). Despite this focus on the subjectivity of the journalist, interviewing and reporting in France were linked to a 'modern conception of news' and journalistic practice originating from the Anglo-American context. Chalaby suggests that from around 1896 Anglo-American models of news were introduced, firstly by American journalists in France. 'Since then, Anglo-American influence has been constant in the French journalistic field' (1996: 318).

Despite this, it is fair to say that the ground upon which a norm of objectivity might take root was not fertile. Chalaby suggests that it is due to the fact that the journalistic field in France is more closely bound to the literary field and its norms. In the Anglo-American world this link to literature was less strong (but not unknown) with the press seen as a 'medium of information'. Literary capital and standing was thus more important in France: 'The journalistic practice most literary in character was the most prestigious' (1996: 315). As Schudson argues, the 'space that would be occupied by "objectivity" as a professional value in American journalism was already occupied in European journalism', mainly by a 'self-understanding that journalists were high literary creators and cosmopolitan political thinkers' (2001: 166).

Other significant differences in national context, such as regulation of the press in France, which stifled the development of news delivery, are worth keeping in mind. As with the case in Italy, French politics was not a story of two parties in parliament. This lack of bipartisanship meant that a convenient definition of impartiality and balance by providing equal time was not going to work. The nature of political struggle in France meant that partisanship was more varied and militant. Following the commercialization argument concerning the emergence of objectivity in journalism, Chalaby sees financial independence gained through advertising as a crucial part of the 'development of a journalism of information based on the discursive norms of neutrality and objectivity' (1996: 320). But he also notes that advertising was not well developed in France in the late nineteenth century.

Objectivity and the British connection

Like Chalaby, Denis McQuail points to the English press as a template for modern journalism. McQuail details how *The Times* came to define an idea of the press:

> In the liberal political and commercial climate of the later nineteenth century, the main impulse toward objectivity was provided by the rise and consolidation of the elite or 'bourgeois' newspaper, on the model of *The Times* (London). This type of newspaper became character-ized by legal freedom; independence from the state; competence and professionalism of its staff; a high degree of informativeness; and a self-chosen responsibility to society in general and, in particular to an educated business and professional middle class, whose interests it represented and advanced. The requirements of business, public administration, and a reformed and participant politics placed a premium on information which was not only extensive but also up-to-date, continuous, accurate, and useful. (McQuail 1986: 3)

The *Times* 'model', for want of a better term, fuses commercial independence with public service ideals, as embodied in the idea of the fourth estate (Chalaby 1996: 320–1). In the early nine-teenth century, much as in the US, British newspapers 'were beginning to free themselves from financial dependence on gov-ernment', largely through advertising (Conboy 2004: 113). It has much to offer as an exemplar in this sense, and Conboy declares *The Times* the 'single most important contributor to the estab-lishment of a discourse of the liberal function of journalism as a Fourth Estate' (2004: 119). But, as Martin Conboy and James Curran note, this reading does not give due credit to the con-tribution of the radical press in Britain (Conboy 2004: 88–108; Curran & Seaton 2003: 8–16), or give a full explanation of how *The Times* managed a 'conversion to the cause of liberal reform' (Conboy 2004: 115).

Issues exist with treating *The Times* as a model for North American journalism, and vice versa. Schudson argues that Chalaby treats the American and British cases as more similar than warranted. 'The British case may be a kind of half-way house between American professionalism and continental traditions of party-governed journalism with high literary aspirations' (2001: 167). Hallin and Mancini are also wary of attempts to discuss an Anglo-American model of journalism in singular terms (2004: 11). One of the difficulties for the idea of an 'Anglo-American' tradition of journalism is that, despite the tendency to see *The Times* in terms of objectivity, the objectivity norm is in fact difficult to situate in UK print journalism. Mark Hampton suggests that while 'the concept of "objectivity" in British journalism history is often taken as part of the intellectual heritage of a transatlantic journalistic tradition . . . the ideal's existence in Britain has generally been assumed rather than demonstrated' (2008: 479). While he is not opposed to a construct of Anglo-American journalism per se, he questions whether the two traditions are in fact isomorphic. From this starting point he carries out a careful comparison: 'To the extent that something we might call "objectivity" prevailed as a British journalistic norm, it need not conform, of course, to the American norm'.

> Especially among British print journalists, not only did the word 'objective' rarely appear in discussion, but journalistic ideals very clearly departed from their American counterparts. Rather than objectivity, notions of truth, independence and 'fair play' held greater appeal to 20th-century British journalists. Unlike 'objectivity', moreover, these alternative concepts, while admirable from a citizen's perspective, do not constitute a professional ritual of the sort that can help to distinguish the journalist from the non-journalist. Nor do they proscribe partisanship. (2008: 478)

Hampton explores the suggestion that objectivity was not generalized in the British context: 'instead, it remained relevant only in much more specific institutional contexts'. British objectivity, when instituted, also took unique forms, with little 'contradiction between truthfulness and commitment to specific political principles' (2008: 483). Hampton nominates editorial independence as a more powerful term in British print journalism than objectivity.

The British Broadcasting Corporation

Objectivity has a long tradition in UK broadcast journalism through the British Broadcasting Corporation (BBC, established 1 January 1927), where it is promoted as a 'precious quality, not to be compromised' (BBC News 2002). As a result it will be useful to focus on the BBC and its commitment to objectivity, but more importantly to discuss the link between objectivity and the norm of impartiality promoted by the organization.

In his BBC Trust report on safeguarding impartiality in the twenty-first century, Richard Tait notes that the BBC 'was never officially told to be impartial' (2007: 25). Its commitment to impartiality, itself an innovation in the nascent area of public broadcasting, was formed in the context of strong government control over the new broadcasting company, as well as the attempt to loosen these controls to allow it to deal with so-called controversial matters. Historically, the most significant event is the general strike of 1926. The strike over miners' wages and conditions defined politics in the UK at that time. In 1925 mine owners threatened to reduce wages. Mine, railway and transport unions united in resistance. The Government forestalled a crisis by instituting a nine-month subsidy. During this time a Royal Commission would investigate, and a report was delivered in March 1926 (Trades Union Congress 2004).

Labour politicians and leaders of the Trades Union Congress were worried about the implications of a general strike, with fears that radical forces in the party (inspired by the events of the 1917 revolution in Russia) would come to the fore. When a strike commenced on 3 May, news was integral to the dispute. Printers were among those who ceased work. Workers at the *Daily Mail* had earlier refused to publish a leading article, 'For King and Country', which suggested the strike was more than an industrial dispute and painted the strikers as revolutionaries. Mail trains were cancelled, and paper supply was restricted. As Asa Briggs notes, 'most of the great national newspapers ceased publication in the regular and reliable form to which their readers were accustomed' (1961: 367).

In this context, the new broadcaster, established only four years earlier in 1922 as the British Broadcasting Company, could have been commandeered by the Government to maintain social and constitutional order (which was feasible under legal authority) (Briggs 1961: 361). It was already under tight control, with restrictions in place on all subjects of political and religious controversy. In addition, because of concerns over unfair competition with established news interests, restrictions on news were in place. At the time of the strike, the BBC broadcast news from other agencies in one bulletin at 7pm, to ensure that sales figures for the press would be unaffected (Allan 1997: 310). In short, the Postmaster-General kept a close reign on the BBC in relation to any matter deemed controversial.

The general strike provided an important opportunity to demonstrate what the organization could do at a crucial juncture in its history. As Tracey notes, 'The BBC was pressed on both sides by the newspaper owners and the politicians, and it was in this context of a badly underdeveloped news service that the BBC found itself in the May of 1926 the major national source of news' (2003: 8). As Stuart Allan puts it, 'the public turned to the wireless for reports on the crisis; the BBC responded with up to five bulletins a day, most of which included at least some material it had gathered itself' (1997: 310).

Seizing the opportunity, the BBC Director-General John Reith and the BBC Chairman prior to incorporation (and Vice-Chairman afterwards), Lord Gainford, defined an alternative path, and maintained press freedom by committing to impartiality. Impartiality, activated as a principle to get around political and commercial sensitivities, arose in the context of the general strike as a way to ensure the Government applied no censorship pressure; but it also meant, in the view of some researchers, that the BBC censored itself by refusing to report anything which might help the strikers.

In terms of objectivity, the transcript of the first bulletin on 4 May was significant.

> The BBC fully realize [sic] the gravity of its responsibility to all sections of the public, and will do its best to discharge it in the most impartial spirit that circumstances permit. In the last issue of the newspapers, allusion is principally made to the possibility of wholesale oscillations. As to that we express no opinion, but we would ask the public to take as serious a view as we do ourselves of the necessity of plain objective news being audible to everybody. (Quoted in Tracey 2003: 13)

A focus on an objective news service was a way to negotiate different interests. Impartiality as a concept could only be partly useful here, and the performance of the BBC could not be impartial in all cases. After all, the government would release policies and act, and the BBC was obliged to respond accordingly. Reith, while having little sympathy for the mine owners or organized labour (Briggs 1961: 363), is regarded to have shared the government viewpoint. Interestingly, statements from church leaders were not broadcast because of the capacity for embarrassing the government (which could lead to reprisals for the BBC). The BBC understood the reality of the official government line, as expressed in this passage from a policy memo signed by Lord Gainford.

> As the Government are sure that they are right both on the facts of the dispute and on the constitutional issues, any steps which we may take to communicate the truth dispassionately should be to the advantage of the Government. (Quoted in Tracey 2003: 14)

Even if impartiality was compromised in this way – or as Tracey puts it, defined constitutionally rather than politically (2003: 19) – at least the information was objective and factual: 'a conscious effort was made to distinguish between agency copy and government copy; and many of the items broadcast were objective in the sense that they were accurate reports of verifiable events'.

For Tracey 'the General Strike certainly left the BBC as a major news source . . . More than anything the events of May 1926 clarified the context within which "impartiality" functions – involving an almost total, if oblique, accommodation to government needs and interests' (2003: 22). While no labour or trade-union speaker was put to air (a proposal was vetoed by the government), speeches from trade union leaders were quoted, which was not the case in the government newspaper the *British Gazette*. Briggs feels that fabrication was avoided, but there were misleading reports that were not always corrected. There was a 'certain natural bias towards the Government side' (Briggs 1961: 374).

The BBC became a public corporation in January 1927, but restrictions on the reporting of controversial matters remained, and aspects of the corporation and its financing were still overseen by the Postmaster-General. Impartiality became a catch-phrase to achieve public trust. It was also linked to the BBC trying to show that it could act independently and responsibly, within the rules of government influence. Slowly the news service developed. Allan describes how by 1934 steps were afoot to make the BBC news an independent department, and the corporate ethic of neutrality was again important to this development (even though much of the news still came from other agencies).

Through the 1940s, objectivity arose as an important value for overseas broadcasts. A 1946 white paper on broadcasting stated 'great care should be taken to ensure the complete objectivity of the News bulletins which will form the kernel of all overseas broadcasting' (Briggs 1985: 313). Objectivity became a key value for the overseas news service. The commitment to 'impartiality as a professional and public duty' was so strong at this time that the first television newscasts were without an announcer, for fear that the authoritativeness and detached impartiality of the news would be compromised (Allan 1997: 312). Impartiality was ingrained in the very discourse of broadcasting such that it was one of the conditions placed on the new Independent Television News (ITN) by the Television Act of 1954. Accuracy and impartiality thus became catchwords for the entire broadcasting system. It continued to be a point of regulation, but also a way to assert and extend the independence of the media through strict editorial standards.

By the time of the Suez Crisis of 1956, impartiality was once again a key way for the BBC to prove itself in the reporting of controversial matters and maintain its autonomy. The Board of Governors, investigating accusations of bias, determined that the 'obligation for impartiality, objectivity and for telling the truth had been fulfilled' (Allan 1997: 318). The BBC commitment to impartiality thus has a long history, and is contested because of its links to conservative and middle-class views. Nevertheless, both objectivity and impartiality are central to what has been seen as a BBC ethos. The BBC is a unique institution in terms of objectivity in that it pursues it as an organizational norm (and because it was a monopoly in the UK for so long it virtually became a professional norm for broadcast news and current affairs).

Turning to the present day, objectivity does not appear in the 2006 Royal Charter. The current version of the 'BBC Mission and Values' statement on the website does not mention objectivity (British Broadcasting Corporation 2011a). The norm is invoked in speeches by executive staff where a regular link is made between practising objectivity and maintaining trust in the BBC (see chapter 7).

The British case points to complexities in any clear construction of Anglo-American journalism. While the British experience in public broadcasting was exported across the Commonwealth of Nations, even there differences are evident. Hackett and Zhao argue that Canada forms a kind of half-way example between the US and UK. There, the labour press of the late 1800s formed a key stepping stone in the development of objectivity by asserting its 'non-partisan, non-sectarian' character (1998: 23). Upon their arrival the cheap dailies diluted the radical democratic discourse of the labour press, but retained the claim to offer independent and impartial information. In the late nineteenth century Canadian press interests began to focus objectivity as part of a move towards respectability and responsibility, often modelled on the British press (Ward 2004: 239). In the twentieth century, the establishment of the Canadian Press (CP) news agency in 1917 helped 'spread the gospel of objectivity' (Ward 2004: 247). The Canadian Broadcasting Corporation (CBC, established in 1936) aligned itself closely with news agencies and 'depended on the "objectivity" of the agency versions of events' (Petersen 1993: 156). The CBC adopted objectivity as a strict, organizational norm, with the press and newly founded journalism schools contributing to the 'culture of objectivity' of the post-World War II period (Hackett & Zhao 1998: 39–40; Albota 1991).

Australia

In Australia, the national broadcaster, the Australian Broadcasting Corporation (ABC), has objectivity written into its governing legislation, the Australian Broadcasting Corporation Act 1983 (CTH). Section 8(1)c explains it is the duty of the board 'to ensure that the gathering and presentation by the Corporation of news and information is accurate and impartial according to the recognised standards of objective journalism'.

In Australia, the then Australian Broadcasting Commission (ABC, established 1 July 1932) was, through agreements with Australian press and other agencies, subject to restrictions on the quantity of news to be taken and the time of day it could be broadcast – largely to protect the market for newspapers and their access to the 'cream' of news. Neville Petersen sees the press of the day as being partisan in nature, and aggressive in pursuing their monopolistic interests (1985: 77). Newspaper proprietors were not held to act in the public interest, with the government expecting them to exercise influence over news coverage. While the agencies had a more 'objective' style, suited to their politically diverse audiences, some critics questioned the idea that the news agencies were neutral (Petersen 1985: 77). Furthermore, news was not a high priority for the nascent commission (Petersen 1993: 51), although the agreements with the press (and coverage of the ABC) were a special concern of the second ABC Chairman (1934–5) William James Cleary, along with General Manager Charles Moses. With the appointment of ABC News Editor Michael Francis (Frank) Dixon in 1936, however, and Warren Denning as Federal rounds-man in 1939 (who also served as the ABC liaison in Canberra, thus complicating ABC–government relations), slow progress was being made towards the creation of the ABC as an independent news service in an environment dominated by established press interests, and a government concerned by the media's power to influence opinion and the course of politics (Petersen 1993: 58). 'Objective' and fair reporting of government statements was crucial to gaining government support. The Australian government was relatively disinterested in the independence of the ABC news services until the relations with press proprietors turned sour over the reporting and restriction of important news in wartime. Concentration of ownership meant that 'too few voices had too much power' (Petersen 1985: 77). When an independent news service was unexpectedly recommended in July 1946, it was in the context of labour government dissatisfaction with the newspapers and their supply of news to the ABC.

Objectivity under the chairmanship of Cleary was not an organizational norm, but tied in a piecemeal way to the delivery of particular services to ensure the satisfaction of either press-clients or ministers. It was reactive, with impartiality more a defensive position. News was not as central to the ABC then as it is now. The commitments to objectivity at that time were tied to the provision of a new national news service to the newspapers in 1942 (Petersen 1993: 165). In this sense, even within the public broadcasting context, there is a link between objectivity and the commercialization argument regarding the development of objectivity in this period (see chapter 1).

In terms of political coverage, this pre-1946 period has been described under a policy of 'news not views'. While initially appearing to imply a separation of fact and comment, it was an informal policy that gave priority to the government of the day as the creator of the news, and gave the opposition the status of only having an opinion on the news (Petersen 1993: 127). The risk of course was that the ABC would be turned into a de facto 'official channel' for ministers (1993: 190).

Objectivity in the late 1930s was not, in Peterson's view, tied to the professionalization of journalism as an occupation per se, although individual journalists did promote objective practices, and the Australian Journalists' Association (AJA) promoted factual, truth-based reporting, a 'non-partisan pursuit of factual accuracy' (Petersen 1993: 73). The first AJA code of practice (which does not mention objectivity) dates from 1944.

In the context of almost continuous concern and debate over the performance of the ABC, a conception of the broadcaster as an independent and 'socially responsible' purveyor of news arose. Petersen notes that this conception of objectivity fell short of a fully developed objectivity norm in some important ways. The 1932 ABC Act did not prescribe impartiality and the focus of discussion was a 'factual news service' and public information rather than a more developed ideal (1993: 93). Even ABC attempts at impartiality in the 1930s were tentative, either sticking to balance of time between parties, or leaning towards refusing to carry political content altogether (Thomas 1980: 83). The ABC faced pressure to cooperate on matters to do with the national interest as defined by the government, especially US–Australian relations in the late 1930s and early 1940s (Thomas 1980: 78). Nevertheless, the ABC imagined its role in distinct terms and Cleary pursued a more direct public service and enlightenment role (Thomas 1980: 58–9).

Following the commitments to objectivity in relation to the provision of the national news service to commercial broadcasters made in 1942, and recommendations by the Parliamentary Standing Committee on Broadcasting to endorse independence and the provision of objective and dispassionate news as fundamental principles (1946: 1), objectivity began to take a more central role at the ABC. In mid-1946, under the Chairmanship of Richard Boyer (1945–61), objectivity was more tightly codified into a 'News and Spoken Transmissions' editorial directive based on an ethos of 'aiding citizenship', 'the stimulating of independent judgements on the problems of life – social, political, philosophic – and of independent appreciation of cultural values' (Australian Broadcasting Commission 1946). The directive placed special emphasis on the selection and presentation of news 'with a degree of objectivity not called for in other organisations'. This objectivity should apply to the priority of news in a bulletin and word length, and that these should be guided by the public interest. It should be 'impossible to determine by listening to the news what the attitude of the news selector should be'. Consistent with the idea of the 'invisible frame' (see Introduction), 'the function of judgement should be left to the listener'.

The handling of issues of balance formed a special focus in the directive. In spoken transmissions full discussion of contentious subjects did not rely on immediate counter, provided that over a reasonable period of time care is taken to present alternative views. In news, equivalent prominence and equivalent wordage to conflicting points of view was required. In relation to politics, the 'news not views' policy was also maintained but modified. The actions of government were deemed more newsworthy but decisions about including the statements of members or ministers were to be based on the public interest. Opposition comment was not required to be sought on factual accounts of the carrying out of policy, but should be sought when new policies were presented or old ones defended.

In the ABC case objectivity can be mapped between press interests, the government and the ABC. Petersen argues that the ABC was criticized by the press for its objectivity – which was seen as a product of news management by the government, 'the antithesis of the traditional press role of being the watchdog against the government on behalf of the people' (1985: 82). 'The shock expressed by the press was undoubtedly genuine because there had been no strong objective news tradition in Australia until this time' (1985: 82). There was, 'apparently no strong press tradition of "objectivity" before 1939' (1985: 83; see also Cryle 1995). In terms of print journalism, researchers suggest it did not become a strong norm in the press in Australia until the 1950s (McKnight 2001).

'Asian values' in journalism

'Asian values' in a range of areas, not just the media, have been the subject of debate since the 1970s (Xu 2005: 9). While not as developed as an area of research into the objectivity norm, objectivity does appear in debates around Asian values in journalism. As P. Kharel notes, 'Western professional standards, its objectivity and financial ability to keep up with the news wherever it is happening, all reflect directly in Asian journalism' (Kharel 1996: 34). While the discussion of Asian values in journalism can take a binary form (East/West, First World/Third World), and get caught up in debates around national identity and globalization, the terms of debate have also been questioned and deconstructed. Participants in the debate have drawn distinctions between the substance and forms of journalism, asked questions about fixed definitions of 'Asia' and 'Asian', and have problematized any simplistic dichotomies of libertarian and authoritarian theories of the press, the individual versus the community, freedom versus control, the marketplace and social consequences (see Masterton 1996).

The debate has also seen a tension between the 'particular' and the 'universal'. The 'particular' focus on distinctly 'Asian' media values falls in some instances on principles of harmony and respect, and trust in leadership, often linked to Confucianism as well as religious traditions of Buddhism, Islam and Hinduism (Nasution 1996: 53). Ideals of human development, cohesion and cultural integrity are also mentioned (Lowe 1996: 35). Xiaoge Xu puts the focus on 'group orientation, filial piety, hard work, and placing community or nation above individuals' (2005: 2). The focus on 'universalism' falls on news values such as truth, objectivity, social equity and non-violence (Masterton 1996: 172). As Chin-Chuan Lee notes, 'are there Asian values? Of course there are, but what are they, and relative to what? Javanese values as opposed to Indian values? Malaysian Chinese values as opposed to Malaysian Malay values?' (Lee 1996: 63).

There is a strong affinity between debates on Asian media values and developmental journalism and communication theories. In echo of Peter Golding's argument regarding the transmission of the ideology of media professionalism to the Third World, there is also recognition that 'media professionalism is a product of Western middle-class liberalism', especially in its insistence on the 'segregation of facts from values', an important feature of objectivity debates (Lee 1996: 62).

Kharel attempts to shift the debate around Asian values in

journalism by suggesting that 'perhaps the question is how much modern journalistic values are practised in Asia' (Kharel 1996: 32). This leads to re-examining Western media and communication concepts in light of 'Asian' practices (see Xu 2005). Taking Hong Kong as one example, Lee notes 'Hong Kong Journalists find it easier to accept the abstract ideals of professionalism (such as objective reporting) than to implement its practical norms (balanced reporting)' (Lee 1996: 62). However, a study of the 1998 elections in Hong Kong, the first after handover, shows the media did a reasonable job of balance between pro-democracy and pro-China forces. 'TV coverage of the 1998 Legco [Legislative Council] election was basically objective in giving balanced reporting to the various political groups as far as their political leanings are concerned, although the coverage seemed biased towards giving greater presence to prominent politicians' (Nip & To 1999: 249).

Conclusion

This discussion has not sought to offer a comprehensive mapping of objectivity across the globe, nor a fully developed post-colonial critique of objectivity. What it has sought to do is open up some analytic problems associated with the question, 'Is objectivity a universal journalism norm?' Of all of the questions posed by this book, it is perhaps the most difficult to answer, and possibly unanswerable. The question is about norms, and for this reason there are competing views on whether norms are always particular, contingent and ethnospecific, or whether they can be turned into imperatives or models for professional work. Another difficulty has to do with the concept of 'universal' itself. As noted in the Introduction, while it may be possible to approach objectivity in journalism as a trans-national norm that has distinct, recognizable form, universality raises a different set of issues around how the norm operates, its similarities and differences, across different times and places.

While it is compelling to suggest that objectivity is an Anglo-American norm, with the US as the centre of a ripple effect across the globe, this does not address the questions raised by its 'diffusion'. What should we make of the case of India, for example, where official discourse on objectivity suggests that objectivity does not have to mean neutrality? As Prime Minister Dr. Manmohan Singh suggested at the Ramnath Goenka Journalism Awards in 2006:

> freedom of press is more than just the freedom of publishers and editors. It is the freedom of society to have its voice heard. The exercise of this freedom does require . . . a 'journalism of courage'. . . . I submit to you that a 'journalism of courage' also implies taking sides. Objectivity does not imply neutrality. It implies respect for truth and facts, and a willingness to take positions, howsoever contrarian or contentious. (Singh 2006)

India's political system and its linguistic diversity offer a very different context for objectivity. This example illustrates how difficult it is to project any consistent process of diffusion, even across former British colonies. The conditions that led to the projection of the ideal of objectivity in the US are not replicated in the UK or Australia.

While the political system, and the function of the media in that system, can provide a sense of how objectivity works in that culture, such an analysis can fall short by directing our attention away from practice, towards the normative system or model in place. Certainly, it allows fundamental issues such as whether objectivity is aligned with neutrality, central to freedom of the press, or necessary to professional journalism, to be debated and disputed. But this focus, I would argue, has also led to an overemphasis on objectivity as discussed by practitioners and media organizations, at the expense of, say, discussions of audience or reader views. Here, the discussion of models or media systems works at the expense of an appreciation of the specificity of how one achieves objectivity in journalism.

In an area of inquiry that is dominated by professional codes of ethics and content analyses of bias, drawing on a concept of objectivity that is still strongly linked to science and positivism, there is a growing awareness of the need for a different approach: one that studies objectivity in journalism as a culturally and textually negotiated *performance* that is actualized according to the conventions of different styles of journalism, encompassing professional and regulatory issues, but also those to do with reader, audience or user expectations. Approaching journalistic objectivity as a culturally negotiated practice allows greater emphasis on issues of persuasion, style, format and genre, but also the politics of standpoint and perspective, and the questions of judgement and interpretation involved in the practice of objectivity.

While debate over the possibility and impossibility of objectivity in journalism is ongoing, objectivity continues to play a central role in media and journalism in linking concepts of truth, accuracy, impartiality and independence, either for the purpose of supporting democratic deliberation, or as an object of critique for movements seeking a new compact between writer and reader or viewer. Objectivity in journalism, it could be said, works within a matrix or cluster of terms. At different times it interacts with terms such as impartiality, transparency, accountability and accuracy, taking on different inflections. In this cluster of terms, however, objectivity remains of special interest. It provides a field of debate that ranges across philosophy, ethics and political economy. It has enabled scholars and practitioners to reflect on the very nature of journalism and media practice, and posit important questions about the sociology, philosophy and ethics of media.

Standards of journalism do not stand above history, and what is good or bad practice needs to be continually reinvented, not just through robust and rigorous discussion in the profession, but through dialogue with new theoretical perspectives and cultural change. The roles the media can play in society are very important. As well as being commercial enterprises (or run like them) media outlets are important institutions in our public life. With this role comes special public responsibilities, for both organizations and the journalists that work for them. In the interests of maintaining this role, and credibility in it, the professional commitments of journalists need to be aired and debated to be made meaningful in the present and future. The debate around journalistic objectivity tells us that it is not enough to 'wheel out' and defend traditional principles simply because they are traditional. Nor should we shelter behind insider status. A process of public education and legitimation is important. To be accountable, the media must attempt, to an even greater degree than might be expected, to lay bare the logic behind the positions they take, and the judgements they make. Media scholars can help by teasing out the political and cultural issues tied up with our current media practice.

References

ABC Editorial Policies (2008) *Short Looks at Some Big Concepts That Govern the ABC*, Australian Broadcasting Corporation, accessed 26 November 2011 at: <http://www.abc.net.au/corp/pubs/documents/200806_reformatted_key_words.pdf>.

Aday, S., Livingston, S. & Hebert, M. (2005) Embedding the Truth: A Cross-Cultural Analysis of Objectivity and Television Coverage of the Iraq War. *The Harvard International Journal of Press/Politics* 10(1), 3–21.

Agnew, S. T. (1969) On the National Media. Mid-West Regional Republican Committee Meeting, Des Moines, IA, 13 November, accessed 1 May 2012 at: <http://faculty.smu.edu/dsimon/Change-Agnew.html>.

Ajami, F. (2001) What the Muslim World Is Watching. *The New York Times*, 18 November, accessed 27 April 2012 at: <http://www.nytimes.com/2001/11/18/magazine/what-the-muslim-world-is-watching.html?pagewanted=all>.

Akhterov, V. (2011) Voiceless Glasnost: Responding to Government Pressures and Lack of a Free Press Tradition in Russia. In: Fortner, R. S. & Fackler, P. M. (eds.) *The Handbook of Global Communication and Media Ethics, Vol. II.* Wiley-Blackwell, Malden, MA, pp. 677–99.

Al-Jazeera (2010) *Code of Ethics*, Al-Jazeera, accessed 15 December 2011 at: <http://www.aljazeera.com/aboutus/2006/11/2008525185733692771.html>.

Al-Jazeera Press Office (2007) Release: News Presenters. *Al-Jazeera*, 8 October, accessed 27 April 2012 at: <http://www.aljazeera.com/aboutus/2007/10/2008525185536833890.html>.

Albota, R. (1991) Dan McArthur's Concept of Objectivity for the CBC News Service. In: Lockhead, R. (ed.) *Beyond the Printed Word: The Evolution of Canada's Broadcast News Heritage*. Quarry Press, Kingston, ON, pp. 223–35.

Allan, S. (1995) News, Truth and Postmodernity: Unravelling the Will to Facticity. In: Adam, B. & Allan, S. (eds.) *Theorizing Culture: An Interdisciplinary Critique after Postmodernism*. New York University Press, New York.

Allan, S. (1997) News and the Public Sphere: Towards a History of Objectivity

References

and Impartiality. In: Bromley, M. & O'Malley, T. (eds.) *A Journalism Reader*. Routledge, London, pp. 297–329.

Allan, S. (2006) *Online News: Journalism and the Internet*. Open University Press, Maidenhead.

Allan, S. (2007) Citizen Journalism and the Rise of 'Mass Self-Communication': Reporting the London Bombings. *Global Media Journal: Australian Edition* 1(2), 1–20.

Allan, S. (2010) *News Culture*. Open University Press, Maidenhead.

Allan, S. & Matheson, D. (2004) Online Journalism in the Information Age. *Knowledge, Work & Society* 2(3), 73–94.

Altschull, J. H. (1990) *From Milton to McLuhan: The Ideas behind American Journalism*. Longman, New York.

Amanpour, C. (1996) Television's Role in Foreign Policy. *The Quill* 84(3), 16–17.

Australian Broadcasting Commission (1946) Directives – News and Spoken Transmissions, from Minutes of the 169th Meeting of the Commission, 5–7 June 1946, no. 5399, Sydney.

Awad, G. (2005) Aljazeera.net: Identity Choices and the Logic of the Media. In: Zayani, M. (ed.) *The Al Jazeera Phenomenon: Critical Perspectives on New Arab Media*. Paradigm Publishers, Boulder, CO, pp. 80–90.

Ayish, M. I. (2002) Political Communication on Arab World Television: Evolving Patterns. *Political Communication* 19(2), 137–54.

Bagdikian, B. H. (1972) The Politics of American Newspapers. *Columbia Journalism Review* 10(6), 8–13.

Baggini, J. (2003) *The Philosophy of Journalism*, openDemocracy, accessed 12 April 2012 at: <http://www.opendemocracy.net/print/1218>.

Baldasty, G. J. (1992) *The Commercialization of News in the Nineteenth Century*. University of Wisconsin Press, Madison, WI.

Barkho, L. (2010) *News from the BBC, CNN, and Al-Jazeera: How the Three Broadcasters Cover the Middle East*. Hampton Press, Cresskill, NJ.

Barnes, A. (1965) Writing the Story. In: Roderick, C. A. & Revill, L. (eds.) *The Journalist's Craft: A Guide to Modern Practice*. Angus & Robertson, Sydney, pp. 72–80.

Barth, A. (1951) Washington Roundup. *Guild Reporter* XVIII(5), 8.

Barthes, R. (1986) The Reality Effect. In: *The Rustle of Language*. Basil Blackwell, Oxford, pp. 141–8.

Bayley, E. R. (1981) *Joe McCarthy and the Press*. University of Wisconsin Press, Madison, WI.

BBC Monitoring Africa (2003) Safrican Broadcasting News Chief Raps Liberal Views on Media Freedom, 5 June.

BBC News (2002) *Alphabetical Checklist*, British Broadcasting Corporation, accessed 12 December, 2011, <http://news.bbc.co.uk/2/hi/programmes/radio_newsroom/1099593.stm#o>.

231

References

Beasley, M. H. & Mirando, J. A. (2005) Objectivity and Journalism Education. In: Knowlton, S. R. & Freeman, K. L. (eds.) *Fair and Balanced: A History of Journalistic Objectivity*. Vision Press, Northport, AL, pp. 180–91.

Beckerman, G. (2004) God Is My Co-Author. *Columbia Journalism Review* 43(3), 32–4.

Bell, M. (1997) TV News: How Far Should We Go? *British Journalism Review* 8(7), 7–16.

Bell, M. (1998a) The Journalism of Attachment. In: Kieran, M. (ed.) *Media Ethics*. Routledge, London, pp. 15–22.

Bell, M. (1998b) The Truth Is Our Currency. *The Harvard International Journal of Press/Politics* 3(1), 102–9.

Belsey, C. (1980) *Critical Practice*. Methuen, London.

Bennett, W. L. (1988) *News: The Politics of Illusion*. Longman, New York.

Berganza-Conde, M. R., Oller-Alonso, M. & Meier, K. (2010) Journalistic Roles and Objectivity in Spanish and Swiss Journalism. An Applied Model of Analysis of Journalism Culture. *Revista Latina de Comunicación Social* 13(65), 1–12.

Berger, P. L. & Luckmann, T. (1971) *The Social Construction of Reality: A Treatise in the Sociology of Knowledge*. Penguin Books, Harmondsworth.

Berkowitz, D. & Eko, L. (2007) Blasphemy as Sacred Rite/Right: 'The Mohammed Cartoons Affair' and the Maintenance of Journalistic Ideology. *Journalism Studies* 8(5), 779–97.

Berry, S. J. (2005) Why Objectivity Still Matters. *Nieman Reports* 59(2), 15–16.

Blackburn, S. (2008) *The Oxford Dictionary of Philosophy*. Oxford University Press. Oxford Reference Online, accessed 5 October 2011 at: <http://www.oxfordreference.com/pub/views/home.html>.

Blankenburg, W. B. & Walden, R. (1977) Objectivity, Interpretation, and Economy in Reporting. *Journalism Quarterly* 54(3), 591–5.

Bledstein, B. J. (1976) *The Culture of Professionalism: The Middle Class and the Development of Higher Education in America*. Norton, New York.

Blumler, J. G. & Gurevitch, M. (1995) *The Crisis of Public Communication*. Routledge, London.

Bolter, J. D. & Grusin, R. A. (1999) *Remediation: Understanding New Media*. MIT Press, Cambridge, MA.

Bolton, T. (2006) News on the Net: A Critical Analysis of the Potential of Online Alternative Journalism to Challenge the Dominance of Mainstream News Media. *Scan: Journal of Media Arts Culture* 3(1), accessed 27 April 2012 at: <http://scan.net.au/scan/journal/print.php?journal_id=71&j_id=7>.

Bonney, B. & Wilson, H. (1983) *Australia's Commercial Media*. Macmillan, South Melbourne.

Bowler, M. (2006) Displacement and Degradation. *The Nelson Mail (NZ)*, 25 October.

References

Bowman, L. (2006) Reformulating 'Objectivity': Charting the Possibilities for Proactive Journalism in the Modern Era. *Journalism Studies* 7(4), 628–43.

Boyce, G. (1978) The Fourth Estate: The Reappraisal of a Concept. In: Boyce, G., Curran, J. & Wingate, P. (eds.) *Newspaper History: From the Seventeenth Century to the Present Day*. Constable, London, pp. 19–40.

Boylan, J. (1986) Declarations of Independence. *Columbia Journalism Review* 25(4), 29–45.

Briggs, A. (1961) *The Birth of Broadcasting. The History of Broadcasting in the United Kingdom, Volume I*. Oxford University Press, London.

Briggs, A. (1985) *The BBC: The First Fifty Years*. Oxford University Press, New York.

Brisbane, A. S. (2012a) Should the Times Be a Truth Vigilante, *The New York Times*, 12 January 2012, accessed 27 April 2012 at: <http://publiceditor.blogs. nytimes.com/2012/01/12/should-the-times-be-a-truth-vigilante/>.

Brisbane, A. S. (2012b) Update to My Previous Post on Truth Vigilantes, *The New York Times*, 12 January 2012, accessed 27 April 2012 at: <http://pub liceditor.blogs.nytimes.com/2012/01/12/update-to-my-previous-post-on-truth-vigilantes/>.

British Broadcasting Corporation (2011a) *BBC Mission and Values*, accessed 2 December 2011 at: <http://www.bbc.co.uk/info/purpose/>.

British Broadcasting Corporation (2011b) *Editorial Guidelines – Guidelines – Section 11: War, Terror and Emergencies – Accuracy and Impartiality*, accessed 2 December 2011 at: <http://www.bbc.co.uk/editorialguidelines/ page/guidelines-war-practices-accuracy/>.

Bromley, M. (2003) Objectivity and the Other Orwell: The Tabloidism of the *Daily Mirror* and Journalistic Authenticity. *Media History* 9(2), 123–35.

Brucker, H. (1937) *The Changing American Newspaper*. Columbia University Press, New York.

Brucker, H. (1949) *Freedom of Information*. Macmillan, New York.

Bruns, A. (2005) *Gatewatching: Collaborative Online News Production*. Peter Lang, New York.

Bruns, A. (2006) Wikinews: The Next Generation of Alternative Online News? *Scan: Journal of Media Arts Culture* 3(1), accessed 27 April 2012 at: <http:// scan.net.au/scan/journal/display.php?%20journal_id=69>.

Burnham, D. & Young, H. (2007) *Kant's Critique of Pure Reason*. Edinburgh University Press, Edinburgh.

Byford, M. (2004) Speech Given at the Newspaper Society Annual Lunch, 4 May. Accessed 27 April 2012 at: <http://www.bbc.co.uk/pressoffice/speeches/ stories/byford_newspaper_soc.shtml>.

Calcutt, A. & Hammond, P. (2011) *Journalism Studies: A Critical Introduction*. Routledge, London.

Campbell, G. (2006) Bruce Jesson Memorial Lecture, November 21. Accessed 1 November 2011 at: <http://www.brucejesson.com/sites/default/files/Bruce%20

References

Jesson%20Memorial%20Lecture%202006%20-%20Gordon%20Campbell. pdf>.

Canberra Times (1998) Debate on Truth, Justice and a Proprietor's Way. *Canberra Times*, 26 May.

Canel, M. J. & Piqué, A. M. (1998) Journalists in Emerging Democracies: The Case of Spain. In: Weaver, D. H. (ed.) *The Global Journalist: News People around the World*. Hampton Press, Cresskill, NJ, pp. 299–319.

Carey, J. W. (1982) Review Essay: The Discovery of Objectivity. *American Journal of Sociology* 87(5), 1182–8.

Carey, J. W. (1989) *Communication as Culture: Essays on Media and Society*. Unwin Hyman, Boston, MA.

Carey, J. W. (1997 [1969]) The Communications Revolution and the Professional Communicator. In: Munson, E. S. & Warren, C. A. (eds.) *James Carey: A Critical Reader*. University of Minnesota Press, Minneapolis, MN, pp. 128–43.

Carey, J. W. (1997 [1986]) The Dark Continent of American Journalism. In: Munson, E. S. & Warren, C. A. (eds.) *James Carey: A Critical Reader*. University of Minnesota Press, Minneapolis, MN, pp. 144–88.

Carey, J. W. (1999 [1987]) Journalists Just Leave: The Ethics of an Anomalous Profession. In: Baird, R. M., Loges, W. E. & Rosenbaum, S. E. (eds.) *The Media and Morality*. Prometheus Books, Amherst, NY, pp. 39–54.

Carroll, W. (1955) The Seven Deadly Virtues. *Nieman Reports* 9(3), 25–30.

Cater, D. (1950) The Captive Press. *The Reporter* 2(June 6), 17–20.

Cater, D. (1959) *Fourth Branch of Government*. Houghton Mifflin, Boston, MA.

Chalaby, J. K. (1996) Journalism as an Anglo-American Invention: A Comparison of the Development of French and Anglo-American Journalism, 1830s–1920s. *European Journal of Communication* 11(3), 303–26.

Chalaby, J. K. (1998) *The Invention of Journalism*. Macmillan, Basingstoke.

Christians, C. G., Rotzoll, K. B., Fackler, M., Richardson, K. B. & Woods, R. H. (2005) *Media Ethics: Cases and Moral Reasoning*. Pearson, Boston, MA.

Conboy, M. (2002) *The Press and Popular Culture*. Sage, London.

Conboy, M. (2004) *Journalism: A Critical History*. Sage, London.

Conboy, M. (2010) *The Language of Newspapers: Socio-Historical Perspectives*. Continuum, London.

Crawford, N. A. (1924) *The Ethics of Journalism*. A. A. Knopf, New York.

Cryle, D. (1995) Journalism and Objectivity: A Colonial Viewpoint. *Australian Studies in Journalism* 4, 90–7.

Cunningham, B. (2003) Re-Thinking Objectivity. *Columbia Journalism Review* 42(2), 24–32.

Curran, J. & Park, M.-J. (2000) *De-Westernizing Media Studies*. Routledge, London.

Curran, J. & Seaton, J. (2003) *Power without Responsibility: The Press, Broadcasting, and New Media in Britain*. Routledge, London.

References

D'Agostino, F. (1993) Transcendence and Conversation: Two Conceptions of Objectivity. *American Philosophical Quarterly* 30(2), 87–108.

Danermark, B., Ekström, M., Jakobsen, L. & Karlsson, J. C. (2001) *Explaining Society: Critical Realism in the Social Sciences*. Routledge, London.

Daston, L. & Galison, P. (2007) *Objectivity*. Zone Books, New York.

Davies, N. (2008) *Flat Earth News: An Award-Winning Reporter Exposes Falsehood, Distortion and Propaganda in the Global Media*. Chatto & Windus, London.

Davis, E. (1952) News and the Whole Truth. *Atlantic Monthly* 190 (August), 32–8.

Davis, M. (1997) *Gangland: Cultural Elites and the New Generationalism*. Allen & Unwin, St. Leonards, New South Wales.

Davies, D. R. (2005) The Challenges of Civil Rights and Joseph McCarthy. In: Knowlton, S. R. & Freeman K. L. (eds.) *Fair and Balanced: A History of Journalistic Objectivity*. Vision Press, Northport, AL, pp. 206–20.

Dawson, N. V. & Gregory, F. (2009) Correspondence and Coherence in Science: A Brief Historical Perspective. *Judgment and Decision Making* 4(2), 126–33.

de Albuquerque, A. (2005) Another 'Fourth Branch': Press and Political Culture in Brazil. *Journalism* 6(4), 486–504.

Dearing, J. W. & Rogers, E. M. (1996) *Agenda-Setting*. Sage, Thousand Oaks, CA.

Debatin, B. (2011) Ethical Implications of Blogging. In: Fortner, R. S. & Fackler, P. M. (eds.) *The Handbook of Global Communication and Media Ethics, Vol. II*. Wiley-Blackwell, Malden, MA, pp. 823–44.

Deleuze, G. (1991) *Empiricism and Subjectivity: An Essay on Hume's Theory of Human Nature*. Columbia University Press, New York.

Dennis, E. E. (1989) *Reshaping the Media: Mass Communication in an Information Age*. Sage, Newbury Park, CA.

Dennis, E. E. & Merrill, J. C. (1984) Journalistic Objectivity. In: Dennis, E. E. & Merrill, J. C. (eds.) *Basic Issues in Mass Communication: A Debate*. Macmillan Publishing Company, New York, pp. 103–18.

Deverell, R. S. (1996) On Subjectivity: What You Can See Depends on Where You Stand and How 'Short' You Are. In: Alia, V., Brennan, B. & Hoffmaster, B. (eds.) *Deadlines and Diversity: Journalism Ethics in a Changing World*. Fernwood Publishing, Halifax, NS, pp. 59–69.

Dicken-Garcia, H. (1989) *Journalistic Standards in Nineteenth-Century America*. University of Wisconsin Press, Madison, WI.

Dicken-Garcia, H. (2005) The Transition from the Partisan to the Penny Press. In Knowlton, S. R. & Freeman, K. L. (eds.) *Fair and Balanced: A History of Journalistic Objectivity*. Vision Press, Northport, AL, pp. 90–9.

Donsbach, W. (1995) Lapdogs, Watchdogs, Junkyard Dogs. *Media Studies Journal* 9(4), 17–30.

Donsbach, W. & Klett, B. (1993) Subjective Objectivity: How Journalists in Four Countries Define a Key Term of Their Profession. *International Communication Gazette* 51(1), 53–83.

du Fresne, K. (2007) A Traditional Notion Undermined. *The Nelson Mail (NZ)*, 19 September.

Dunkley, C. (1997) Whose News Is It Anyway? *Financial Times [London (UK)]* 20 September, accessed 1 September 2005 at: <http://serbianlinks.freehosting.net/whosnews.htm>.

Dunlevy, M. (1998) Objectivity. In: Breen, M. (ed.) *Journalism: Theory and Practice*. Macleay Press, Paddington, NSW, pp. 119–38.

Durham, M. G. (1998) On the Relevance of Standpoint Epistemology to the Practice of Journalism: The Case for 'Strong Objectivity'. *Communication Theory* 8(2), 117–40.

Dwyer, T. & Martin, F. (2010) Updating Diversity of Voice Arguments for Online News Media. *Global Media Journal (Australian Edition)*, 4(1), accessed 15 December 2011 at: <http://www.commarts.uws.edu.au/gmjau/v4_2010_1/dwyer_martin_RA.html>.

El-Nawawy, M. (2004) Why Al-Jazeera Is the Most Popular Network in the Arab World. *Television Quarterly* 34(1), 10–15.

El-Nawawy, M. & Iskandar, A. (2003) *Al-Jazeera: The Story of the Network That Is Rattling Governments and Redefining Modern Journalism*. Westview Press, Cambridge, MA.

Emery, E. (1972) *The Press and America: An Interpretative History of the Mass Media*. Prentice-Hall, Englewood Cliffs, NJ.

Esser, F. (1998) Editorial Structures and Work Principles in British and German Newsrooms. *European Journal of Communication* 13(3), 375–405.

Evans, H. (1983) *Good Times, Bad Times*. Weidenfeld and Nicolson, London.

Fallows, J. M. (1996) *Breaking the News: How the Media Undermine American Democracy*. Pantheon Books, New York.

Fawcett, L. (2011) Why Peace Journalism Isn't News. In: Berkowitz, D. A. (ed.) *Cultural Meaning of News: A Text-Reader*. Sage, Los Angeles, CA, pp. 245–56.

Ferré, J. P. (2009) A Short History of Media Ethics in the United States. In: Wilkins, L. & Christians, C. G. (eds.) *Handbook of Mass Media Ethics*. Routledge, New York, pp. 15–27.

Fielding, H. (1806) *The Works of Henry Fielding, Esq.* J. Johnson, London.

Foucault, M. (1980) Truth and Power. In: Gordon, C. (ed.) *Power/Knowledge: Selected Interviews and Other Writings, 1972–1977*. Pantheon, New York, pp. 109–33.

Fray, P. (2011) Editors, Journalists and Audiences: Towards a New Compact, *The Sydney Morning Herald*, 17 November 2011, accessed 25 April 2012 at: <http://www.smh.com.au/national/editors-journalists-and-audiences-towards-a-new-compact-20111116-1nizh.html>.

Gans, H. J. (1979) *Deciding What's News: A Study of CBS Evening News, NBC Nightly News, Newsweek, and Time*. Pantheon Books, New York.

References

Gauthier, G. (1993) In Defence of a Supposedly Outdated Notion: The Range of Application of Journalistic Objectivity. *Canadian Journal of Communication* 18(4), 497–506, accessed 27 April 2012 at: <http://www.cjc-online.ca/viewarticle.php?id=201>.

Gitlin, T. (2003 [1980]) *The Whole World Is Watching: Mass Media in the Making & Unmaking of the New Left.* University of California Press, Berkeley, CA.

Glasgow University Media Group (1976) *Bad News.* Routledge & Kegan Paul, London.

Glasser, T. L. (1992) Objectivity and News Bias. In: Cohen, E. D. (ed.) *Philosophical Issues in Journalism.* Oxford, New York, pp. 176–83.

Golding, P. (1977) Media Professionalism in the Third World: The Transfer of an Ideology. In: Curran, J., Gurevitch, M. & Wollacott, J. (eds.) *Mass Communication and Society.* Edward Arnold, in association with The Open University Press, London.

Hackett, R. A. (1984) Decline of a Paradigm: Bias and Objectivity in News Media Studies. *Critical Studies in Mass Communication* 1(3), 229–59.

Hackett, R. A. (1996) An Exaggerated Death: Prefatory Comments on 'Objectivity' in Journalism. In: Alia, V., Brennan, B. & Hoffmaster, B. C. (eds.) *Deadlines and Diversity: Journalism Ethics in a Changing World.* Fernwood, Halifax, NS, pp. 40–3.

Hackett, R. A. & Zhao, Y. (1998) *Sustaining Democracy?: Journalism and the Politics of Objectivity.* Garamond Press, Toronto.

Hacking, I. (2000) *The Social Construction of What?* Harvard University Press, Cambridge, MA.

Hafez, K. (2002) Journalism Ethics Revisited: A Comparison of Ethics Codes in Europe, North Africa, the Middle East, and Muslim Asia. *Political Communication* 19(2), 225–50.

Hahn, M. & Thompson, H. S. (1997) *Writing on the Wall: An Interview with Hunter S. Thompson,* accessed 12 February 2012 at: <http://www.theatlantic.com/past/docs/unbound/graffiti/hunter.htm>.

Hall, S. (1973) Determinations of News Photographs. In: Cohen, S. & Young, J. (eds.) *The Manufacture of News.* Sage, Beverly Hills, CA, pp. 176–90.

Hall, S. (1977) Culture, the Media and the 'Ideological Effect'. In: Curran, J., Gurevitch, M. & Woollacott, J. (eds.) *Mass Communication and Society.* Edward Arnold, in association with the Open University Press, London, pp. 315–48.

Hallin, D. C. (1986) *The 'Uncensored War': The Media and Vietnam.* University of California Press, Berkeley, CA.

Hallin, D. C. & Mancini, P. (1984) Speaking of the President: Political Structure and Representational Form in U.S. and Italian Television News. *Theory and Society* 13(6), 829–50.

Hallin, D. C. & Mancini, P. (2004) *Comparing Media Systems: Three Models of Media and Politics.* Cambridge University Press, Cambridge.

Hallin, D. C. & Mancini, P. (eds.) (2012) *Comparing Media Systems beyond the Western World*. Cambridge University Press, Cambridge.

Hampton, M. (2008) The 'Objectivity' Ideal and Its Limitations in 20th-Century British Journalism. *Journalism Studies* 9(4), 477–93.

Hanitzsch, T. (2004) Journalists as Peacekeeping Force? Peace Journalism and Mass Communication Theory. *Journalism Studies* 5(4), 483–95.

Hanitzsch, T. (2007) Deconstructing Journalism Culture: Toward a Universal Theory. *Communication Theory* 17(4), 367–85.

Harber, A. (2003) Credibility and Authority Are Qualities the SABC Needs. *All Africa Global Media*, 13 June, accessed 27 April 2012 at: <http://allafrica.com/stories/200306130416.html>.

Harding, S. (1991) *Whose Science? Whose Knowledge? Thinking from Women's Lives*. Cornell University Press, Ithaca, NY.

Harding, S. (1993) Rethinking Standpoint Epistemology: What Is 'Strong Objectivity'. In: Alcoff, L. & Potter, E. (eds.) *Feminist Epistemologies*. Routledge, New York, pp. 49–82.

Hargreaves, I. (2005) *Journalism: A Very Short Introduction*. Oxford University Press, Oxford.

Harless, J. D. (1990) Media Ethics, Ideology, and Personal Constructs: Mapping Professional Enigmas. *Journal of Mass Media Ethics* 5(4), 217–32.

Harrington, H. F. & Frankenberg, T. T. (1924) *Essentials in Journalism*. Revised Edition. Ginn & Company, Boston.

Harrison, J. (2005) *News*. Routledge, London.

Hartley, J. (1982) *Understanding News*. Methuen, London.

Hartley, J. (1992) *The Politics of Pictures: The Creation of the Public in the Age of Popular Media*. Routledge, London.

Hartley, J. (1996) *Popular Reality: Journalism, Modernity, Popular Culture*. Arnold, London.

Hartley, J. (2000) Communicative Democracy in a Redactional Society: The Future of Journalism Studies. *Journalism* 1(1), 39–48.

Hayashi, K. (2011) Questioning Journalism Ethics in the Global Age: How Japanese News Media Report and Support Immigration Law Revision. In: Fortner, R. S. & Fackler, P. M. (eds.) *The Handbook of Global Communication and Media Ethics, Vol. II*. Wiley-Blackwell, Malden, MA, pp. 534–53.

Hemánus, P. (1976) Objectivity in News Transmission. *Journal of Communication* 26(4), 102–7.

Herman, E. S. & Chomsky, N. (1988) *Manufacturing Consent: The Political Economy of the Mass Media*. Pantheon Books, New York.

Hjørland, B. (2005) Empiricism, Rationalism and Positivism in Library and Information Science. *Journal of Documentation* 61(1), 130–55.

Holbert, R. L. & Zubric, S. J. (2000) A Comparative Analysis: Objective and Public Journalism Techniques. *Newspaper Research Journal* 21(4), 50–67.

References

Hulteng, J. L. (1973) *The Opinion Function: Editorial and Interpretive Writing for the News Media.* Harper & Row, New York.

Hume, M. (1997) *Whose War Is It Anyway?: The Dangers of the Journalism of Attachment.* BM InformInc, London.

Iggers, J. (1998) *Good News, Bad News: Journalism Ethics and the Public Interest.* Westview, Boulder, CO.

Ingelhart, L. E. (1987) *Press Freedoms: A Descriptive Calendar of Concepts, Interpretations, Events, and Court Actions, from 4000 BC to the Present.* Greenwood Press, New York.

Irvine, D. (2011) *Al-Jazeera's D.C. Bureau Chief: 'I Don't Know What Objective Journalism Is'*, Accuracy In Media, accessed 13 December 2011 at: <http://www.aim.org/don-irvine-blog/al-jazeeras-d-c-bureau-chief-i-dont-know-what-objective-journalism-is/>.

Irwin, W. (1969 [1911]) *The American Newspaper.* Iowa State University Press, Ames, IA.

Ivison, D. (2003) Arguing About Ethics. In: Lumby, C. & Probyn, E. (eds.) *Remote Control: New Media, New Ethics.* Cambridge University Press, Cambridge, pp. 25–41.

James, W. (1998 [1907]) *Pragmatism (a New Name for Some Old Ways of Thinking). A Series of Lectures by William James, 1906–1907.* Arc Manor, Rockville, MD.

Janowitz, M. (1975) Professional Models in Journalism: The Gatekeeper and the Advocate. *Journalism Quarterly* 52(4), 618–62.

Janowitz, M. (1977) The Journalistic Profession and the Mass Media. In: Ben-David, J. & Clark, T. N. (eds.) *Culture and Its Creators: Essays in Honor of Edward Shils.* University of Chicago Press, Chicago, IL, pp. 72–96.

Johnson, T. & Fahmy, S. (2006) *See No Evil, Hear No Evil, Judge as Evil?: Examining the Degree to Which Users of Al-Jazeera English-Language Website Transfer Credibility Views to its Satellite Network Counterpart*, presented at International Communication Association, 2006 Annual Meeting, 1–39.

Jones, P. (2011) *From Fourth Estate to Media Populism*, presented at: Representation and Its Discontents, 25 February, The University of Sydney, Australia, accessed 27 April 2012 at: <http: sydney.edu.au/arts/sdi/papers/PJ_populism.pdf>.

Josephi, B. (2007) Internationalizing the Journalistic Professional Model: Imperatives and Impediments. *Global Media and Communication* 3(4), 300–6.

Kant, I. (1997 [1781]) *Critique of Pure Reason.* Cambridge University Press, Cambridge.

Kaplan, R. L. (2002) *Politics and the American Press: The Rise of Objectivity, 1865–1920.* Cambridge University Press, Cambridge.

Keane, J. (2011) *Democracy in the Age of Google, Facebook and Wikileaks*, 18 May, presented at: The University of Melbourne, Australia, accessed 27 April

2012 at: <http://johnkeane.net/18/topics-of-interest/democracy-21st-century/democracy-in-the-age-of-google-facebook-and-wikileaks-2>.

Keil, R. (2005) An American Original. *American Journalism Review* 27(2), 60–2.

Kelly, B. M. (2005) Objectivity and the Trappings of Professionalism, 1900–1950. In: Knowlton, S. R. & Freeman, K. L. (eds.) *Fair and Balanced: A History of Journalistic Objectivity*. Vision Press, Northport, AL, pp. 149–66.

Kessler, L. & McDonald, D. (1989) *Mastering the Message: Media Writing with Substance and Style*. Wadsworth, Belmont, CA.

Kharel, P. (1996) Session 2: Asian Values in Journalism: Do they Exist? In: M. Masterton (comp.), *Asian Values in Journalism*. Asian Media, Information and Communication Centre, Singapore, pp. 29–34.

Kielbowicz, R. B. (1987) News Gathering by Mail in the Age of the Telegraph: Adapting to a New Technology. *Technology and Culture* 28(1), 26–41.

Kieran, M. (1997) *Media Ethics: A Philosophical Approach*. Praeger, Westport, CT.

Kingston, M. (2003) Diary of a Webdiarist: Ethics Goes Online. In: Lumby, C. & Probyn, E. (eds.) *Remote Control: New Media, New Ethics*. Cambridge University Press, Cambridge, pp. 159–72.

Kinsley, M. (2006) The Twilight of Objectivity: How Opinion Journalism Could Change the Face of the News, *Slate*, accessed 12 February 2012 at: <http://www.slate.com/id/2139042>.

Klaidman, S. & Beauchamp, T. L. (1987) *The Virtuous Journalist*. Oxford University Press, New York.

Klotzer, C. L. (2009) The Myth of Objectivity. *St Louis Journalism Review* 38(311), 8.

Knowlton, S. R. (2005a) A History of Journalistic Objectivity. In: Knowlton, S. R. & Freeman, K. L. (eds.) *Fair and Balanced: A History of Journalistic Objectivity*. Vision Press, Northport, AL, pp. 3–5.

Knowlton, S. R. (2005b) Into the 1960s and Into the Crucible. In: Knowlton, S. R. & Freeman, K. L. (eds.) *Fair and Balanced: A History of Journalistic Objectivity*. Vision Press, Northport, AL, pp. 221–35.

Knowlton, S. R. & Freeman, K. L. (eds.) (2005) *Fair and Balanced: A History of Journalistic Objectivity*. Vision Press, Northport, AL.

Koch, T. (1990) *The News as Myth: Fact and Context in Journalism*. Greenwood Press, Westport, CT.

Köcher, R. (1986) Bloodhounds or Missionaries: Role Definitions of German and British Journalists. *European Journal of Communication* 1(1), 43–64.

Koppel, T. (2010) Ted Koppel: Olbermann, O'Reilly and the Death of Real News. *The Washington Post*, 14 November, accessed 27 April 2012 at: <http://www.washingtonpost.com/wp-dyn/content/article/2010/11/12/AR2010111202857_pf.html>.

Kramer, M. (1995) Breakable Rules for Literary Journalists. In: Sims, N. &

References

Kramer, M. (eds.) *Literary Journalism: A New Collection of the Best American Nonfiction*. Ballantine Books, New York, pp. 21–34.

Kramer, M. H. (2007) *Objectivity and the Rule of Law*. Cambridge University Press, New York.

Kurspahic, K. (1995) Neutrality vs. Objectivity in Bosnia. *Media Studies Journal* 9(4), 91–8.

Kurspahic, K. (2003) Objectivity without Neutrality. *Nieman Reports* 57(1), 79–81.

Lahey, T. A. (1924) *The Morals of Newspaper Making*. University Press, Notre Dame, IN.

Lasica, J. D. (2005) The Cost of Ethics: Influence Peddling in the Blogosphere. *Online Journalism Review*, accessed 27 April 2012 at: <http://www.ojr.org/ojr/stories/050217lasica/>.

Latham, K. (2000) Nothing but the Truth: News Media, Power and Hegemony in South China. *The China Quarterly* No. 163 (September), 633–54.

Layton, S. (1998) Pacific Island Journalists. In: Weaver, D. H. (ed.), *The Global Journalist: News People Around the World*. Hampton Press, Cresskill, NJ, pp. 125–40.

Lee, C.-C. (1990) Mass Media: Of China, About China. In: Lee, C.-C. (ed.) *Voices of China: The Interplay of Politics and Journalism*. Guildford, New York, pp. 3–29.

Lee, C.-C. (1996) Session 3: Social and Cultural Influences on Journalism Values in Asia? In: M. Masterton (comp.), *Asian Values in Journalism*. Asian Media, Information and Communication Centre, Singapore, pp. 58–64.

Li, L. (1994) The Historical Fate of 'Objective Reporting' in China. In: Lee, C.-C. (ed.) *China's Media, Media's China*. Westview, Boulder, CO, pp. 225–37.

Lichtenberg, J. (1991a) In Defense of Objectivity. In: Curran, J. & Gurevitch, M. (eds.) *Mass Media and Society*. Edward Arnold, London, pp. 216–31.

Lichtenberg, J. (1991b) Objectivity and Its Enemies. *The Responsive Community* 2(1), 59–69.

Lippmann, W. (1914) *Drift and Mastery: An Attempt to Diagnose the Current Unrest*. H. Holt & Co., New York.

Lippmann, W. (1920) *Liberty and the News*. Harcourt, Brace & Howe, New York.

Lippmann, W. (1922) *Public Opinion*. Harcourt, Brace & Company, New York.

Lippmann, W. & Merz, C. (1920) A Test of the News: An Examination of the News Reports in the New York Times on Aspects of the Russian Revolution of Special Importance to Americans March 1917–March 1920. *New Republic* XXIII Part II [Supplement] (296), 1–42.

Lovink, G. (2007) *Zero Comments: Blogging and Critical Internet Culture*. Taylor and Francis, New York.

Lowe, B. (1996) Session 2: Asian Values in Journalism: Do they Exist? In:

References

M. Masterton (comp.), *Asian Values in Journalism*. Asian Media, Information and Communication Centre, Singapore, pp. 34–39.

Loyn, D. (2007) Good Journalism or Peace Journalism?, *Conflict & Communication Online*, 6(2), 1–10, accessed 27 April 2012 at: <http://cco.regener-online.de/2007_2/pdf/loyn.pdf>.

Lynch, J. (2007) Peace Journalism and Its Discontents, *Conflict & Communication Online*, 6(2), 1–13, accessed 27 April 2012 at: <http://www.cco.regener-online.de/2007_2/pdf/lynch.pdf>.

Lynch, J. & Conflict & Peace Forums (2002) *Reporting the World: A Practical Checklist for the Ethical Reporting of Conflicts in the 21st Century, Produced by Journalists, for Journalists*. Conflict & Peace Forums, Taplow.

Lynch, J. & Galtung, J. (2010) *Reporting Conflict: New Directions in Peace Journalism*. University of Queensland Press, St Lucia, QLD.

Lynch, J. & McGoldrick, A. (2005) *Peace Journalism*. Hawthorn, Stroud.

Lynch, M. (2006) *Voices of the New Arab Public: Iraq, Al-Jazeera, and Middle East Politics Today*. Columbia University Press, New York.

Macaulay, T. B. (1828) Hallam's Constitutional History. *The Edinburgh Review* 48 (September).

MacDougall, C. D. (1938) *Interpretative Reporting*. The Macmillan Company, New York.

MacDougall, C. D. (1947) What Newspaper Publishers Should Know About Professors of Journalism. *Journalism Quarterly* 24(1), 1–8.

Machan, T. R. (2004) *Objectivity: Recovering Determinate Reality in Philosophy, Science, and Everyday Life*. Ashgate, Aldershot.

Mancini, P. (2000) Political Complexity and Alternative Models of Journalism: The Italian Case. In: Curran, J. & Park, M.-J. (eds.) *De-Westernizing Media Studies*. Routledge, London, pp. 265–78.

Maras, S. (2012) *Contesting the Public Interest: The Selling of the Pentagon as a Case Study in Objectivity*, presented at: Australia and New Zealand Communication Association Annual Conference, Adelaide, South Australia, 4–6 July.

Markel, L. (1953) The Case for 'Interpretation'. *The Bulletin of the American Society of Newspaper Editors* (353), 1–2.

Masterton, M. (ed.) (1996) *Asian Values in Journalism*. Asian Media, Information and Communication Centre, Singapore.

Mattelart, A. (1980) *Mass Media, Ideologies, and the Revolutionary Movement*. Harvester, Brighton.

May, R. (1953) Is the Press Unfair to McCarthy? *The New Republic* 128, 10–12.

Mazwai, T. (2002) Journalists Are Affected by Religions, Cultural Beliefs. *Business Day*, 16 September.

McCombs, M. E. & Shaw, D. (1972) The Agenda-Setting Function of Mass Media. *Public Opinion Quarterly* 36(2), 176–87.

McDonald, D. (1975 [1971]) Is Objectivity Possible? In: Merrill, J. C. & Barney,

References

R. D. (eds.) *Ethics and the Press: Readings in Mass Media Morality.* Hastings House, New York, pp. 69–88.

McGill, D. (2004) *The Fading Mystique of an Objective Press.* The McGill Report, accessed 12 February 2012 at: <http://www.mcgillreport.org/objectivity.htm>.

McGill, D. (2008) *The True Promise of Citizen Journalism.* The McGill Report, accessed 22 December 2011 at: <http://www.mcgillreport.org/truepromise>.

McGoldrick, A. (2006) War Journalism and 'Objectivity', *Conflict & Communication Online,* 5(2), 1–7, accessed 27 April 2012 at: <http://www.cco.regener-online.de/2006_2/pdf/mcgoldrick.pdf>.

McKnight, D. (2001) Facts Versus Stories: From Objective to Interpretive Reporting. *Media International Australia incorporating Culture and Policy* No. 99 (May), 49–58.

McLaughlin, G. (2002) War, Objectivity, and the Journalism of Attachment. In: *The War Correspondent.* Pluto Press, London, pp. 153–81.

McNair, B. (2000) Power, Profit, Corruption, and Lies: The Russian Media in the 1990s. In: Curran, J. & Park, M.-J. (eds.) *De-Westernizing Media Studies.* Routledge, London, pp. 79–94.

McQuail, D. (1986) From Bias to Objectivity and Back: Competing Paradigms for News Analysis and a Pluralistic Alternative. In: McCormack, T. (ed.) *Studies in Communications: A Research Annual.* JAI Press, Greenwich, CT, pp. 1–36.

McQuail, D. (1992) *Media Performance: Mass Communication and the Public Interest.* Sage, London.

Media Alliance (2010) *Life in the Clickstream II.* Media Entertainment & Arts Alliance, accessed 27 April 2012 at: <http://www.thefutureofjournalism.org.au/foj_report_vii.pdf>.

Media Entertainment & Arts Alliance (1999) *Media Alliance Code of Ethics.* Media Entertainment & Arts Alliance, accessed 24 November 2011 at: <http://www.alliance.org.au/code-of-ethics.html>.

Merritt, D. & Rosen, J. (1998) Imagining Public Journalism: An Editor and a Scholar Reflect on the Birth of an Idea. In: Lambeth, E. B., Meyer, P. & Thorson, E. (eds.) *Assessing Public Journalism.* University of Missouri Press, Columbia, MO, pp. 36–56.

Methvin, E. H. (1975 [1970]) Objectivity and the Tactics of Terrorists. In: Merrill, J. C. & Barney, R. D. (eds.) *Ethics and the Press: Readings in Mass Media Morality.* Hastings House, New York, pp. 199–205.

Meyer, P. (1995) *Public Journalism and the Problem of Objectivity,* accessed 28 February 2005 at: <http://www.unc.edu/~pmeyer/ire95pj.htm>.

Miles, H. (2005) *Al-Jazeera: How Arab TV News Challenged the World.* Abacus, London.

Mill, J. S. (1997 [1859]) Of the Liberty of Thought and Discussion. In: Bromley, M. & O'Malley, T. (eds.) *A Journalism Reader.* Routledge, London.

References

Min, J. K. (2005) Journalism as a Conversation. *Nieman Reports* 59(4), 17–19.

Mindich, D. T. Z. (1998) *Just the Facts: How 'Objectivity' Came to Define American Journalism*. New York University Press, New York.

Miraldi, R. (1990) *Muckraking and Objectivity: Journalism's Colliding Traditions*. Greenwood Press, New York.

Mirando, J. A. (1993) *Journalism's First Textbook: Creating a News Reporting Body of Knowledge*, presented at 76th Annual Meeting of the Association for Education in Journalism and Mass Communication, Kansas City, Missouri, 11–14 August.

Mirando, J. A. (2001) Embracing Objectivity Early On: Journalism Textbooks of the 1800s. *Journal of Mass Media Ethics* 16(1), 23–32.

Morgan, W. (1992) Balance and Related Concepts: A Few Thoughts. *Canadian Journal of Communication* 17(1), accessed 27 April 2012 at: <http://www.cjc-online.ca/index.php/journal/article/view/652/558>.

Morrison, A. & Tremewan, P. (1992) The Myth of Objectivity. In: Comrie, M. & McGregor, J. (eds.) *Whose News?* Dunmore Press, Palmerston North, pp. 114–32.

Mott, F. L. (1953) Objective News *Versus* Qualified Report. In: *The News in America*. Cambridge University Press, Cambridge, pp. 67–87.

Moussa, M. B. (2007) Review of *Al-Jazeera: The Inside Story of the Arab News Channel That Is Challenging the West*, by Hugh Miles, *Canadian Journal of Communication*, 32(1), 149–52, accessed 27 April 2012 at: <http://www.cjc-online.ca/index.php/journal/article/download/1731/1847>.

Myrick, H. A. (2002) The Search for Objectivity in Journalism. *USA Today* 131(2690), 50–52.

Nagel, T. (1986) *The View from Nowhere*. Oxford University Press, New York.

Nasution, Z. (1996) Session 3: Social and Cultural Influences on Journalism Values in Asia? In: M. Masterton (comp.), *Asian Values in Journalism*. Asian Media, Information and Communication Centre, Singapore, pp. 52–55.

National Union of Journalists [UK] (2011) *NUJ Code of Conduct*, National Union of Journalists, accessed 24 November 2011 at: <http://www.nuj.org.uk/innerPagenuj.html?docid=174>.

Nieman Fellows (1950) Reporting 'Background'. *Nieman Reports* 4(2), 29–32.

Nip, J. Y. M. & To, Y.-M. (1999) Television Coverage: Objectivity and Public Service. In: Kuan, H.-C., Lau, S.-K., Kin-Sheun, L. & Wong, T. K.-Y. (eds.) *Power Transfer and Electoral Politics: The First Legislative Election in the Hong Kong Special Administrative Region*. Chinese University Press, Hong Kong, pp. 215–52.

Nolan, D. & Marjoribanks, T. (2006) Objectivity, Impartiality and the Governance of Journalism. In: Colic-Peisker, V., Tilbury, F. & McNamara, B. (eds.) The Australian Sociological Association 2006 Conference Proceedings. University of Western Australia and Murdoch University, 4–7 December, accessed 27 April 2012 at: <http://www.tasa.org.au/conferences/

conferencepapers06/papers/Culture,%20Media%20and%20Communication/
Nolan,Marjoribanks.pdf>.

Norris, P. (2000) *A Virtuous Circle: Political Communications in Postindustrial Societies*. Cambridge University Press, Cambridge.

Novack, G. E. (1968) *Empiricism and Its Evolution: A Marxist View*. Pathfinder Press, New York.

Novick, P. (1988) *That Noble Dream: The 'Objectivity Question' and the American Historical Profession*. Cambridge University Press, Cambridge.

Noyes, N., Jr. (1953) Design for Impressionistic School of Reporting. *Editor & Publisher* 9 May, 11, 63.

O'Donnell, P. (2007) Journalism and Philosophy: Remembering Clem Lloyd. In: Heekeren, M. V. (ed.) *Australian Media Traditions 2007*, Bathurst, Australia, accessed 27 April 2012 at: <http://www.csu.edu.au/special/amt/publication/odonnell.pdf>.

Ochs, A. S. (1896) Business Announcement. *New York Times*, 19 August, p. 4.

Ognianova, E. & Endersby, J. W. (1996) Objectivity Revisited: A Spatial Model of Political Ideology and Mass Communication. *Journalism & Mass Communication Monographs* 159 (October), 1–32.

Olasky, M. (1996) Biblical Objectivity, *World Magazine*, accessed 14 November 2011 at: <http://www.worldmag.com/world/olasky/truthc1.html>.

Olasky, M. (2006) *New Journalistic Standards (Including Biblical Objectivity) Coming*, accessed 14 November 2011 at: <http://www.humanevents.com/article.php?print=yes& id=12309>.

Olbermann, K. (2010) *False Promise of 'Objectivity' Proves 'Truth' Superior to 'Fact'*, Countdown with Keith Olbermann, accessed 16 December 2011 at: <http://video.msnbc.msn.com/countdown-with-keith-olbermann/4020522 140205221>.

Orwell, G. (1965 [1947]) Why I Write. In: *Decline of the English Murder, and Other Essays*. Penguin Books, Harmondsworth, pp. 180–8.

Overholser, G. (2006) *On Behalf of Journalism: A Manifesto for Change*, accessed 21 November 2011 at: <http://www.annenbergpublicpolicycenter.org/Overholser/20061011_JournStudy.pdf>.

Park, R. E. (1923) The Natural History of the Newspaper. *The American Journal of Sociology* 29(3), 273–89.

Park, R. E. (1940) News as a Form of Knowledge: A Chapter in the Sociology of Knowledge. *The American Journal of Sociology* 45(5), 669–86.

Parliamentary Standing Commitee on Broadcasting (1946) *14th Report: The Broadcasting of News*. Document no. 63, 5 July. Parliamentary Standing Commitee on Broadcasting, Canberra.

Pavlik, J. V. (2001) *Journalism and New Media*. Columbia University Press, New York.

Pax, S. (2003) *The Baghdad Blog*. Atlantic on behalf of Guardian Newspapers, London.

Pearson, M. & Polden, M. (2011) *The Journalists Guide to Media Law*. Allen & Unwin, Crows Nest, NSW.

Petersen, N. (1985) The ABC, the State and Journalistic Objectivity, 1932–42. *Australian Journalism Review* 7(1& 2), 74–86.

Petersen, N. (1993) *News Not Views: The ABC, the Press, & Politics 1932–1947*. Hale and Iremonger, Sydney.

Phillips, E. B. (1977) Approaches to Objectivity: Journalistic Versus Social Science Perspectives. In: Kline, G. F., Hirsch, P. M. & Morris, P. V. (eds.) *Strategies for Communication Research*. Sage, Beverly Hills, CA, pp. 63–77.

Phillips, G. & Lindgren, M. (2006) *The Australian Broadcast Journalism Manual*. Oxford University Press, South Melbourne, Vic.

Pilger, J. (2006) *War by Media. Breaking the Silence: War, Lies and Empire*, presented at: Heyman Center for the Humanities at Columbia University, New York, 14 April, accessed 11 February 2008 at: <http://www.johnpilger.com/page.asp?partid=267>.

Polish Journalists' Association (SDP), et al. (1995) *Media Ethics Charter*, EthicNet: Journalism Ethics, accessed 3 May 2012 at: <http://ethicnet.uta.fi/poland/media_ethics_charter>.

Porwancher, A. (2011) Objectivity's Prophet: Adolph S. Ochs and the New York Times, 1896–1935. *Journalism History* 36(4), 186–95.

Pray, I. C. (1855) *Memoirs of James Gordon Bennett and His Times*. Stringer and Townsend, New York.

Putnam, H. (1984) The Craving for Objectivity. *New Literary History* 15(2), 229–39.

Pyle, R. (2005) *19th-Century Papers Shed New Light on Origin of the Associated Press*, accessed 20 September 2011 at: <http://www.ap.org/pages/about/whatsnew/wn_013106a.html>.

Reeb, R. H. (1999) *Taking Journalism Seriously: 'Objectivity' as a Partisan Cause*. University Press of America, Lanham, MD.

Reese, S. D. (1990) The News Paradigm and the Ideology of Objectivity: A Socialist at the *Wall Street Journal*. *Critical Studies in Mass Communication* 7, 390–409.

Reese, S. D. (2008) Theorizing a Globalized Journalism. In: Löffelholz, M. & Weaver, D. (eds.) *Global Journalism Research: Theories, Methods, Findings, Future*. Blackwell, Malden, MA, pp. 240–52.

Reifenberg, J. (1982) The New York Times. In: Rice, M. & Cooney, W. J. A. (eds.) *Reporting U.S.–European Relations: Four Nations, Four Newspapers*. Pergamon Press, New York, pp. 24–61.

Reston, J. B. (1945) The Job of the Reporter. In: Garst, R. E. (ed.) *The Newspaper, Its Making and Its Meaning*. C. Scribner's Sons, New York, pp. 92–108.

Rettberg, J. W. (2008) *Blogging*. Polity, Cambridge.

Richards, I. (2005) *Quagmires and Quandaries: Exploring Journalism Ethics*. University of New South Wales Press, Sydney, NSW.

References

Ricketson, M. (2001) Gang of Two. *The Australian*, 13 June.

Righter, R. (1978) *Whose News?: Politics, the Press and the Third World.* Burnett Books in association with André Deutsch, London.

Romano, C. (1986) The Grisly Truth About Bare Facts. In: Manoff, R. K. & Schudson, M. (eds.) *Reading the News.* Pantheon Books, New York, pp. 38–78.

Rorty, R. (1991) *Objectivity, Relativism, and Truth.* Cambridge University Press, Cambridge.

Rorty, R. (1998) *Truth and Progress.* Cambridge University Press, New York.

Rosen, J. (1993) Beyond Objectivity. *Nieman Reports* 47(4), 48–53.

Rosen, J. (1994) Making Things More Public: On the Political Responsibility of the Media Intellectual. *Critical Studies in Mass Communication* 11(4), 363–88.

Rosen, J. (2003) *The View from Nowhere*, Pressthink: Ghost of Democracy in the Media Machine, accessed 18 February 2012 at: <http://archive.pressthink.org/2003/09/18/jennings.html>.

Rosen, J. (2004a) *What Time Is It in Political Journalism?*, Pressthink: Ghost of Democracy in the Media Machine, accessed 18 February 2012 at: <http://archive.pressthink.org/2004/02/23/gopnik_time.html>.

Rosen, J. (2004b) *Journalism Is Itself a Religion: Special Essay on Launch of the Revealer*, Pressthink: Ghost of Democracy in the Media Machine, accessed 14 November 2011 at: <http://archive.pressthink.org/2004/01/07/press_religion.html>.

Rosen, J. (2010a) *Objectivity as a Form of Persuasion: A Few Notes for Marcus Brauchli*, Pressthink: Ghost of Democracy in the Media Machine, accessed 18 February 2012 at: <http://archive.pressthink.org/2010/07/07/obj_persuasion.html>.

Rosen, J. (2010b) *The View from Nowhere: Questions and Answers*, Pressthink: Ghost of Democracy in the Media Machine, accessed 18 February 2012 at: <http://pressthink.org/2010/11/the-view-from-nowhere-questions-and-answers/>.

Rosenthal, A. M. (1969) In *New York Times Company records (Box 70, in the Editorial Policy [General] folder for 1967–1970).* New York Public Library.

Ross, C. G. (1911) *The Writing of News: A Handbook.* Henry Holt and Company, New York.

Rosteck, T. (1989) Irony, Argument, and Reportage in Television Documentary: *See It Now* Versus Senator McCarthy. *Quarterly Journal of Speech* 75 (3 August), 277–98.

Rule, P. C. (1971) CBS, the White House and the Myth of Objectivity. *America* 22 May, 541–2.

Rusbridger, A. (2007) *Ombudsmen in the Digital Future*, presented at: Conference of the Organization of News Ombudsmen, Harvard University, Cambridge, MA, 21 May, accessed 27 April 2012 at: <http://newsombudsmen.org/rusbridger.html>.

References

Russell, N. (1995) Public Journalism: An Old Game with a New Name?, *Media*, 2(1), 16–17.

Ryan, M. (2001) Journalistic Ethics, Objectivity, Existential Journalism, Standpoint Epistemology, and Public Journalism. *Journal of Mass Media Ethics* 16(1), 3–22.

Saad, L. (2002) *Al-Jazeera: Arabs Rate Its Objectivity*, Gallup, 23 April, accessed 27 April 2012 at: <http://www.gallup.com/poll/5857/aljazeera-arabs-rate-its-objectivity.aspx>.

Sambrook, R. (2004) *America – Holding onto Objectivity*, presented at: The Poliak Lecture, Columbia University, 27 April, accessed 24 November 2011 at: <http://www.bbc.co.uk/print/pressoffice/speeches/stories/sambrook_poliak.shtml>.

Sánchez-Aranda, J. J. & Barrera, C. (2003) The Birth of Modern Newsrooms in the Spanish Press. *Journalism Studies* 4(4), 489–500.

Santos, J. P. (1997) (Re)Imagining America. In: Dennis, E. E. & Pease, E. C. (eds.) *The Media in Black and White*. Transaction Books, New Brunswick, NJ, pp. 121–7.

Sargent, G. (2012) What Are Newspapers For? *The Washington Post*, accessed 27 April 2012 at: <http://www.washingtonpost.com/blogs/plum-line/post/what-are-newspapers-for/2012/01/12/gIQAuUCqtP_blog.html>.

Schiller, D. (1979) An Historical Approach to Objectivity and Professionalism in American Newsgathering. *Journal of Communication* 29(4), 46–57.

Schiller, D. (1981) *Objectivity and the News: The Public and the Rise of Commercial Journalism*. University of Pennsylvania Press, Philadelphia, PA.

Schudson, M. (1978) *Discovering the News: A Social History of American Newspapers*. Basic Books, New York.

Schudson, M. (1995) *The Power of News*. Harvard University Press, Cambridge, MA.

Schudson, M. (2001) The Objectivity Norm in American Journalism. *Journalism* 2(2), 149–70.

Schudson, M. (2008) The 'Lippmann-Dewey Debate' and the Invention of Walter Lippmann as an Anti-Democrat 1986–1996. *International Journal of Communication* 2, 1031–42.

Schudson, M. & Anderson, C. (2009) Objectivity, Professionalism, and Truth Seeking in Journalism. In: Wahl-Jorgensen, K. & Hanitzsch, T. (eds.) *The Handbook of Journalism Studies*. Routledge, New York, pp. 88–101.

Schultz, J. (1998) *Reviving the Fourth Estate: Democracy, Accountability and the Media*. Cambridge University Press, Cambridge.

Seaton, J. (2005) *Carnage and the Media: The Making and Breaking of News about Violence*. Allen Lane, London.

Shapiro, B. J. (2000) *A Culture of Fact: England, 1550–1720*. Cornell University Press, Ithaca, NY.

References

Shaw, D. L. (1967) News Bias and the Telegraph: A Study of Historical Change. *Journalism Quarterly* 44(1), 3–12.

Shepard, A. C. (1994) The Gospel of Public Journalism. *American Journalism Review* 16(7), 29–34.

Sherwin, A. (2010) Mark Thompson: Britain Needs a Channel Like Fox News. *The Guardian*, 17 December, accessed 27 April 2012 at: <http://www.guard ian.co.uk/media/2010/dec/17/mark-thompson-bbc-fox-news/print>.

Shi, D. E. (1995) *Facing Facts: Realism in American Thought and Culture, 1850–1920.* Oxford University Press, New York.

Shuman, E. L. (1894) *Steps into Journalism: Helps and Hints for Young Writers.* Correspondence School of Journalism, Evanston, IL.

Siebert, F. S., Peterson, T. & Schramm, W. (1956) *Four Theories of the Press: The Authoritarian, Libertarian, Social Responsibility and Soviet Communist Concepts of What the Press Should Be and Do.* University of Illinois Press, Urbana, IL.

Sigal, L. V. (1973) *Reporters and Officials: The Organization and Politics of Newsmaking.* D. C. Heath, Lexington, MA.

Sinclair, U. (1919) *The Brass Check, a Study of American Journalism.* The author, Pasadena, CA.

Singh, M. (2006) PM Gives Away the Goenka Journalism Awards. Express media awards. New Delhi, 12 April, accessed 1 May 2012 at: <http://pmindia. nic.in/speech-details.php?nodeid=301>.

Smith, A. (1978) The Long Road to Objectivity and Back Again. In: Boyce, G., Curran, J. & Wingate, P. (eds.) *Newspaper History: From the Seventeenth Century to the Present Day.* Constable & Company, London, pp. 153–71.

Society of Professional Journalists (1973) *Code of Ethics Sigma Delta Chi [1973],* Center for the Study of Ethics in the Professions, accessed 24 November 2011 at: <http://ethics.iit.edu/indexOfCodes-2.php?key=18_479_762>.

Society of Professional Journalists (1996) *Society of Professional Journalists – Code of Ethics [September 1996],* Center for the Study of Ethics in the Professions, accessed 24 November 2011 at: <http://ethics.iit.edu/indexOf- Codes-2.php?key=18_479_764>.

Spivak, C. (2010) The Fact Checking Explosion. *American Journalism Review* 32(4).

Starkey, G. (2007) *Balance and Bias in Journalism: Representation, Regulation and Democracy.* Palgrave Macmillan, Basingstoke.

Stensaas, H. S. (1986) Development of the Objectivity Ethic in US Daily Newspapers. *Journal of Mass Media Ethics* 2(1), 50–60.

Stoker, K. (1995) Existential Objectivity: Freeing Journalists to Be Ethical. *Journal of Mass Media Ethics* 10(1), 5–22.

Streckfuss, R. (1990) Objectivity in Journalism: A Search and a Reassessment. *Journalism Quarterly* 67(4), 973–83.

Strout, R. L. (1950) Ordeal by Publicity. *The Christian Science Monitor*, 27 May.

References

Sugiyama, M. (2000) Media and Power in Japan. In: Curran, J. & Park, M.-J. (eds.) *De-Westernizing Media Studies*. Routledge, London, pp. 191–201.

Taflinger, R. F. (1996) The Myth of Objectivity in Journalism: A Commentary, accessed 13 June 2012, <http://public.wsu.edu/~taflinge/mythobj.html>.

Tait, R. (2007) *From Seesaw to Wagon Wheel: Safeguarding Impartiality in the 21st Century*, BBC Trust, accessed 27 April 2012 at: <http://www.bbc.co.uk/ bbctrust/our_work/other/century21.shtml>.

Taylor, C. A. & Condit, C. M. (1988) Objectivity and Elites: A Creation Science Trial. *Critical Studies in Mass Communication* 5(4), 293–312.

Tharoor, I. (2011) Why the US Needs Al Jazeera, *Time US*, accessed 22 February 2012 at: <http://www.time.com/time/nation/article/0,8599,205293 4,00.html>.

The Economist (2011) Impartiality: The Foxification of News. *The Economist*, 7 July, accessed 27 April 2012 at: <http://www.economist.com/node/18904 112>.

The New York Times (1952) Better Reporting Held Modern Need. *The New York Times*, 27 August.

The New York Times Company (2005) *The New York Times Company Policy on Ethics in Journalism*, accessed 23 October 2011 at: <http://www.nytco. com/press/ethics.html>.

The Times [London]. (1852) The Earl of Derby Remarked with Considerable . . . *The Times*, 7 February.

Thomas, A. (1980) *Broadcast and Be Damned: The ABC's First Two Decades*. Melbourne University Press, Melbourne.

Thompson, H. S. (1973) *Fear and Loathing: On the Campaign Trail '72*. Straight Arrow Books, San Francisco, CA.

Thompson, H. S. (1994) *Better Than Sex: Confessions of a Political Junkie*. Random House, New York.

Thompson, M. (2005) *Broadcasting and the Idea of the Public*, presented at Worth Abbey Gaudium Et Spes Conference, 5 July, accessed 27 April 2012 at: <http://www.bbc.co.uk/print/pressoffice/speeches/stories/thompson_catholic. shtml>.

Thompson, M. (2006) *Whose Side Are We On?*, presented at: International Press Institute World Congress, Edinburgh, 28 May, accessed 27 April 2012 at: <http://www.bbc.co.uk/pressoffice/speeches/stories/thompson_ipi.shtml>.

Thorsen, E. (2008) Journalistic Objectivity Redefined? Wikinews and the Neutral Point of View. *New Media & Society* 10(6), 935–54.

Tiffen, R. (2010) The Press. In: Turner, G. & Cunningham, S. (eds.) *Media and Communications in Australia*. Allen & Unwin, Crows Nest, NSW, pp. 81–96.

Tracey, M. (2003) *BBC and the Reporting of the General Strike: Introduction to the Microfilm Edition by Michael Tracey*, East Ardsley, Wakefield, accessed 27 April 2012 at: <http://www.microform.co.uk/guides/R97608.pdf>.

References

Trades Union Congress (2004) *The Build Up*, TUC History Online, accessed 2 December 2011 at: <http://www.unionhistory.info/generalstrike/buildup.php>.

Tucher, A. (1994) *Froth & Scum: Truth, Beauty, Goodness, and the Ax Murder in America's First Mass Medium*. University of North Carolina Press, Chapel Hill, NC.

Tuchman, G. (1972) Objectivity as Strategic Ritual: An Examination of Newsmen's Notions of Objectivity. *The American Journal of Sociology* 77(4), 660–79.

Tuchman, G. (1978) *Making News: A Study in the Construction of Reality*. Free Press, New York.

Tumber, H. & Prentoulis, M. (2003) Journalists Under Fire: Subcultures, Objectivity and Emotional Literacy. In: Thussu, D. K. & Freedman, D. (eds.) *War and the Media: Reporting Conflict 24/7*. Sage, London, pp. 215–30.

Turner, G. (1996) Post-Journalism: News and Current Affairs Programming in the Late '80s to the Present'. *Media International Australia* No. 82 (November), 78–91.

van Ginneken, J. (1998) *Understanding Global News: A Critical Introduction*. Sage, London.

Voloshinov, V. N. (1973 [1929]) *Marxism and the Philosophy of Language*. Seminar Press, New York.

Voltmer, K. (2012) How Far Can Media Systems Travel? Applying Hallin and Mancini's Comparative Framework outside the Western World. In: Hallin, D. C. & Mancini, P. (eds.) *Comparing Media Systems beyond the Western World*. Cambridge University Press, Cambridge, pp. 224–45.

Vos, T. P. (2012) 'Homo Journalisticus': Journalism Education's Role in Articulating the Objectivity Norm. *Journalism* 13(4), 435–49.

Waisbord, S. (2000) Media in South America: Between the Rock of the State and the Hard Place of the Market. In Curran, J. & Park, M.-J. (eds.) *De-Westernizing Media Studies*. Routledge, London, pp. 50–62.

Wall, M. (2005) 'Blogs of War'. *Journalism* 6(2), 153–72.

Ward, S. J. (1998) An Answer to Martin Bell: Objectivity and Attachment in Journalism. *The Harvard International Journal of Press/Politics* 3(3), 121–5.

Ward, S. J. A. (2004) *The Invention of Journalism Ethics: The Path to Objectivity and Beyond*. McGill-Queen's University Press, Montreal & Kingston.

Ward, S. J. A. (2011) Multidimensional Objectivity for Global Journalism. In: Fortner, R. S. & Fackler, M. (eds.) *The Handbook of Global Communication and Media Ethics, Vol. I*. Wiley-Blackwell, Malden, MA, pp. 215–33.

Wark, M. (1994) *Virtual Geography: Living with Global Media Events*. Indiana University Press, Bloomington, IN.

Weaver, D. H. (1998) *The Global Journalist: News People around the World*. Hampton Press, Cresskill, NJ.

References

Weaver, P. H. (1975 [1974]) The New Journalism and the Old. In: Merrill, J. C. & Barney, R. D. (eds.) *Ethics and the Press: Readings in Mass Media Morality.* Hastings House, New York, pp. 89–107.

Weinberger, D. (2009) *Transparency Is the New Objectivity,* Joho the Blog, accessed 16 December 2011 at: <http://www.hyperorg.com/blogger/2009/07/19/transparency-is-the-new-objectivity/>.

Westerhåhl, J. (1983) Objective News Reporting: General Premises. *Communication Research* 10(3), 403–24.

White, A. R. (1971) *Truth.* Macmillan, London.

White, L. & Leigh, R. D. (1946) *Peoples Speaking to Peoples: A Report on International Mass Communication from the Commission on Freedom of the Press.* University of Chicago Press, Chicago, IL.

White, P. R. R. (2000) Media Objectivity and the Rhetoric of News Story Structure. In: Ventola, E. (ed.) *Discourse and Community: Doing Functional Linguistics.* Gunter Narr Verlag, Tübingen, pp. 379–97.

Wiebe, R. H. (1967) *The Search for Order, 1877–1920.* Hill and Wang, New York.

Wikinews (2010) *Wikinews: Neutral Point of View,* accessed 22 December 2011 at: <http://en.wikinews.org/wiki/Wikinews:Neutral_point_of_view>.

Williams, J. H. (2005) The American Revolution and the Death of Objectivity. In: Knowlton, S. R. & Freeman, K. L. (eds.) *Fair and Balanced: A History of Journalistic Objectivity.* Vision Press, Northport, AL, pp. 51–63.

Williams, W. & Martin, F. L. (1911) *The Practice of Journalism: A Treatise on Newspaper Making.* E. W. Stephens Publishing Co., Columbia, MO.

Windschuttle, K. (1998) Journalism Versus Cultural Studies. *Australian Studies in Journalism* 7, 3–31.

Winston, B. (1999) How Are Media Born? In: Marris, P. & Thornham, S. (eds.) *Media Studies: A Reader.* Edinburgh University Press, Edinburgh, pp. 786–801.

Wolfe, T. (ed.) (1973) *The New Journalism, with an Anthology Edited by Tom Wolfe and E. W. Johnson.* Picador, London.

Wright, N. T. (1992) *The New Testament and the People of God.* Fortress Press, Minneapolis, MN.

Xinhua News Agency (1994) Amended Text of 'Norms of Professional Ethics of Journalists'. *BBC Monitoring Service: Asia Pacific,* 14 June.

Xu, X. (2005) *Demystifying Asian Values in Journalism.* Marshall Cavendish Academic, Singapore.

Zayani, M. (ed.) (2005) *The Al Jazeera Phenomenon: Critical Perspectives on New Arab Media.* Paradigm Publishers, Boulder, CO.

Zelizer, B. (1993) Journalists as Interpretive Communities. *Critical Studies in Mass Communication* 10(3), 219–37.

Zelizer, B. (2004) *Taking Journalism Seriously: News and the Academy.* Sage, Thousand Oaks, CA.

References

Zhao, Y. (2012) Understanding China's Media System in a World Historical Context. In: Hallin, D. C. & Mancini, P. (eds.) *Comparing Media Systems beyond the Western World*. Cambridge University Press, Cambridge, pp. 143–73.

Index

254

Index

Index

Index

Index

Index

Index